P J Lynch
Trout Creek

God's Underground

God's Underground

BY

FATHER "GEORGE"

as told to

GRETTA PALMER

APPLETON-CENTURY-CROFTS, INC.

New York

My own identity and that of some characters in my story cannot be publicly disclosed: for many of those with whom I have had friendly contact in the Christian Underground are hostages of the USSR and its quisling states today.

The Author

FOREWORD

I FIRST came to know the author of this book a little over two years ago: since then I have had both direct and indirect contact with him—not only in America, but also in China, which we both visited last spring. He is a Croat priest who spent eighteen months incognito as an officer attached to the Red Army, six of these traveling inside Russia itself.

I know that the story of this spiritual Odyssey behind the Iron Curtain is authentic. (Indeed, it is the very authenticity of his account which makes it necessary for this priest to use an assumed name: the need for anonymity increases in direct ratio to the fear and tyranny of a political milieu.) I know the author's real name and his diocese and I have been given confirmation of his experiences from Church authorities.

When I heard some of Father George's stories of underground religion in Soviet Russia, I felt that these anecdotes . . . so vivid, so touching . . . deserved a wider audience. And so I put him in touch some months ago with Gretta Palmer, one of my friends. She became his collaborator on this book.

What they tell is not altogether new to the few who have already had religious contacts with Russia; but it will be very new and intensely interesting to the vast majority of readers whose knowledge of today's Russia is limited to the broadcasts of commentators and political analysts.

For the strong, unbroken spirituality of the Russian people under the Communist persecution is one of the important truths of our era. Word of it has been circulated through confidential sources for some time; more such information gets out of Russia than is generally believed . . . far more than the general public hears. (It is interesting that no one ever speaks of Russia as having an Iron *Door;* it is always merely an Iron Curtain. A door of iron could not be pierced, but it is fairly easy to get behind a curtain.) The contributor of this Foreword has received from religious, but non-Catholic sources, the names of MVD agents who have been streaming into western Europe disguised as priests. A year after I first heard of this, the facts were confirmed by the intelligence department of one of the major democratic states. Other such data has come my way in recent years; all of it supports the facts recounted in *God's Underground.*

Father George is the first to make public not only details of the mysterious spiritual activity inside Russia, but also the manner in which he secured this knowledge. There are countless records of political refugees from Russia; here is the first record of a religious refugee.

This book will disabuse the minds of those who, fed on propaganda, believe that Russia is friendly to religion. True, there has been a recognition of the Orthodox Church in Moscow, but only at the price of political subservience to the foreign policy of the Communists. This new church, the stooge of Communism, has been neatly called by one of the European newspapers "a religious Cominform in the service of atheistic imperialism." Along with this recognition of a politically dominated church is to be noted an intensification of Soviet *anti-religious* propaganda. On June the 29th, 1948, *Pravda* declared that the Central Committee of the Communist Party favored the intensification of atheistic activity. On June 15th, 1948, *Bolshevik* warned that "all sorts of prejudices and superstitions have revived among the people as the result of neglect of propaganda." On June 11th the Soviet Teachers' newspaper *Uchitelskaya Gazeta* contained directions telling the teachers of the USSR how atheistic propaganda was to be carried on in the schools. No protest was ever lodged against this decision by the politically dominated Orthodox Church of Russia.

It is known from underground sources, independent of Father George, that there are many orthodox priests and laymen in Russia who do not recognize the validity of the puppet church, and who are carrying on their religious life quite independently. More remarkable still is the religious group gathered from the Catholic, Orthodox and Protestant Churches who call themselves the *Yurodivy,* which means "born fools." These saintly people, self-condemned to Soviet concentration camps, try to follow to the best of their ability the example of Christ in Gethsemane, realizing that evil can be overcome not by opposing it physically but by absorbing it spiritually. They take upon themselves the evils of the tyrannical system, as if to absorb them in their own sacrificial lives without retaliation, as Christ in the Garden drank the Chalice of His Passion to the very dregs lest the Chalice, falling to the ground, should spill upon the earth a drop of evil. So the *Yurodivys* take upon themselves the iniquities and sins of their fellowmen.

In these concentration camps they tell a new version of the story of St. George and the Dragon. St. George, they say, was about to slay the dragon when Christ stepped in and bid St. George hold his sword because the Dragon was *not yet* full of iniquity. If he were killed too early, there would still be evil left upon the earth; only when the cup of iniquity is filled will Christ step aside and allow St. George to slay the Dragon. This story is expressive of the deep and profound appreciation of the Passion of Christ in the present-day Russia, a continuation of the pre-Bolshevik religious tradition of that country. This spirit found its expression in St. Nilus, the Arch priest Avvakum, St. Tychon, St. Seraphim and, more lately, in Father Yelchaninov, who said: "We must not live superficially, but with the greatest possible tension of all our forces, both physical and spiritual. When we expend the maximum of our powers, we do not exhaust ourselves; we increase the sources of our strength."

Father George brings this religious tradition of Russia up-to-date, showing that just as there was once a catacomb beneath pagan Rome, so there is a catacomb above the earth in Russia; in it are priests bringing the Sacraments to the people, carrying blessed earth to place over their graves, and marrying religiously those who were married only civilly before. None of these priests are registered under the stooge ecclesiasticism of Moscow, whose sole purpose is to rend, if possible, the seamless Robe of Christ. In addition to this organized group of secret Christians there is also there a hard core of millions of anti-Communists who are organized only in spirit. They have their own secret methods of communicating with one another, such as the very interesting code of the melons which Father George narrates.

There is a stronger Christian Fifth Column in Russia than there is a Communist Fifth Column in the rest of the world. Only three per cent of the population of Russia belongs to the Communist Party; that means that there are less than six million out of two hundred million people who belong to the only Russian party that is permitted to exist. The vast majority of the Russian people harbor the same hope and aspirations as Christian people throughout the world. As the Godless in America are the friends of the Godless in Russia, so the Godlike in America are the allies of the Godlike in Russia.

Communism is within a lifetime of disintegration, for evil, by its nature, is self-defeating. The number of desertions from the Russian Army during World War II was a great scandal to Communism, resulting when Stalin made the mistake of letting his soldiers see Europe. Even in these days of cold war, there are twenty-five thousand desertions a year to the American Zone alone. But these desertions are usually for political or economic reasons; the greatest potential for desertion are the religious people of Russia who, though willing to desert Communism, would never desert Russia, preferring to stay and suffer in order to make it what its fathers believed it one day would be: Holy Russia.

Some of Russia's noblest souls are shipped off to concentration camps every month. Perhaps one of the greatest indications of the political tragedy of the world today is the movement of trains, shuttling such exiles and refugees about the world. It is peculiar what an important role trains have played in contemporary history—there is in all literature nothing on this subject comparable to a chapter which appears in *The Dark Side of the Moon,* a book introduced to the public by T. S. Eliot in 1947. In it is the awful description of the prisoners being hurried off to Siberia. While awaiting their trains, the corpses of small children froze in the snow, and their mothers vainly tried to restore them to life by covering up the little bodies with their own. As these trains left Poland a priest used to come every morning, raise a silver crucifix in the light of the Eastern sun and give to the unfortunate people the last blessing that they would receive on the face of this earth.

China also is a country where the tragedy of trains is evident: to stand alongside her railroad tracks and watch the apparently hopeless mass of humanity climbing aboard to seek refuge in the south of China is the strongest refutation of Communism. These people in flight are not capitalists, nor bourgeoisie, nor great landowners: if the Communists in the north were giving them abundance and plenty and a share of land, the poor would not flee from such prosperity. Yet, no one ever sees a crowded train going to the north of China.

Crowded trains stream from the north of China to the south, and from the satellite countries of Europe to Siberia; but they always return empty. There is not a single American Communist, proclaiming that Russia is the paradise of the world, who would take a train to Russia in order to live there the rest of his life; but if it were not for the Communist tyranny forbidding travel outside of Russia, there would not be trains enough to carry out the self-exiled. We know of no American Communist who has ever jumped out of a window in order to get back to Russia; but it is known that Russians *have* jumped out of windows to stay in America.

Father George makes a distinction throughout his book which is important for the understanding of Russia: namely, the difference between the superimposed ideology and the Russian people. The Russian people are among the finest on the face of God's earth. They are perhaps the profoundest of all metaphysicians; they have a deeper insight into suffering and expiation than any other people, with the possible exception of the Spaniards; the Russians have a consciousness of a Messianic mission to unite the East and the West which is found in no other people, except among the pre-Christian Jews.

It is about the Russian people that Father George writes, and he writes hopefully. One gets the impression from this book that Russia is like an egg—there is life inside of it and the potency for new life, but before that life can manifest itself, the shell must be broken. Nowhere does Father George hint or suggest, and at no time may any true Christian suggest that that hard shell of Communist materialism must be broken by war. Its shell can be cracked from within by the warmth of Divine charity, and this book suggests that already the new life is beginning to hatch—if we but add the warmth and charity of our prayers, for prayer is like a cloud that is carried by the invisible wind over mountains and Iron Curtains alike, that it may finally drop its beneficent secrets onto the suffering Russian earth beneath.

FULTON J. SHEEN

PREFACE

I HAVE little confidence in the neat barriers which men build around their fears. There was the Maginot Line. And before that, there was a Great Wall of China. Both of them crumbled, unused, because the invader had powerful allies inside the barricades. The Trojan Horse, in one form or another, has always been smuggled inside the city's walls before the frontal assault begins. Politicians build walls to keep the future out; but they never succeed. And so it will be with the Iron Curtain.

The Soviets have set up a ring of vassal states to protect them from—what? Armies? Atom bombs? No. To protect their people from a political idea and a moral truth. The idea they fear is the Christian concept that every individual man is sacred. All civil rights are based on that. The moral truth they would keep out is this: right and wrong are unchanging realities, which no man can rescind to win a war or to build a state.

But the Russian people have learned these forbidden ideas and fallen in love with them. The Christian zealots in the USSR form a hard core of men braced for martyrdom; and around them are other significant sections of the population who consider themselves prisoners in their own country and who long as ardently for liberation as any underground Frenchmen or Hollanders longed for release from the Nazi occupation troops.

The various resistance movements meet and merge in the religious underground. The clearest-eyed of all the rebels inside Russia are those who fight the Communists on moral grounds.

This is why Stalin has begun to wage a bacteriological warfare of the spirit, and why irreligion is being spread like a vast sickness through east Europe. Everywhere he has ordered his henchmen to cripple the Church—to introduce atheist teaching in the schools, to destroy the Christian press and the religious lay organizations. Stalin knows, if the West does not, that when you have once deprived people of the freedom of religion, other freedoms follow fast. For when you destroy faith, you destroy the roots of human decency.

Europe is sick today. But Europe is not a continent in despair. For there are maquis of the faith there, who await the day when the Iron Curtain will be rolled back, as the stone was once rolled from the tomb.

At Monte Cassino I have seen new flowers springing out of the bomb crater—flowers no one in the countryside had ever seen there before the war. Life took new and lovelier forms in the spring that followed the peace.

I believe that in the spiritual world a similar miracle is coming. Spring is beginning to break through the strangling ice inside the hearts of men. And spring will come first in the country where the winter of cruelty and disbelief has been the longest. As irreligion spreads on the western borders of the Soviet, faith is coming back in the Soviet itself.

I have seen dozens of omens of the change as my travels crisscrossed the Russian border during the war and in the two years after it. The people of Russia have begun to believe again: and that is the greatest single fact about our world today.

George Spencer has written that "peoples, like individuals, can return to the Faith by three methods: miracles, punishments, prayers." All three have assuredly played a part in the still unfinished drama of which I write. All three continue: the miracles are in God's hands, the punishments are in the Russian authorities'. But the prayers are our affair. I beg of you, whoever you may be . . . Catholic, Protestant, Jew, Moslem . . . to join in the four-word aspiration whose repetition will one day make this people free:

"Spasitiel Mira, Spasi Rossiou"
"Savior of the World, save Russia."

New York City,
Feast of St. Thérèse of Lisieux,
October 3, 1948.

CONTENTS

CHAPTER 1

The Soviet Offers Peace Terms to God

SITTING in the garden of a Soviet Legation on a starlit night, I heard the new minister send up a little trial balloon, and I knew history was being made in that garden. While the fireflies signaled their morse code against the blackness, and the smell of cut grass sweetened the summer air, he delivered to me a message which had been hammered out somewhere in the secret conference chambers of the godless state.

"The Nazis," he said, "did a very stupid thing when they began to persecute the Jews. They made enemies of all the Jews throughout the world. Of course. But they did a more dangerous thing than that; they made enemies of the best Christians, too. They antagonized the kind of people, in every camp, who are selfless enough to live for an ideal. No movement can afford to do that. In order to win, it is always necessary to have a sense of moral superiority over the enemy."

He was a man of forty-odd, dark, shrewd, mannerly and eager to discuss the problems of the day in terms of ultimate values. Talk with a well-indoctrinated Communist is always interesting to a Catholic; we are almost the only two kinds of men in the world today who know that philosophy matters. While the diplomat touched lightly on a dozen concrete facts about Russia and the West, his real desire was to discuss with me the necessity for an absolute. For the Absolute called God.

The Russian lit one of his long cigarettes. In the light of the match I saw that he was frowning, choosing his words with care.

"We Communists," he said, "have drawn our strength around the world from the idealists, the young men and women who fell in love with the dream of a better future for mankind. That is good; fanatics are the only followers worth having in a revolutionary age. We do not envy the capitalists their timeservers, or the opportunists who cling to the old system for what advancement and prosperity it can offer them. They are deadwood. Capitalism is doomed because it lacks an appeal to man's idealism.

"But the capitalists are not our only enemy. There is also your Church."

He paused. "We do not wish to make the mistake of the Nazis," he said. "We do not want the idealists to be against us. Capitalists can be bought. But men like you cannot be bought. Men like the priests in the Nazi concentration camps cannot be bought. We do not want selfless men against us; we feel that they belong on our side, not with the regime of reaction.

"We are willing to make generous concessions in order to do away with this barrier that exists between the Russian authorities and the men who really follow Christ."

"That is enormously interesting, Comrade," I said. "Why do you speak of it to me?"

"Because you have won a certain prominence by your attacks on the Nazis," he said. "They have been pitched in idealistic terms: not in terms of nationalism, not on a basis of expediency, but in terms of right and wrong. You steer by a compass not too different from our own. Your north, to which the needle returns, is God. Our north is a future world of peace and plenty. But both of us judge every event by a compass that is unaffected by our personal interests. I am talking to you because I believe that you will understand me and give me help."

I waited. He flung his cigarette into the darkness and paused.

"We Communists are pragmatists," he said. "We have a stubborn dream and we will not renounce it. But we are quite willing to use any one of a thousand different routes for reaching it. If Pavlov's conditioning would help us to usher in the classless society and make it secure, we should import every psychiatrist of his school from the entire world. If Freud's theories could do it, we'd deify Freud. If it could be done by applying any sociological device, we would expend a fortune to introduce it into all our towns. And if religion is necessary to usher in the securely Communist state, we shall allow religion and even encourage it."

"Yes?" I asked gently.

"I am an atheist," he said. "So are all the Communist Party leaders. But we have discovered a curious thing: the masses are not at home in the atheism which seems so satisfactory to us. They do not feel superior to the believer, as we had thought they would after a few years of atheist education. They feel uneasy in his presence.

"When our government servants have been sent abroad, we give them a special reindoctrination course on their return to eliminate any capitalist or Trotskyite notions they may have picked up. These are easily removed, for the most part. But we have been less successful in destroying the awe which some of them have felt in the churches they have visited. And some of our most devoted young people are confused when they run into this matter of 'right' or 'wrong.' We can't afford to have such questions bothering them. If they are so easily upset by their first contact with religious thought we must face the fact that religion is a basic human need and, somehow, provide for it."

"Can you do that, my friend?" I asked him. "Your philosophers deny that the two systems can be reconciled. So do ours."

"We need not recant openly. The French Revolution opposed God, but its antireligious laws were later allowed to lapse. History can repeat itself.

"We are certainly not eager to import an alien scale of values to confuse our people. But it is just possible that religion is a necessary evil. (I speak frankly. . . . You will not take offense.) The conscience of the individual may be a better watchdog of loyalty than all the secret police."

"And what do you wish me to do?" I asked.

He leaned towards me very earnestly.

"I wish you to do this, Father George. I wish you to communicate, through discreet channels, the things that I have told you to the heads of your Church. I wish you to tell me what they say. And then I want you to go to Moscow and discuss this matter with the authorities there."

This talk, in 1940, was the first formal admission made to a foreigner that the war on religion was failing. The diplomat was not, of course, completely frank. His government was still hoping to save face.

I took the message to the Church authorities, as I had been asked to do.

I had not been altogether surprised when the new Soviet minister had approached me through discreet channels a few days before. As a young man I had been a doctor and later a professor. My special field was sociology. It happened that my particular area of study was the Soviet experiment.

What caught my lasting interest, what was utterly, fantastically, brazenly new about the Soviet, was its materialistic philosophy. Through it, the Marxists raised atheism to the status of a national faith. Only France had seriously tried such a thing before, and only for thirty days. The leaders of the Soviet persisted, year after year, in trying to build a great power without recognizing the Source of all power; they hoped to enforce laws without permitting their citizens to admit the existence of the God on whose justice the respect for human law is always based.

Even the pre-Christian world had never attempted that. Even the harshest rulers of the past, the Mongol Emperors, the Goths, and Huns, acknowledged man's weakness by a few gestures of humility. They offered a pinch of incense, a garlanded bullock, a heap of autumn fruit, before the Mystery of which men are aware. But the Marxists had set up a new and dreadful shrine; Collective Man was enthroned in the tabernacle where God alone is ever at His ease.

Just such an experiment in social blasphemy was being carried on a few miles from my home. I saw that atheism, a false and sterile form of thought, could not long occupy the creative Russian mind. For these, my neighbors, love life ardently; their very melancholy is rooted in longing for experience more intense than this world can provide. No people were ever less fitted to live inside the dull and dialectical cage of materialism than the poetic, great-hearted Russians whom I know and love.

If New York State had declared atheism its official religion, the people of Connecticut might find themselves asking, rather oftener than they do today, such questions as, "Am I certain that a God exists? And if He does, is He good? Does His goodness give the individual citizen rights no state may rightly overrule? Is this a universe whose moral laws have permanent validity, outside of any social change which may occur?"

Studying such problems as these and reading what answers other men have found to them led me on from the low rungs of logic to the topless stairway of theology. Rather late in life for such a decision, I became a Catholic priest.

I could read Russian; in *Pravda, Izvestia, Antireligionznik, Bolshevik* and a score of other Government publications I had followed the attempt of the Russian authorities to send God to Siberia along with thousands of His priests. Studying, reading, talking to refugees and tourists from the east, I had kept in close touch with developments inside the Marxist state right up to the outbreak of the war in 1939.

Atheism was the very foundation of that state.

Shortly after the Revolution one of its leaders, V. Stepanov, the translator of Marx, laid down the line that was to be followed for over a quarter of a century of Russian history: "We need a resolute struggle against the priest, whether he be called the pastor, the abbot, the rabbi, the patriarch, the mullah or the Pope. At a certain stage this struggle must be transformed into the struggle against God, whether he be called Jehovah, Jesus, Buddha or Allah."

The Communist leaders of the twenties threw all their giant resources into this campaign: the propaganda efforts of other modern governments seem, in comparison, mere skirmishes compared with a world war. The Russian authorities used their despotic control over press, radio, book publishing and over the entire school system of the USSR to stamp out the people's belief in God. It allotted millions of rubles to a propaganda designed to make atheism popular. It changed the work habits of its entire economy, so that only a fraction of the population would be free on Sunday; it then imposed harsh penalties, including prison sentences, on those who stayed away from work to attend church. It closed all seminaries so that the clergy must, in time, die out without being replaced. It made the teaching of religion to the young a serious crime.

It did more than that: lest persuasion should not be enough, the USSR made war on religion by means of the Terror. How many men have been killed for Christ in Russia will never, perhaps, be known: the Greek Orthodox Church reveres as martyrs fifty-eight bishops and over one thousand priests who lost their lives before 1923. Many times that number have been killed since then.

It seemed evident to me that the battle against God could not succeed inside the USSR. To a group of sceptical friends in Croatia I said, "The Soviet has waged a twenty-two year battle with Christ and it has lost. The authorities dare not face the full meaning of this fact: that without atheism, the whole Marxist scheme cannot survive.

"But the leaders won't accept that fact yet. They will try to believe that they can jettison atheism and remain Marxists, in contradiction to all that they themselves have said.

"Soon the USSR will try to come to terms with God. The hidden spirituality of the Russians will emerge. In the distraction of the war with the West, the Communist Party may lose its grip and the real Russia, the good and Holy Russia, come to light."

My viewpoint was no secret. I openly predicted that the USSR could not, in case of war, continue its unpopular internal war against the Faith.

The Soviet minister had made the opening move. I was being asked to forward to the proper authorities a question Moscow wished to have answered: On what terms can the Communist state have peace with the Catholic world? Thus I found myself in 1940 carrying from that legation garden a message to my superiors.

After delivering it, I began an intensive study of the Russian religious viewpoints of the day. I soon discovered that a kind of schizophrenia on the subject had developed in the highest Soviet circles. One group had arrived, coldly and cynically, at the viewpoint expressed by the ambassador. The second group of officials believed that atheism must always remain the cornerstone of Marxist belief and that the campaign against the churches must go on. A third group, whose wishes seem to have prevailed in 1948, saw that religion must indeed be given to the ideal-hungry people; but they hoped it could be channeled through a puppet-church whose teachings could be perverted so as never to conflict with the political purposes of the state. A fourth group (whose leaders were later to be my friends) had become secret believers in God; these men from government posts began to organize an anti-Communist resistance movement inside the Soviet.

Those were the currents among the top-level members of the Communist Party. But while they debated the question "Shall we let God into Russia?" the question answered itself. The love of God, which knows no limits of political expediency, had already found its way into the Russian hearts.

I did not need to learn this from any legation. I knew it already. But my certainty was made more firm after my country was invaded and I was forced to live incognito as a Partisan soldier attached to the Red Army of the Ukraine. In this disguise I visited Russia and stayed for six months, billeted with the officers of the Russian Army. But in 1940, besides being a priest, I was an editor and a professor of sociology in a Catholic university in my eastern European home.

CHAPTER 2

Christian Youth Goes Underground

WHEN Jugo-Slavia was attacked in April, 1941, the Christian youth leaders in Zagreb and Belgrade were already black-listed by half a dozen separate branches of the Nazi secret police. They had harbored refugee Jews from Austria—that in itself would have made them suspect. They had denounced the Nazis a hundred times in their speeches and writings. And, worst of all, they were a Christian lay organization, with a Catholic majority but many Protestant members. That was fatal, for each of the modern tyrannies has had the same ideal—to make religion a dead letter and set up the swastika, the fasces or the hammer and sickle in place of the eternal Cross.

We all saw that the antireligious persecution of the Germans would be more severe than the Fascists'; in the Nazi-occupied zone we went underground as soon as the country was attacked. To make it harder for the Gestapo to trace us, several Catholic youth leaders and I left our homes for Trebinje, assuming new identities and carrying false identity cards forged for us by obliging friends in the police headquarters.

For my own part, I decided that I could best help my endangered young friends by abandoning my clerical dress. It was the beginning, for me, of a strange career of secrecy. I have borne nine separate names since 1941. I have assumed the nationality of three countries which are not my own. I have claimed as occupation, doctor, sanitation chief, factory worker, plumber and professor.

Now, in Trebinje, I learned some of the difficulties an underground priest must face.

There is the Mass, said daily by Catholic priests wherever they may be. Normally this is offered only in churches or chapels; but it is not for the underground priest to rejoice in the candle-girt altar, the beauty of stained glass, the touch of silk vestments. I have said my Mass alone and late at night in poor lodginghouses in many Balkan towns. I have said it in the frozen dugouts of the winter forest, fearful of Red Army sentries who marched a few yards away and who must not, at any cost, guess my identity. I have said Mass nightly in a prison cell in Prague.

The wine which is essential for the sacrifice was concealed in an iodine bottle hidden among my medicines when I adopted my most frequent incognito of a doctor. The Hosts were mixed among my aspirins. Priests celebrate the Mass fasting; in these years I have often had to wait without food from midnight until six in the evening of the following day.

And there is the "office," a collection of psalms and prayers which change with the days of the liturgical year and are printed in Latin in the Breviary. Every priest spends an hour a day saying his office: I have carried my Breviary inside a tear in my coat, and wrapped in newspapers, and inside a binocular case. And even in the book jacket of a Russian volume by Stalin.

There will be many such underground priests under the Red terror which is gripping eastern Europe today. But in 1941 our disguise was a new thing in modern times. And it was still the Nazis and the Fascists whom we had to fear.

We especially feared the Nazis; we expected their occupation of the country to be more severe, their espionage cleverer than that of the Italians. And we were right. I had been only a little time in Trebinje when a Catholic boy who had a window-washing job in the Nazi Army Headquarters came to me. He had overheard instructions given to an informer by the secret police. My present identity was known. The Gestapo were searching for me.

Very well. I should move to the area which Italy had hastily annexed, Dalmatia. The border patrols between the zones were lax. I set out on a bicycle, a knapsack on my back and pedaled to the Adriatic.

The towns of southern Croatia were overflowing with enemies of the Reich that year. Jews, Social Democrats, and after June, Communists as well, had all come to the same realization: the Fascists might wish their extinction as eagerly as the Nazis, but Mussolini's agents were far less apt than Hitler's to have their names copied, in accurate triplicate, in the files of the secret police.

The Fascist invaders may have been bunglers but it did not take them long to decide which institution was their main obstacle here: they declared a war on Catholicism.

It seemed, at first, a fairly temperate war. There were

no mass arrests of priests and nuns, there was no defiling of convents. The churches remained open. But placards went up on every other building announcing that, henceforth, sermons must be preached in Italian, a language unintelligible to the people. Priests could not preach the faith effectively in a tongue of which their congregations understood no word. Widespread defiance of the order swept through the priesthood; it became a usual Sunday-morning sight to find a group of Italian soldiers gathered menacingly about the sacristy doors of the churches. As the priests came out, those who had not spoken in Italian were beaten and abused.

Then a more serious blow was struck; all local Catholic papers were suspended and all Catholic schools and seminaries were closed. Christian lay organizations of every sort were banned; the authorities suggested that members of these could occupy themselves by joining Fascist organizations, instead. Students from the south were no longer allowed to go to Zagreb, in the German zone, to the national Catholic university.

Some of the young Catholics came to me.

"Can we organize a resistance movement of the mind?" asked Emil, a militant member of the Christian youth movement. "Can we organize a Catholic university here?"

"Of course," I said. "Give me a few days to look around."

I decided to take advantage of the fact that the churches were open and that the public was visiting them as never before. At all hours of the day the grieving people approached the altars for a few minutes of prayer. With everyone going to church, a few more visitors would not attract attention.

A congregation of monks had their community adjoining a large church in the very center of the town; they were willing to have my clandestine university set up in their refectory. The rest was easy; every morning, by twos or threes, my students entered the church, prayed for a moment and then, when they dared, stole into the sacristy that led to our meeting place.

We met here, about fifty young men and women, for six to eight hours a day for many months. Were we studying Secret Service techniques—methods of assassination—how to manufacture bombs? No. Our weapons against tyranny were the writings of St. Thomas Aquinas and Duns Scotus, Plato and Aristotle and St. Augustine. We studied economics and sociology. We read about the sufferings of the Fathers of the Early Church.

Through the shutters of our windows we could see the sun gleam on the Fascist bayonets, as the sentries passed up and down. We got to understand the history of the Early Christians better then, for we, too, were a hunted, hated sect. We grew so bold, in our fervent faith, that we even dared to sing the old Gregorian chants as we opened our sessions; the Black Shirts, passing by, thought that they were listening to the voices of a few cloistered and harmless monks. They did not know that inside those monastery walls were the young Partisans of the faith who would one day drive the Fascists from their soil.

When Hitler attacked Russia in June, the Communists joined and nearly swamped the local resistance groups of a more militant type than ours. I heard of it at once, for many of my students were also activists; I have no doubt that they did their share in sending troop trains off the rails and carrying on the other harassing, deadly activities of guerrilla warfare. These activities were not my affair; as a priest, my only work was to spread the knowledge and practice of religion. But in the more violent resistance groups, some of my students met young Communists who asked if they, too, could attend the secret university.

"Certainly," I said. "Bring them in."

Half a dozen Marxists thus joined our school. They had, of course, to learn the principles of thought (logic) and the premises of thought (philosophy) along with the rest. Under such an examination their shallow Marxist beliefs could not stand up; some of the Communists became uneasy after they had lost one or two classroom arguments and stayed away. A few continued to come.

One night one of these, the leader of the local Communist youth organization, waited for me after class.

"Father," he said, "I want to learn more than Christian philosophy. I want to learn the facts of Christian religion. And my wife does, too. We have been unsettled in our Communism ever since the Nazi pact was signed. And now I am sure the Communists are wrong and you are right. Will you instruct me so that I can join your Church?"

I began instruction that night. We met in the ramshackle tenement where the young couple lived. We spoke in darkness so that no visitors would come. I began the instruction, as priests usually do, with the five proofs of God established by Thomas Aquinas.

We met at odd hours. He had his Party business and his work in the resistance groups. I had my long lectures to prepare. Both of us had constantly to fear detection by the Black Shirts, and now, by the Communists as well.

But in the following months I saw the lovely, familiar miracle of a soul opening to the light of faith as a flower opens to the sun. I saw these two supple, brilliant young minds grow strong and healthy on the food of truth instead of the husks that had starved them for so long.

When they broke with the Party, it was a less bitter thing than it might have been in peacetime. The Christians and the Communists were allies in the dangerous missions of the resistance movement. "It is a joy," the boy said to me, "to live, at last, in a universe that makes sense."

I remembered my conversation with the Soviet diplomat the year before. I felt immensely happy. For if one intelligent Communist had found his way to the truth, in spite of a lifelong education of lies, might not others also find the way—and find it soon?

The situation in Dalmatia, when I arrived there, was difficult and confusing. I had been wise to cross the border, I decided. Dalmatia, a Croatian-speaking country, was occupied by the Italian Fascists, who were somewhat less severe than the Nazis in the north. The laxity of the Black Shirt guards was greater than I had expected. I even dared, sometimes, to wear clerical dress. Their strategy of persecution was to make ours a one-day religion, to let the people's love of God die out gradually, with no spectacular martyrdoms to fan the faith alive. The restrictions were, on the surface, so mild that few protests were made. Although Christian lay organizations were disbanded and the Church press destroyed and religious teaching in the schools was banned, Catholics who cared to go to church could do so openly. The Fascists did not even trouble, after awhile, to enforce the law against use of the Croatian language in public.

But under the surface the Italian strategy was a more evil thing than outright persecution would have been. The Fascists, following the old, hateful conqueror's rule of "divide and conquer," were trying by bribery and propaganda to make trouble between Orthodox Serb and Catholic Croat, in the hope that our Christian resistance would be diverted and split. Mihailovitch, the Serbian leader, helped in this when he launched a military campaign against a few Croatian villages. Unless someone spoke out, there was a grave danger that the Croats would plan reprisals and continue the civil war.

When I was asked to give a series of Christmas sermons in one of the largest churches in Split, I had a grave question to decide. If I avoided all talk of politics, the Fascists would not trouble me: I could continue the clandestine university as a reward for my discretion. On the other hand, it was possible that a single voice raised against hatred might prevent an anti-Orthodox drive from catching fire among the Catholics. I decided to speak out.

My sermons were preached in Croatian and they were a plea for friendship with the anti-Fascist Serbs. I pointed out that the gigantic evils of the Nazi and Fascist systems sprang from the insolent desire to set the State on a higher altar than the Christian God. The Orthodox were a religious people, a Christian people; they were also our fellow countrymen in a moment of desperate national crisis. We must not divert our energies merely to fight an old and indecisive quarrel with them.

As for the Russians, they, like the Nazis and the Fascists, had a totalitarian state. But they were not the enemy who threatened us in 1941. They were, for the moment, fighting on the side of the angels. In this tragic hour the invaders were our enemy; until they had been driven off our soil other quarrels must be deferred.

My sermons attracted many non-Catholic groups; all political meetings had been banned and word soon spread around among the exiles that it was possible to enjoy the rare experience of hearing an attack on our conquerors by simply getting up early enough on Sunday morning to attend a Catholic Mass. The Jews, the Communists, the Social Democrats crowded into the church, and after the first few sermons even the dilatory Fascist secret police had learned that treason was being spoken from my pulpit.

One night, as I was putting on my vestments in the sacristy, a young Christian worker slipped in to tell me that the church was encircled by Black Shirt guards. The Fascists had sent spies who were prepared to take down every incriminating word I said and then to arrest the entire congregation on a charge of plotting against the regime.

As I mounted the pulpit steps I felt the tension in the church. Crowds filled the aisles and overflowed into the doorways. These people must not be delivered up to the police. I fixed my eyes on a young man sitting near the pulpit, a notebook in his hand: an informer. He was there to report my sermon? Very well. I should preach a sermon for him—one I had never thought about until that moment.

Praying for help, I launched into a forty-five minute description of the miracle of Fatima, wrought by Our Lady in Portugal in 1917. Part of the revelation made by the Virgin Mary at this time predicted that "Russia will be converted and an era of peace will be given to the world"—but only after a second world war, in which "Russia will spread its errors throughout the world, giving rise to wars and persecutions against the Church. The good will suffer martyrdom and the Holy Father will suffer much. Different nations will be destroyed." My sermon attacked stateism and atheism as usual, but it saw the enemy in a red shirt, not a black one this day.

I watched the young informer. He began eagerly taking down my words; then, as the sermon developed, a puzzled look came into his eyes. He put his notebook aside. He slipped outside, through the crowd. I knew then that he and the others planted in the congregation had gone to tell the Fascist soldiers to disband.

But another Sunday came when I had to flout the Fascist police and to speak against their effort to revive old, bitter divisions among the Serbs and Croats. On the Orthodox Christmas—the seventh of January—I preached a sermon urging that we Roman Catholics should join our prayers to those of the Serbians in their celebration of the Nativity.

This sermon finally exhausted the patience of the Fascist police. They decided to get me out of Dalmatia; but they hoped to do it without the public clamor that might have followed an arrest from the pulpit. One day in February, 1943, I was summoned to the Italian Army Headquarters and told that I must leave the Italian-occupied area at once. I should be put on a train for the German zone the following day.

That was the end of the clandestine university and almost the end of my cassock-wearing days. I must now go underground in earnest. I must begin tomorrow.

On the train heading for Zagreb I entered the men's lavatory a priest, conspicuously dressed in black. I changed into a gray suit. I struggled to open the grimy, dust-locked window. As the train passed by the edge of a river I tossed my bundle into the water. It was to be three years before I could wear my clerical black again.

The Germans let me pass the frontier without difficulty: they were not too scrupulous in the examination of passports at this imaginary line between the Army zones. In Zagreb I hurried from the station to the home of a young Christian youth friend. He urged me to be his guest, but I dared not endanger him by my presence for more than twenty-four hours. The second night I spent with another member of the underground. In this way I moved about, learning the new meeting places, renewing old contacts, hearing word of old friends whose arrest had occurred in my absence, wondering what work I could take up next.

I dared not make any plans. The Gestapo would surely find me within a month. And they would hardly be as lenient as the Black Shirts.

But God's ways are better than any we can devise. One morning a member of the underground met me at the arranged meeting place (a bench in a park on the outskirts of the town) and said to me: "The Slovakian consul wishes to speak with you. He wants you to go into his country to help the anti-Nazi Catholics there."

This startled me: it had the earmarks of a trap. Slovakia was an ally of the Germans at that time. True, the little country had declared war under pressure. But a man who held an official position such as the consul's must have the approval of the Nazis.

"He is friendly to us," the student assured me. But he was young enough to be an easy dupe.

Nonetheless, I agreed to meet the consul in a room behind an obscure tailoring shop. At once he explained his work.

"I am in this job," he said, "because I know of no other way in which I can do more for the Allied cause. My Slovakian people will not long remain on the side of the Nazis; you will see. There is to be an uprising, and while it is being prepared many of us must masquerade as collaborators. I, alas, am one of them.

"We need help. We need help, especially, among the devout Catholics inside Slovakia. Their fear of the Communists is, as you know, very great. And the Nazis are taking advantage of this: they are reversing their usual attitude of persecution of the Church and are trying, instead, to turn the war into a Christian Crusade against the Reds. Duplicity could hardly go further. At this very moment they are murdering nuns and defiling altars across the Polish border. But in Slovakia the policy is different; they hope to kill the Slovakian Church with kindness.

"This is dangerous. We need someone to rally the Catholic youth, to remind them that the Nazis are the major threat today, that the Communists must wait. It is a job for a priest who knows how to talk to hot-blooded young men. Father, will you go to Bratislava and help us?"

"But how?" I asked. "The Nazis know me too well."

"I will arrange a false identity for you," he promised. "You speak our language; I shall draw up a Slovakian passport. Do you wish to go as a professor?"

I thought rapidly. The less the resemblance between my new identity and my old one, the better. And I had studied medicine years ago.

"No," I said. "Call me a physician."

And so I left Croatia, bearing a new passport, a new name, a new profession. I marched past the Slovak guards at the frontier. A Nazi troop train bound for Russia was on the next siding. I started to pass, as if I had no quarrel with them or with the Swastika that floated over the customhouse.

One of the Storm Troopers stopped me.

"You are a medical doctor?" he asked.

"Yes," I told him.

"Good," he said. "You can change the bandage on this cut. I haven't had time to go back to the Army doctor."

My first patient in many years was a German soldier nicked by a bullet some Slovakian patriot had fired.

Resistance movements are of two kinds in a sad century like ours when some of our best and bravest patriots live the lives of hunted outlaws. There is a wartime resistance movement, the kind of underground to which our Catholic groups in Dalmatia had belonged. In such a case the maquis can count on the sympathy of four-fifths of his own countrymen.

There is also the kind of underground which is active in a country divided within itself. Then the maquis cannot rely with any certainty on their own people, for their people are divided. Their own inner conflict is difficult, for they are plotting against their countrymen and are supported by a moral belief alone. They are prey to the dreadful doubts that come to any protesting minority at such a time; they must ask themselves, "Am I being a traitor to my country, and in a time of war?"

Such underground groups were numerous in Slovakia when I arrived there in the summer of 1944 and made contact with them.

"Slovakia has become an ally of the Germans under force," the boys in the Resistance told each other. "The people do not wish the Nazis to win the war." But then the other portion of their divided minds would answer them, "Yes. But who is on the other side? Russia, whose philosophy is quite as evil as the Nazis'. And France and England, who sold us out at Munich. Is there really so great a choice that I must give my blood to favor one side against the other?"

Many of the best men of the country were paralyzed by this line of thought. This was why the Slovakian consul in Zagreb had sent me here. I could sympathize with the inward struggles of these students and young workers —the group who became, as always, my particular friends. Willing to run every risk, to make every needed sacrifice for the right, they were still bewildered by a situation which seemed to ask them to surrender their lives for one of two great evils.

I rented a room in a poor section of Bratislava and established contact with the young men who had been active in our student groups before the war. It does not cost much to live as a member of the Christian underground, where a windfall for one member is immediately shared with all the rest and where, whenever penury threatened us, we prayed for help and knew that it would come.

I met first with a small group of young Catholic men and women who were willing enough to die for their beliefs, but were by no means sure that those beliefs were embodied in the Allied military cause. Our meetings were very secret: we had to fear some of the Slovakian police and government agents, but even more the Gestapo men whom the Germans had sent in to be sure of this reluctant ally.

The young revolutionists were confused. They reviewed the situation for me: Nazi propaganda filled every newspaper, flooded every radio program, was spread by every speaker who was given a license to mount a platform and address a crowd. Hatred of Communism was the theme of most of this propaganda, and even these Christian Slovaks found it hard to disagree with Government speakers who told them what they themselves believed about the menace of the Soviet and then went on to plead for their assistance to the one power which was ready to destroy the Soviet.

Our Christian underground began with a dozen men and two young women. One night we would gather on the outskirts of the city in a secluded mansion owned by one of the outstanding merchants of the country. The next meeting might take place behind the city's poorest water-front sailors' saloon. We invited to every meeting one or two "outsiders" whom we wished to convince; then, in order that they might not betray us, we always broke up the gathering as if we expected never to meet again. Word of the next meeting was passed around among the most trustworthy members when they briefly met at an appointed spot: a café washroom, a particular row of seats in a motion-picture theater, a newsstand on a busy corner.

In such sessions there was no time for the leisurely, Scholastic lectures of the underground university I had organized in Dalmatia; the Slovakians had to forge a policy rapidly enough to act on it. We needed a policy not only towards the Nazis but also towards our scarcely less dangerous allies, the Russians.

The Nazis were our overlords in Slovakia here and now. We dared not submit to them or acknowledge their victory. If they won the war, then all Europe would be lost to Christianity. But the Russians had as allies the British and the Americans—especially the Americans, who were flooding their country with Lend-Lease supplies. I believed at that time that President Roosevelt would exact a *quid pro quo* from Stalin for this enormous flow of goods. I hoped that the postwar settlement would insist that Russia fling open her doors to the Four Freedoms, including the freedom of the Christian Churches to contend openly for the soul and sympathy of the Russian people.

In order to reassure my students that in forging their policy they had the official backing of the Church against the Nazi and Fascist war on religion, I read them the Papal Encyclicals of 1937 and 1940, in which the Holy Father accused Hitler himself of "treading the steps of Judas"; called Mussolini's anti-Jewish manifesto "a true apostasy"; and attacked the whole philosophy which yields to the state the ultimate power over man.

Meanwhile, though we co-operated with the Russians against the Nazi invader, we could never allow our viewpoint to be corrupted by either philosophy. We could not be naïve enough to think the new Soviet policy of "religious toleration" meant that the Communist leaders had become genuinely friendly to our Church.

Scepticism towards the Communists' religious about-face was made easier for us by the news from the young Christians at home with whom we were constantly in touch. Now, in 1944, they sent us strange reports of the Communist bands headed by Tito.

As far back as April, 1941, when Germany and Italy invaded our country from all sides, Tito's patriotism had been curiously quiescent. Tito had been Hitler's most enthusiastic collaborationist in all of Nazi-occupied Jugo-Slavia until June, 1941, when the Nazis attacked the Soviet.

But a genuine Jugo-Slav Partisan movement was already in existence. I know, because the Christian youth movement with which I was closely associated formed an important branch. Our Christian students and workers had not waited until June of '41 to discover that Nazism was an evil thing. Their names had been blacklisted by the Gestapo and the Fascists for years before the war.

By 1943, when my discussions with the youth group in Bratislava began, Tito's official atheism was notorious. Especially in Croatia, the frankly sacrilegious behavior of his Partisans alienated the devout villagers. The faith of the Croats was not shaken when they heard the Communist soldiers sing, "*Nasha kapa sa tri roga, Poda glase protif Boga*" ("We raise our caps against God"); they were repelled. When the Partisans appeared, with their military caps topped by a big red star, the villagers ran to protect the churches from these men who blasphemed at the priests and preached atheism at the altars.

And so a change of front was decreed. Tito introduced

the same cynical policy of "religious collaboration" as Stalin himself had used when he allowed the Russian churches to reopen at the beginning of the war. But Tito's men did not do the thing by halves; their orders were to win the sympathy of the population by a crusade of fervent mock religiosity.

The peasants were given no warning to distrust the Partisans by the heads of the Church in Jugo-Slavia; the hierarchy knew too well that the enemy of the moment, the man from whose defeat we must not be distracted, was Hitler. Tito's Partisans were fighting the Nazis, and it was important that they should have the villagers' support in driving the invader out. So Archbishop Stepinac said nothing against Tito.

The archbishop had opposed the anti-Christian principles of the Nazi state since 1934. Before the war, the hundreds of Jewish refugees who came to him were provided with papers, food and help in getting passage money for Canada, South America, Africa and Australia. Others whom he could not get away, he sheltered in the Capuchin Friars' monastery in Slovenia. Time and again, the archbishop expressed his horror of the Nazi atrocities from the pulpit in a crowded Cathedral. In reprisal, the German Army ordered him confined to his palace. The Storm Troopers intensified their anti-Catholic campaign. In some areas, more than three-fourths of the priests were jailed or killed.

Archbishop Stepinac never approved of the policies of Pavelic, the pro-Nazi dictator, as the Tito regime has attempted to prove in the postwar trials. But he refused to whitewash the same evils when they were performed after the war by the Red Fascists instead of the Brown. His protests against the Gestapo and Pavelic brought him only house arrest. And after the war against the Germans had been won, it remained only for the victorious Tito Partisans to add the sacrilege of jailing him.

Curious scenes occurred in 1944 when the Communist Partisans entered a village in the deeply Christian areas. The soldiers came well stocked with holy pictures and Rosaries. Their leaders would approach a small child and say, "Well, little one. And have you said your prayers today?"

If the child shook his head, the soldiers folded the child's hand about a picture of the Holy Virgin or one of the Saints. The children were soon hurrying home, anxious to show off their new treasures to their families.

"Who gave you that?"

"The Comrades, the Tito Comrades, and they asked me to say a prayer for Tito."

The mothers would open their eyes in surprise and say, "Well! The Tito Partisans have changed. They cannot be so bad. They are not atheists any more."

These soldiers were taught to slip Rosaries into the hands of the old people, with the same plea for prayers for Tito. And the old ones, too, were saying, "The Communists have changed."

Many of the simple village priests were baffled by the behavior of the Communists when they had captured a village. Frequently the Commanding Officer's first call would be to the church. The priest would often tremble, thinking they had come to commit the same sacrileges as they had last year. Instead, the officer might say to him, "Father, tomorrow our entire Red Partisan unit will come to Mass." Communist Partisans, armed to the teeth, would fill the village churches and kneel as if in prayer.

Sometimes the propaganda succeeded; the villagers

and even the priests were won over. More often it failed. More often with their peasant shrewdness the villagers and priests said, "It is a comedy they are playing. It is a mass sacrilege."

CHAPTER 3

I Join the Partisans

OUR Balkan underground incurred constant risks of Nazi detection as we met to hammer out a program of resistance to moral and intellectual bombardment by our German conquerors. We could not have been so effective in combating the Nazis if it had not been for the existence, long before the war began, of a Christian youth movement.

In Croatia, Slovenia, and now here in Slovakia I found myself rejoicing in the presence of many clear-eyed men and women who belonged to the world-wide movement known as "Jeunesse des Ouvriers Chrétiens." These "Jocistes," as they were called, had existed since Canon Joseph Cardijn of Belgium called the movement into being in 1926; they now claimed over one hundred thousand members in France alone, and new groups had formed rapidly throughout eastern Europe. The Jocistes of France showed our Balkan youth the way to meet the Nazi invader long before Hitler turned east.

Disciplined, dedicated and energetic, the Jocistes are no pious psalm-singing group; they have always fought for social justice on any unpopular front they found, and their faith flowered into works of a practical nature. They consistently opposed all racial discrimination and fought every political movement which would subordinate the rights of the individual to the interests of the state. No Jociste accepted a factory job that might hasten a Nazi victory. These devout young leaders were sent to the French concentration camps, frequently to those where no priest was numbered among the prisoners. When the pattern of prison persecution in France became clear, special and secret permission was granted to the imprisoned Jocistes: they were allowed to carry about their necks and under their shirts small hidden boxes containing a single consecrated Host, to be administered to the dying when no priest was available.

In the first years of the war the two Jociste leaders in France died martyrs' deaths inside the camps. The first one contracted a fatal case of typhus from a dying inmate to whom he was giving the Host. The second was performing the same rite when a Nazi guard saw what he was doing and shot him in the act.

Our own Jocistes had hairbreadth escapes in those days of study in Bratislava. Once, as the group of forty or fifty of us were conferring in the cellar of an ancient warehouse, the guard we had posted at the entrance gave the low whistle which signaled danger. We scrambled rapidly to our feet, the girls snatched the kerchiefs from about their heads and turned them into dust cloths, and the men began to shift about the old barrels and boxes that had gathered dust in the cellar for half a century.

Our visitor was the owner of the factory, who rarely inspected the place and who was surprised by the sounds of conversation which had floated up to him through the radiator pipes.

"Good day," said Jan cheerfully. "Come to help us work? This is going to make a fine air-raid shelter when we get through with it."

"Oh," said the owner, doubtfully. "*That's* what's going on. But why didn't the authorities warn me or ask my permission?"

"Red tape, I guess," said Jan. "All I know is our volunteer air-raid workers were told to come in here and clean it out."

That satisfied him. The next day, to make the story plausible, we arranged for one of our members to report to the owner, regretfully, that a mistake had been made and his cellar would not be needed after all.

Genuine air-raid shelters were to be one of our favorite meeting places later in the year. In the summer months, while it was warm enough, we still held sessions out of doors in the woods a few miles from town.

Usually our secret meetings were kept small, for greater safety. Twenty or thirty of us would gather in the forest to exchange information, to lay plans for the future and, most of all, to strengthen each other by exchanging views with friends of our hearts, from whom we need not hide our secret sympathies.

But one day we dared more. We decided that our spiritual life needed the deep satisfaction of an act of fervent common worship. We decided to hold an all-day Retreat for a larger group of men and women, and in the open air.

It was a bold idea. Already several of our friends had been caught talking "treason" and the Nazis had exported them, as slaves, to Germany. We did not dare to tell the whole group the details of our plan; only the "group leaders," each with eight to twelve followers, were given the hour and place of the meeting. The others could not reveal the secret even under torture, for they did not know it.

We went out like picnickers. Some of the young men carried mandolins or guitars and the girls brought the food for our lunch. In those days of wartime famine they could not carry baskets openly, so they wore broad skirts under which were suspended little packages of fruit and potatoes. Deep in the forest, shortly after dawn, our groups came together. Scouts had searched the terrain to be sure we were alone. Patrols were posted.

This day I did not act as chaplain; instead, a young priest recently ordained was the Retreat master, and I moved about as a member of the crowd, dressed like a workman. I remember the Father's opening discourse well.

His fine young voice rang out: "Brothers! Sisters! We will begin our Retreat by blessing this, our Cathedral. Under the vault of these magnificent trees stretch the aisles of flowers that lead to our secret altar. Let us bless the Lord, who planned and built our Cathedral! Let us bless the Holy Ghost, who brought us here to meet as secretly as the Apostles on whom the Holy Ghost descended in the earliest Pentecost."

From the whole great circle of bowed heads rose the splendid music of the "Veni, Creator Spiritus."

We sang old, forbidden Gregorian chants that day. The young priest, in his working clothes, made a short and fierce and impassioned plea for courage and charity towards our oppressors. Then the students and workers gathered into semicircular groups, kneeling on the ground in a silence of meditation which was not broken until twilight fell.

In the dusk the young girls distributed the food; young men went into the forest to gather wood for the fire, with a terse warning to step softly.

After dinner that night one of our patrols gave us the warning signal, a birdcall. The chaplain winked at us and our voices rose at once in one of the popular songs of the day. The group of worshipers was transformed into an excursion party. Mandolins and guitars were taken up. The intruders were only three peasants carrying axes, who had happened upon our group; but they were strangers and, therefore, possible spies. After they had passed, another birdcall told us that it was safe to return to the silence of our meditation. The day ended when our priest rose to quote the message to the Apostles: "I send you forth to start a great and lasting fire. I came to bring that fire of love to the earth, and it is my will that it should burn."

Another time we gathered a smaller group by the river: we knew all its hidden and capricious curves and found a spot safe from any interruption. I remember how we dipped into the water and then lay, still in our swimming clothes, in a broad circle on the sand. One of our members read aloud the Epistle and the Gospel for the day; I commented on them. Across the broad river, on the other shore, was a gay drinking party; all that they could see was a group of men and women sun-bathing around an older man who squatted on the sand and talked to them. We seemed harmless enough.

And that was the strength of our Jociste conspiracy. That is always its strength. We need not perform the telltale crimes of the men who act as spies for temporal governments; we do not search brief cases or smuggle bombs, and our equipment for our revolutionary work is very easy to transport. All we need is a heart to feel with, a mind stocked with a little knowledge to think with, a tongue to pray with. The Nazis might have searched our knapsacks; they would have found nothing. The weapons by which we hoped to destroy their hated rule were hidden in our hearts.

During 1944 the Allied air raids on Bratislava were frequent; the Germans had moved some of their armament factories to Slovakia, and our city was a legitimate target. I often saw the American planes overhead, low enough to pick out the U.S. insignia on the wings.

We found that the air raids offered us the best of all times for our secret meetings: at that time the Nazi and Slovak guards scattered, the crowds were off the streets and everyone was more concerned with his own safety than with his suspicions of a traitor. We came to regard the air-raid sirens as the convenient signal for our meetings. We did not expect to be hit. The house where we usually met was miles away from the nearest armament plant.

But one memorable day, after the sirens had sounded, the thunder of the motors ground louder than it ever had before. We glanced out of the windows; a four-motored bomber hovered directly overhead. Without a word our comrades separated and ran, two by two, at one-minute intervals, towards the nearest public shelter. There we gathered in a remote corner. In a low voice which strangers could not overhear, I continued my little talk.

It was a long raid. Time and again the American plane circled directly overhead. The earth shook once, twice, five times, which meant that some great bridge or building had come toppling down, fire had begun to ravage the wooden buildings of the old city, men were maimed and dying not many yards away. These are not good things to think about while you are huddled in an air-raid shelter.

At the sound of the loudest concussion, I started to sing. The young voices took up the tune, a patriotic air. Courage can be as contagious as fear; the strained and anxious faces of the several hundred people around us gradually relaxed. A few smiles broke out and soon the whole crowd, the flotsam and jetsam of a city in peril, began to sing.

We were sworn to do whatever we could to keep courage in the hearts of the bewildered and unhappy people outside our groups. We could do pitifully little, but we remembered the traditional Jociste motto: "See. Judge. Act." Seeing was all too easy. We were seeing the horrors modern war unleashes on a civilian population, the presence of soldiers belonging to a brutal foreign power, and the terror of air raids overhead. Yes, there was much for us to "see."

"Judging" was our main preoccupation. It was to judge wisely that we held those anxious secret meetings where we penciled our copies of the Pope's Encyclicals and hammered out our duty as Christians in an anti-Christian world.

But how to "act"? That was more difficult.

I remember one secret meeting which was attended by a visiting bishop. It was during an air raid and we led him to a shelter where a small group might be fairly safe among other refugees. This shelter was an intricate underground affair of several connecting rooms; a small cell formerly used as a wine cellar was set apart from the rest, and here we met.

Under cover of the sound of sirens and crashing bombs we softly sang, "*Veni, veni, Creator, veni.*" Then we gathered at the bishop's feet and attempted to plan, with his guidance, our work for the next few arduous months.

"Resist, of course," he told us. "Always resist. Refuse, no matter what the offered reward might be, to collaborate with the evil which the Nazis represent. But nowadays you can do much more than that. You can act."

Perched on the dusty bins, we listened to this bishop—surely one of the few in history who have addressed a flock while seated on an upturned wine barrel.

"You have a courage in the face of death which men lack if they do not know that there is an afterlife," he said. "You, therefore, must always be the ones to venture first when dangerous work is to be done. You must organize your own squads to rescue the wounded from spots where the city's teams might hesitate to go. You must know more about First Aid than the others. You must, especially, take on yourselves a work of mercy for which no provision has been made. You must set up a registry of the wounded and the missing. Train your most tactful girl members to break the news to the families of those killed in the bombings. Return to such homes to comfort the bereaved."

This was the program of action which our Catholic youth movement carried out throughout those dangerous days. Born in the new catacombs and blessed by our kindly bishop, it saved us from the futile, wasteful hatred and fear which exhausts the emotion of so many victims of mass bombings. Because our members had kept busy and had given their fear a noble outlet they did not end the war with pent-up feelings of resentment against either the Germans, who have leveled so much destruction upon our poor country, or against the Russians, who have betrayed our hopes since the war came to an end.

Word reached us in the spring of 1944 that some French slave laborers were in Slovakia, working in the German arms factories. Word was also sent out to us, by a Catholic workman in one of the plants, that there were Jocistes among them and that they would like to contact the Slovakian cells.

I decided to go myself. Because I had been at many international congresses of the group, I knew the French leaders and I could find out, more easily than any Slovakian member, whether this invitation was a trap.

Ostensibly a plumber come to repair some of the factory pipes, I made my way into the section where the French laborers were at work. Almost immediately my eye caught that of a young man whom I had known before the war as a devoted member of the Jociste movement at Lyons.

"Father," he said. "You have found us! We have a Jociste organization functioning among the deportees. We have made three converts!"

"Magnificent!" I said. "Would you like to meet some Slovakian members?"

"Of course," he said. "But we are guarded."

"We have made a plan," I told him.

This was it. Whenever the flocks of U.S. bombers appeared over the German factories, the sirens gave the signal for the workmen to scatter into the fields and forests. There was always great confusion: the German soldiers were busy manning their anti-aircraft guns, the guards were attempting to drag the most important sections of the machinery into the protected sections. A few workmen could easily slip away.

On such a day we met, during an air raid, at a prearranged spot near the factory. The meeting place, carefully chosen in advance, was at a spot flat on the earth, where we lay concealed by the uncut hay which covered the summer fields. Here we exchanged confidences and made plans for future reunions with our French friends.

During one of these hayfield congresses we Slovakians had grave news to pass to the French. An insurrection against the Germans was being planned for that September of 1944, and widespread fighting would surely break out. Many Slovakian elements were combined in the conspiracy: there were the democrats who felt, as we did, that the Nazis were a greater menace in that hour than the Communists; the Jews whose permanent policy was to judge the Nazis as Enemy No. 1; and, of course, the Communists. To help the last group, Russian Army parachutists had begun to arrive in great secret in the mountains of Slovakia, where they formed guerrilla bands.

When the uprising came, the Germans would surely send in reinforcements from the west and as surely clamp down tighter restrictions on the movements of these slave prisoners.

What did the French factory workers wish to do?

"I would like a crack at fighting the Germans," said Emil, a boy who had been shipped to Slovakia because he refused to join the Nazi militia in Vichy France. "But I don't want to join the Communists if I can help it.

"Are there Partisan bands under a leadership we can accept?"

"Yes," our leader told him. "There are. In the forest are several groups of Partisans whose resistance to Hitler began before the Communists changed sides in 1941. They are seasoned guerrilla fighters and some of them are splendid boys. We know how to put you in touch with them. Do you wish to go?"

The French maquis took a vote that night, huddled under the stars; they decided they would make a bolt for it.

"It is better to die fighting in the forest than to wait here for the firing squad," the leaders agreed.

The Jocistes were few, only eighteen men in all. But they had friends, they assured us, who would want to join. These were anti-Nazi workmen from the factories of Paris, Bordeaux, Lille . . . a few Catholic seminarians and university students . . . a half dozen intellectuals. The forest where the guerrillas fought was not so far away from the one where we were meeting now; with a guide the whole group could make the trip on foot within a week.

We arranged to meet in the same place again the following evening to lay the final plans. As I waited in the shadows, I watched the boys wriggling through the hayfields towards our forest; two by two they rose to their feet and made the short dash across the moonlit pasture to the darkness of our woods. Here our guards passed them on with whispered instructions. At last we all met, deep inside the woods, at the appointed meeting ground.

We dared not light a match that night, but the full moon lit our little congregation. Over a hundred Frenchmen had decided to risk it. On the ground we spread the crude map; here, one by one, the men were shown its features by means of a flashlight shielded by a handkerchief-hood. They made plans for carrying rations for the trip; a few of the Frenchmen had access to the factory stores. They would bring with them what they could carry.

Then the group was ready to disperse, to return for their food and for any tools from which an ingenious guerrilla might hope to hammer out an instrument of war. They were ready to go, and the long procession started the dangerous road back to the factory.

I walked last of all. One by one the men dropped back; it was as a priest that they approached me in this giant confessional of forest arches, whose vaulted roof was studded with the summer stars. After each man had made his confession he went forward, yielding his place to another. It was their last confession before joining in the dangerous life of the forest-maquis; for some of them, it was the last confession of all. The next morning three were caught leaving the factory and were shot. They were the first martyrs of our underground against the German Army. They died a few days before the Reichswehr had become Slovakia's enemy.

In Bratislava that month, the first Russian parachutists contacted some of our members. We received them as friends and experimented with the few words of their language which our young men had picked up. They seemed simple, friendly boys, this advance guard of the Russian Army, naïvely thrilled over the "wealth" of even the shabbiest Slovak working home.

In September the planned insurrection occurred. The Partisans drove the Germans out of the central section of Slovakia, recapturing an area about as large as the state of Connecticut. Within the cities, however, it was from the first a hopeless fight. Unarmed boys could not hope to subdue the tanks and bombers of the Reich. But there were "incidents." Bombs went off along the tracks that carried the German materials of war back to the Reich. Defiant leaflets appeared upon the streets, urging the Slovaks to refuse collaboration. And the uprising served its purpose; it harassed the Germans and forced them to deploy their forces, sending extra regiments of men into Slovakia, away from the Russians in the major thrust.

It also served the less desirable purpose of bringing a fresh group of Gestapo agents into Bratislava.

This doomed my own efforts in the capital. One of my students, whose brother worked for us in a pro-German government bureau, warned me that my assumed identity as a doctor had been detected. The Nazis had asked the local authorities to put me under arrest. There was no time to lose.

Dressed in workingman's clothes and accompanied by two of my students, I set out at once for the town of Nitra. We reached this city at an inauspicious moment: the first friend with whom we established contact gave a low, melancholy whistle.

"What a day you have chosen to appear! The Gestapo is making a house-to-house search for Jews! If they find any strangers in town they will surely arrest them. You must flee."

I realized that my days of usefulness in the cities had come to an end. The pursuit was now too hot; the breath of the Nazi agents was uncomfortably warm. I must join our other friends in the guerrilla. I must put on the soldiers' uniform and become a part of the forest-maquis.

That night three of us set out on foot, taking one of the little roads across the hedges which the German soldiers had not bothered to guard. We were assisted by the moon, which kindly hid her light so that our bulging silhouettes could not be seen by sentries posted outside the gates of the town. I carried on my back the only possessions I was to have for many months to come: what food I had gathered, my toilet articles, a few extra pairs of socks, a clean shirt and my precious medical kit.

It took us six nights of walking to reach the point in the forest for which we had set out; during the days we slept in piles of autumn hay or, towards the end, on the floor of the forest itself. We were heading for the territory held by a group of Partisans not far from Banska Bystrica. When we finally arrived among our friends we threw ourselves down at their campfire, wolfed the rations that they shared with us, and realized that we had won through to some of the best things that this life affords: comrades who would share their last crust or their last round of ammunition with us . . . safety from the German for a time . . . and the right to fly, over our small, mean barracks, the well-loved flag of freedom.

CHAPTER 4

More About Russian "Toleration"

THOSE months in the forest late in '44 are memorable for many things. There was the renewal of old friendships, for some of the French workers whom we had helped to flee from the German-run factory were here. They knew, of course, that I was a priest; it was necessary to swear them individually to secrecy so that I might maintain my anonymity. For I knew this area would soon be visited by the Russian Army. My usefulness would certainly be less if I met the Reds as one of the clerics whom their atheist schoolbooks had taught them to mistrust.

Besides the French, we had many other nationalities among the thirty thousand men in our forest army. We had Slovaks and Czechs and Poles, Serbs and Croats and Slovenes, Hungarians, Ukrainians and Austrians, and a little later many Russians. This Foreign Legion, in spite of its diversity, was fused into an amiable unity. There were no quarrels among our fighters in the forest. Our hatred was expended on the enemy's evil belief. For each other we had nothing but friendship.

The hard life of the forest guerrilla left little time for

study or meditation. We were usually fairly close to the German lines; unless our patrols were alert we might at any time find ourselves encircled and taken prisoner. Our military objectives were to harass the German communications, to gather intelligence about their movements, and to carry out the whole chain of individually petty but collectively vital tasks which make life uncomfortable for an army occupying a hostile countryside.

As a doctor (my official identity) I had plenty of work to do. Our men did not live a life conducive to health; the food we ate was foraged from the sympathetic peasants whose farms were close to us, but it was very meager. From them we obtained supplies, usually potatoes and black bread; it was a tremendous event when we were able to have a cow to slaughter. Sometimes we even killed our famished cavalry horses and ate their meat.

Many of the men had ulcers and abscesses as a result of the rough diet. And there were the casualties of fighting. Our scouts were shot by German patrols and borne back, badly shattered, on the improvised litters their comrades made of branches and overcoats. I dressed their wounds with the simple medicines I carried.

Some maladies were the result of the harsh cold. A winter on the Russian border is no joke; to pass through its rigors without real shelter, and with only an inadequate amount of fat on one's bones, is an experience to be avoided. Frostbite and chilblains were all too common among the ill-clad workmen and students, so many of whom were boys whose city life had never hardened them for such living as this, camping, as we did most of the time, in the open air.

How did we live? We dug into the frozen ground,

making a big hole which we lined with a tracery of branches to keep out the dampness. Around the outside of the hole was a series of small canals through which water could drain off. On this foundation we learned to build a sort of igloo of packed snow, supporting it with heavy branches and leaving a little hole at the top through which the smoke of our campfires could escape. In these snug little houses we passed many nights on our beds of fir and pine or scattered hay.

In the early months we were alone; an army which drew neither provisions nor arms from any of the great Allies. We were suspect to the men of Tito because we were not Communists. And no Partisans of whom Tito disapproved received aid from England or America. It was ironic that our ragged little Slovak units should finally get help from the last place we expected it—from Communist Russia.

And then, indeed, we found our status changed. For now we were given arms and uniforms and rations which Russia had received from America. K rations, C rations, Spam and Ten-In-One became our Lend-Lease luxuries. And the health of the men immeasurably improved.

But that help did not come until February of 1945. In the long cold months that preceded the arrival of the Russians in force, we did what we could alone, with the help of the villagers. These sympathetic peasants not only saved us from starvation, they also tipped us off whenever German units were too close. Our lives depended on keeping contact with the villagers, separated from us by long, snow-covered hills over which we dared not leave footprints or ski prints by which German patrols could trace us to our secret camp.

Mere movement exhausted half our energies that dreadful winter in the hills. We cut our paths through the snowdrifts with a shovel; then, for security, we had to fill them in again, brushing the surface smooth with a broom of fir branches. Thus we traveled painfully through the cold, aware that at any moment a shot might send us to our death.

Our army had no USO, no moving pictures, no courses in orientation, none of the morale builders which accompanied the well-equipped forces of the great powers. Our only entertainment was homemade; we told each other the stories of our lives. We taught each other various languages—and in our international brigade there were enough of these spoken to keep a linguist busy for a lifetime. We had accordions and mouth organs in the camp, and some of the mountain boys had fine voices and knew many of the old peasant songs. For reading, we exchanged the few books that had been brought into the forest in the knapsacks of these oddly assorted men: in the forest I read Tolstoi and Marx in Russian, Mark Twain's *Tom Sawyer* in Greek, Marcel Proust in German and the *Imitation of Christ* in French.

In the forest I celebrated my Mass daily in one of our bunkers—those holes in the ground partially covered over with fir branches and snow. We had a varying congregation, sometimes only half a dozen men, sometimes as many as fifty. But since the whole thing had to be arranged in the greatest secrecy, we dared not invite many men who would, no doubt, have liked to attend. The lives of everyone depended on our keeping from the Russians our great secret: that we had a priest among us. For to the Political Commissars the word would immediately have been translated as "spy."

Our Mass was very precious to us. For organ music we often had the sound of German artillery. For altar candles we had a hooded flashlight. The usual time, the safest, was one hour after midnight. I had retained a carefully concealed Missal; from this I read and commented on the day's Gospel in both French and Russian—everyone among us spoke one or the other of those languages. A French maquis served as my altar boy.

My greatest problem was the obtaining of grape wine, without which Mass cannot be said. I had managed to bring with me a small amount. Finally I had only enough to fill a tiny iodine bottle, which I hid among my medicines. I used only a single drop for each Mass, using a bit of blotting paper at the Offertory. For a cruet I used an ordinary medicine glass.

Americans have said to me, "Couldn't you have admitted that you were a priest, after the official 'freedom of religion' had been declared in Russia?"

The answer is no: the Soviets, even in their wartime toleration of the Church, allowed no Catholic churches to reopen. Religious instruction of the young by Orthodox teachers was still strictly forbidden. Behind that *no* is a fantastic history of Soviet duplicity and trickery since 1919. To see why I did not wish any Red Army liaison officer to know that there was a priest among the Partisans, one must know some of that tale too.

After the killing of priests and nuns by revolutionary mobs, and the burning of churches had died down in the 1920's, the majority of the Russian people still believed. The Communists therefore devised a plan (the first of many) for controlling the Church instead of stamping it out. The Moscow government organized a few corrupt and time-serving priests into what they called the "Living Church." It was headed by a priest named Sergius who apostasized to receive this honor.

The true character of this organization was openly stated in *Working Moscow:* "Our aim is not to 'renovate' the Church, but to abolish it, to eradicate all religion."

Sergius made an act of penitence for his apostasy within a year. The Living Church had rapidly failed for lack of a congregation. Meanwhile bishops, priests and nuns who remained loyal to their true faith were tried, jailed and sometimes sentenced to death.

Trials of priests in Communist-dominated countries nowadays are usually masked; the official charge states that the man of God was involved in "political activity." In the twenties the Russians were more forthright: they openly prosecuted men for the crime of keeping religion alive. In one of the early trials the prosecutor asked a priest: "Did you teach religion to persons under age (under eighteen)?" "Yes." "Did you know this was against the law?" "Yes. But I care more for my conscience than for the law." "Have you preached without submitting your speeches to the Government censor?" "Yes." "Did you continue to say Mass after the Leningrad churches were closed?" "Yes." "Where? When? To whom?" "Often in my room. Sometimes in the cellar of a deserted orphanage, where one hundred and fifty to two hundred persons were present." On such testimony men were exiled or shot.

Such persecution was not the whole of the Communist drive against God. Their real efforts were devoted to indoctrinating youth with the new faith, godlessness. All the propaganda techniques of which they are master, all the power they possess have gone into this campaign.

Children's primers and schoolbooks taught them to scoff at religion. Antireligious posters were hung in the classrooms. Pictures of the Saints and the Blessed Trinity decorated playing cards. Teachers put drops of holy water under the microscope to show children the loathsome-looking bacilli and to repel them. Antireligious traveling shows toured the villages, playing in church buildings; their audiences were served refreshments "including church wine."

In the early years *Pravda* jubilantly reported success:

> In a Kremenching classroom a teacher asked, "How many believe in God?"
>
> Four—five—seven hands went up, then two were lowered.
>
> "How many are against God?"
>
> A whole forest of hands shot up.
>
> "Hurrah," shouted the children. "God has lost!"

But in 1925 worse laws were added. Parents from now on might not take their children to church or teach them prayers in the home: the penalty for disobedience was the removal of the children to a state orphanage.

In the same year, an old Bolshevik named Emil Yaroslavsky was put at the head of a new organization called the Militant Atheists League, with a handsome subsidy. He published a magazine called *Godless,* starting off with a circulation of 350,000. The League printed 70,555 antireligious posters; it devised special holidays with processions and ceremonies ridiculing Christmas, Easter, Yom Kippur and the Moslem feasts. By 1928 it claimed 5,500,000 members and the magazine *Godless* had a circulation of two million readers a month.

Still, 60 per cent of the parents in Moscow continued

to baptize their children, and in some schools 90 per cent of the children appeared "affected" by religion. (These are the estimates made by *Izvestia* in 1929.)

The Five-Year Plan brought more propaganda and persecution to believers. The new six-day week made it impossible for more than a fraction of the population to attend church on Sunday. Religious funerals were strictly forbidden. Taxes on the clergy increased by seven times. More churches were ordered closed. And after 1929 the martyrs belonged to every sect. Until then, the Soviet had concentrated on Orthodox and Catholic Christians. At the start of the Five-Year Plan it widened its field, and persecution of the Protestants and Jews was intensified.

The population resisted these measures. How did they dare? How were they organized? I was not to learn this secret until I myself became a member of God's underground in Russia. But a few incidents in the Soviet press told me, even before the war, that somehow a vital religious movement was kept alive.

Near Kharkov the Comsomol attempted to take over a church. The young Christians resisted and seven Communists were killed. Eight Christians also gave their lives in the struggle. In other villages the will to resist was quite as strong. The congregation remained for eight days and nights in one village church; when a Comsomol girl entered and spat upon the icons, she was killed by the outraged congregation.

Men and women in Russia did not defy the ruthless dictatorship of Stalin for the sake of their businesses, their prerevolutionary property, not even for the right to teach their children non-Marxist truths in any secular field. His secret police stilled all their protests—but with one exception. That exception is the Faith. Ten, twelve, twenty years after the revolution, men and women and even children were still willing to die rather than have their churches closed to them.

In 1932 the fifteen years of atheist propaganda had begun to boomerang. A whole generation of Russian youth, exposed to the false and superficial indoctrination of the Atheists League, had begun to question their masters. Inquiring minds, even among the members of the Comsomol, had weighed the antireligious arguments and found them untrue. Young parents and teachers now refused to pass on to the younger children a philosophy in which they could not believe. The Christian underground made converts even among the Communist Party members from this period on.

Items taken at random from newspapers of any year include such facts as these recorded in 1935: In Pessochnoye, twelve of the fourteen top Communist Party leaders were found to have icons in their homes. In a Leningrad factory, the workers openly read the Bible aloud during their lunch hour. In Ukrainian country districts, teachers allowed pupils to wear crosses to school, with a warning to hide them when an Atheists League inspector came to town.

Antireligious traveling shows began to encounter sabotage: in town after town the electric light system mysteriously broke down at the hour planned for the performance. Bundles of *Godless* remained undistributed, because of sabotage by the postmen. Platforms were torn down secretly, so that antireligious lecturers could not speak from them.

Yaroslavsky admitted in 1937 that one-half to two-thirds of the Russians outside the great cities believed in God. (And his figures were surely lower than the reality.) Although millions of Russians had had no chance to go to church for years, their faith stood firm. And remember that the Soviets had left only 20,000 churches open for 200,000,000 people; the United States, with 130,000,000, has 254,000 churches.

The persecution could not reach all the Russians who defied the law. But it seized on the most eminent offenders; the arrests offered a clue as to what was really going on in the Russian catacombs. The Bishop of Stalingrad was arrested in 1937 for having "given religious instruction to children." Two Leningrad priests were sentenced to death that year for having given shelter to one of the "traveling priests" who defied the secret police to take the sacraments to people far removed from any church. A hundred Protestants in the Kharkas were given a mass trial for having owned copies of the Bible—one of them was sent to Siberia for ten years. And even among the Party Faithful, troubles were increasing.

A new directive in 1937 reminded Young Communist League members that they were liable to expulsion if they attended a church. Nonetheless *Godless* reported that, "Members of the Party and the YCL, as well as Stakhanovites, display absolute indifference to the restoration of religious practices in their families, such as the baptism of children, church weddings, celebration of church holidays." *Antireligioznik* complained that one of its lecturers had been sent to the Donets Basin area; he found local authorities so hostile that they would not give him living quarters or transportation. *Pravda* said, "The activity of the Militant Atheists League has proved fruitless; it has increased dissatisfaction, but not with religion or with the clergy. Among members of collective farms, especially, the dissatisfaction is with official atheism, and it is growing. That is why parents frequently refuse to send their children to school, knowing they will be taught atheism there."

The Central Committee of the Communist Party confessed: "It is much more difficult to uproot religion from the consciousness of the workers than to liberate them from the exploitation of the capitalists."

That is why, when the Germans attacked Russia in 1941, the churches were thrown open and a policy of "religious toleration" was rapidly improving. Sergius, the old apostate from the twenties, sold out the Faith now: he was allowed to move into the German Embassy, as the Nazi ambassador moved out. He made a radio appeal asking the devout of Russia to support Stalin in the new war. The Soviet smiled warmly on his efforts; a government office was set up for friendly liaison with the churches. This was headed by one of the leading officials of the Militant Atheists League, now tactfully disbanded. Several of the antireligious museums were also closed.

In January of 1945 the USSR formally granted the Orthodox Church certain new privileges: it might arrange religious conferences, hold prayer meetings, appoint new ministers, borrow money from a local Soviet source. The Soviet still denied the Church the right of property ownership, the right to publish religious books, the crucial right to give public or private instruction in the faith to those under eighteen.

News of these concessions came to me in the forest: I might have been misled by them if I had not had two striking warnings. I had already learned what Communists meant by "religious toleration" from the behavior of Tito's men in Jugo-Slavia in 1943 and 1944.

And I was lucky enough to stumble upon a Russian general who kindly explained to me, the very month that they were issued, how lightly I should take the latest Soviet peace offering to God.

CHAPTER 5

I Join the Red Army

IT WAS in the far north, during one of the most bitter cold spells of the war. The wind brought tears to our eyes and cut sharply through our great overcoats, lashing our flesh as if with thongs. A visiting Russian commandant and I were on our way to interview the Commanding General of this area; we had to arrange for medical supplies and for better sanitation if the health of the Partisans was to be preserved. We had, with difficulty, obtained an appointment. The commandant seemed pleasant enough; I had not, as yet, had a chance to sound out his political views. And this was no time, in the midst of winter windstorms, to begin.

Our badly rutted road came to an end at a Command Post with the hammer and sickle flying over it. The young sentry, whose head was covered with a fur cap which I envied him, directed us to—of all things—a nearby monastery. We were now on Polish territory; some of the monks had been turned out and their places taken by Russian officers. The general we sought might be there.

We approached the monastery. When we asked for

the general we were led, instead, to the abbot. He welcomed us kindly and gave us a small glass of wine.

"You are very welcome here," he said. The abbot saw that one of us, at least, was a Red Army officer. He went out of his way to praise the kindness which he had received at the hands of the Russian general. The Red soldiers, he said, had not disturbed the few monks who had been allowed to remain. When Holy Saturday had come around, the general had not only permitted the usual procession through the town, but had even passed the word around that he hoped the townspeople would participate.

I was immensely interested in this: had we come upon an example of the much-advertised Soviet tolerance towards religion? Was it real? Or was this general an "underground Christian"? If so, he was very daring.

We left the monastery and finally found the commandant in the refectory. He was a hearty, sanguine man of forty-five or so. He greeted us as comrades, opened a bottle of vodka and offered us cigarettes. Once we had discussed our army business, he pressed us to remain and dine with him. This mess was remarkable: big sausages swimming in a lake of grease, green vegetables! We were unaccustomed to such luxury. After dinner we sat around one of the old-fashioned brick stoves and talked.

The general had the job of pacifying and reorganizing this whole region for eventual absorption into the USSR: his department corresponded to the Allied Military Government of the western front. Since we had arrived with excellent recommendations, this man assumed that we were both Party men.

The general spoke to us quite openly, as fellow Marxists. He urged on us the supreme duty of seeing that the Party was well organized in every little hamlet through which the Army passed. We must see to it that the small towns had in them a "hard core" of militant Party men who would be able to run the political affairs of the section, either openly or behind the scenes. It was especially necessary that we contact reliable Party men in areas where there were "mensheviks" or Socialists and arrange, through liquidation if necessary, that these men should not be in a position to obtain authority later. The presence of the Red Army could enormously assist us in this important task of establishing for all time the local Communist leaders.

"As for religion," the general said, puffing at his cigarette and taking a sip of the harsh Polish vodka, "do not be disturbed, my friends, to see the monks still living here. We know what we are doing. We have not forgotten that there is an utterly irreconcilable feud between religion and our State. Dialectical materialism can never come to terms with Christianity. There has never been a reliable Communist who was not also an atheist, and there never will be. We have not forgotten that.

"But the problem, at the moment, is a special one. We are now taking over a number of Catholic countries, such as this Poland. Their backward people still cling fondly to their religion: if we attack it openly, they will never listen to our propaganda. That is absurd, but true.

"No. Our wisest course—and this has been decided on very high levels in Moscow—is to disarm the first opposition of these people by an apparent change of face. We must let it be believed that the policy has changed, that religious liberty is the policy of the USSR.

I have given strict orders to my men that they are not to destroy the churches here, or even to disturb the monks in that wing we have left them for their home. We *want* them here as a proof to the Polish population that we are not antireligious.

"Now, I myself sometimes go and drink a glass of wine with the old abbot across the way. I have even shown myself at his church on important feast days. We are being much cleverer in this than the Nazis: they alienated the populations they overran in the east by a frontal attack on their religion. You see the results—they are hated everywhere."

My Russian companion nodded his approval. I saw that he was a true Communist—or was trying to give the impression of being one. The general poured a little more vodka into each of our glasses. He seemed very pleased with himself and with his government.

"You will see," he said, "some very strange things happening from now on in this matter of religion. Do not let the Comrades become confused; explain the pattern to members of your cells, as I have explained it to you. We are planning a great many novelties in this area. On Easter, for instance, the Soviet Ambassador to Constantinople is to head the Easter Eve procession, carrying a candle to show his respect for the Oecumenical Patriarch there. Imagine! He is a man who has been a Militant Atheist for thirty years. I know him well. But we can all afford to make these little empty gestures for the sake of the Party. It will not hurt the ambassador to practice a little harmless hankypanky—and the world press will be touched."

(Exactly what the general predicted took place in Constantinople in 1947. For the first time since Czarist days the Russian ambassador participated in the Patriarch's Easter Eve procession in the Cathedral.)

"Let the old people here have their churches," he went on. "Our job is with the youth. We must indoctrinate *them* fully. We must make them completely ours. We must strengthen our hold on the governments that will arise in these countries; thanks to the Yalta agreement it will not matter who wins a majority in the earliest post-war elections, for it was decreed at Yalta that *all* parties must be represented in the new governments. Our men will have to be included; you know what that means. Within a year we shall have infiltrated into every important government post east of Berlin.

"And then, Comrades"—he triumphantly raised his little glass, as if it had been a bumper—"then we can accelerate the rhythm. Wipe out their Christian schools. Tear down their outmoded crucifixes. Abolish the Catholic press and Christian youth organizations and announce to the population that the whole Orthodox religious organization we have set up in Moscow has been a fraud.

"Don't be afraid. The day will come when eastern Europe is atheist. But it is wise, just now, to play a waiting game."

If this proof of Soviet duplicity was discouraging, it was scarcely worse than I had already feared.

During the last months of 1944 our Partisans were fighting alone—back and forth across Hungary, Rumania, Ruthenia, Poland and Russia itself. Sometimes we were close to regular Slovak troops who had deserted from the Germans in a body and joined the Russians. Most of these units had had their chaplain removed by the Communist commissars: priests and ministers were thrown out of the camp. Once, inside the Russian frontier, we came close to a group of regular Slovaks who had just surrendered to the Reds. Their priest was still attached to them.

It was a devastated region. Houses, villages and barns were burnt to the ground. The fields were sown with mines. The farmers worked in danger of their lives. Even the Army had to set up a special First Aid station for victims of the small "personnel bombs." In the room next to it the Slovak priest set up his altar and said his Mass that Sunday.

It might be the last Mass most of these men would hear: rumors that the priest would be sent home were flying through the camp. (For even "toleration" did not make the Red Army approve of a chaplain with the troops.) This day his little chapel was overcrowded, with men kneeling on the ground outside the door. They lined up to take Communion as if it had been a great Feast Day. And this sight was one that the peasants in the neighborhood could not fail to notice.

How well they had noticed it became apparent in the next few days, when a strange procession began to make its way up the muddy road that led to the camp.

Barefooted, kerchiefed women, and old men bent over their walking sticks made a ragtag and bobtail procession heading for our camp. I stared at them from the top of our hill. The most remarkable feature of that long line of march was this: nearly every peasant was accompanied by a child, many of them so small that they were carried in the arms. I went closer to see what they wanted.

To the first Slovak outposts they saw, these people all

addressed the same question: "Where is the *batiushka* (little priest)?" They were sent to the chaplain.

"What do you want?" he asked the first of them.

"*Batiushka*," said a young woman, her face streaked with dust, her eyes smiling. "We have brought the babies for baptism."

"And where are you from?"

They told him. I knew the map of that part of Russia well and I listened to them aghast; some of them had come on foot. They were all ages: boys up to the Army age of fifteen, girls and women of twenty or more. Most of them had had no chance to visit a priest since the revolution of 1919 had occurred! "Toleration" had not raised from the dead sufficient priests for all of Russia.

"But," the priest told them, "my dear friends, you can baptize your children yourselves. Any Christian can baptize a baby in the absence of a priest."

"We know," they said. "We have done it. But we know it is better to have it done properly by a priest, when there is a chance."

"You know," he said, "I am a Roman Catholic priest. Most of you are members of the Orthodox Church."

An older woman rushed forward and threw herself on her knees.

"Do not refuse us," she cried. "You are a priest; that is all that matters. We have suffered so much. Please save the souls of our little ones."

So he baptized the children that day. The next day, more arrived. And the next day, and the next. The word had spread and families brought babies to him from incredible distances. After each ceremony the mothers (for it was usually the mother who came) slipped into the priest's hand an egg, a bit of cheese, a small loaf of bread, giving him the whole of their poverty as thanks. Then they went back across the winding roads into the hills—a drab but glorious procession.

Priests with other Slovak units had the same experience at other encampments inside the Russian border. And the most astonishing thing about these baptismal processions was that they were made up of the parents of the children—not, as one might have supposed, of the grandparents, who might have learned their religion in the old prerevolutionary days. The parents were the youth of the country which had tried to banish Christ forever. And they were coming to the priest on bare and bleeding feet, so poor that their torn rags had no distinguishable color any more, risking the anger of the commissars to have an unnecessary baptism performed!

The soldiers could not be very hospitable to these Russian believers; usually, they had no shelter to offer them, no food, no slight protection from the cold. Had there been only a few, they might have crowded under the walls of the poor huts which served, at least, to break the icy winds. But they were too many for that.

But soon I had a chance to learn to know the devout Russian heart more intimately than through a mass baptism.

In February of 1945 our Partisans were joined to the Fourth Ukrainian Front of the Russian Army. From that time on we became a small international island in a vast sea of Red soldiery. Our movements were planned by Russian marshals and generals. Our supplies came from Moscow (which meant that they came, indirectly, from the U.S.A.). We began to enjoy new luxuries: jeep riding, and meals of canned meat and apple butter and such forgotten luxuries. We were issued spruce new guns and better shoes. We still wore distinguishing uniforms that were different from the Reds', but to these were sometimes added the extravagance of woolen overcoats and fur-lined gloves.

The Russians among whom we lived now were far friendlier and less guarded than the Reds we had known in the early days in the forest. Those first liaison officers had been chosen men, so well indoctrinated in Party beliefs that they could be trusted to associate with outsiders without political chaperonage. Now we met the real Ivan Ivanovitch—the non-Communist Russian who represents at least 95 per cent of the people of that suffering land.

Those Russians lived with us and some died with us. We got to know them better, I believe, than any visitor to Russia can hope to do today. The units we joined were made up of men from every section of the USSR. There were Mongols and Moscovites, White Russians and Caucasians among them. There were peasants from the steppes and factory workers from the big industrial cities. There were intellectuals and illiterates, young and old, men and women.

And they talked to us as they would never have dared to talk at home. For the Iron Curtain is not a postwar invention; ever since the Soviet regime has been in power it has been careful to keep a well-insulated sheet of iron, of distrust, of physical distance between its citizens and those of the West. Until the war came, this was easily done. Visitors to Russia were carefully screened; only the sympathetic or the naïve were, for the most part, allowed to enter. They were conducted around the country in Intourist groups, and they left it with as little knowledge of real conditions as the visitor to New York's

Chinatown gets from the remarks of the barker who conducts the tour. Assuring this ignorance was the main purpose of the Intourist system.

And the iron curtain of fear which kept the visiting foreigner away from the Russians served a second purpose: it saved the Soviet citizens from contamination with the ideas of the West. Almost no foreigner, before the war, could say that he had really known the Russian soul, for almost no foreigner had held a spontaneous conversation with a Russian inside the USSR.

In the forest the Iron Curtain was removed. The political commissars could not supervise the contacts of all the thousands of soldiers, from every part of their country, who mingled with us of the West. Perhaps, too, threats of political punishment no longer seemed so terrifying to men who faced, every day, the possibility of death from battle or from exposure or from hunger. And there was a third factor making intimacy possible: No political indoctrination could convince these Russian comrades that we guerrillas from western Europe were fat, self-satisfied capitalists. Were we not there sharing their perils, suffering the same cold and fear and hunger as themselves? They were bound to trust our friendship, for they saw it proven every day.

So the Communists' policy of segregation broke down, and broke down badly. For the first time in over twenty years a large number of Soviet citizens opened their hearts to men from other lands in camps like ours. Their confidences flowed to me, even more than to the other foreign Partisans in our particular unit—partly because the doctor is, in all lands, a recipient of many confidences, and partly because my training as a priest had taught me how to listen. It proved a useful talent.

The prevailing mood of the Red soldiers, while we talked beside the smoky campfires or toiled our icy way along the treacherous forest trails, was bitter disillusion.

"We have been deceived and lied to," was the commonest remark to be heard in the forest. "The Communists have made fools of us for thirty years."

The conversation with outsiders alone convinced the Russians that the world "outside" was very different than they had been taught in the Soviet schools. Every talk we had with a Red soldier ended with his wondering remark, "They never told us about that." But more destructive of the Communist propaganda than any conversation were the sights the Russian soldiers saw.

I went with Ivan, a Red soldier, to a Hungarian town not far from the fields where we were camped. We were looking for medicines for the troops: someone had told us that an apothecary in the town still had a small stock of much-needed supplies. We lost our way in the unfamiliar streets and entered a poor dwelling to see whether anyone could direct us. A young man let us in. While I explained in Polish what we were looking for, I saw Ivan staring about him with undisguised interest.

He spoke to me in Russian.

"This is the home of a great capitalist," he said. "Ask him what kind of factories he owns."

Surprised, I said to the Pole, "What is your business?"

Our host was a poor man, an assistant in a carpenter's shop. I translated what he had said to Ivan.

"Then he must be very high in politics," said Ivan. "Look how richly furnished this home is!"

I looked about me. It was a drab and poverty-stricken little home—two rooms scantily furnished with a rickety table, two beds, a wardrobe, a homemade rug on the floor, and flimsy curtains at the windows. There was a gas stove and, in one corner, an ancient sewing machine.

"You see?" said Ivan. "He has gas. He has a mirror to see his face. Water runs out from those faucets. He is a rich man."

"My poor Ivan," I said. "He is a workingman, like you. These things are not rare luxuries; they are everyday articles."

"You mean it?" said Ivan. "The poor outside of Russia live like this? Then, by God, I'll have something to say to those lying swine of the Party when I get home again! Why, they told us the workers in the other countries were chained as slaves. But here's a worker and he lives as well as one of our factory managers.

"They have been deceiving us for twenty years!"

Thousands, millions of such scenes of awakening took place along the frontier. Whenever Russian soldiers entered a town, Polish, Slovak, Czech, Hungarian or Rumanian, its poverty seemed to them luxurious and beautiful. Compared with the hideous scarcities of Russia, these pitiful little homes were palaces. A deep rage, the righteous anger of the man who has been badly duped, arose in the hearts of the Russian fighting men.

"These are the poor workers *we* were going to liberate through world revolution," they growled to one another; "these downtrodden masses we've heard about. Why, they live better than we do ourselves! Maybe we are the ones who need to be freed."

Yes. It was what psychiatrists call a "trauma," a shock for peasants in the Red Army to enter these rich villages of Hungary and to find the wine cellars full, the shops offering bread as white as snow, roads paved with asphalt even in the villages. The commonest topic of conversation among them was "Isn't Europe wonderful?" and "Ah, my friends, if only we could live like this at home!"

At one time I had occasion to travel by Red Army train to a Russian Army headquarters east of us to arrange for some added medical supplies for our men. I was in a compartment with a group of officers returning to Moscow: their conversation centered entirely around the extravagance and luxury that they had seen.

A Red colonel spoke up: "I have been in Czecho-Slovakia. It is an amazing country. In one town I saw more than fifty bicycles parked in a rack in a downtown section, with nobody to guard them."

A captain of the Air Force nodded. "Yes," he said, "I can believe it. For I myself have seen Slovak women returning from market with bread, and even meat, in an open shopping bag! Nobody steals it from them on the trip home."

The colonel added, marveling, "I have been in their kitchens. They are wonderful. Things are laid out in bowls, as orderly as the wares in a drugstore."

Later I moved into a car filled with common soldiers of the Red Army traveling, heaped together, on the floor of a freight car. They were talking of the same wonders.

"Comrades," one of them cried out from his dark corner, "I have now been in Poland, Czecho-Slovakia, Hungary and Austria and I know what life can be. If we have to go back now to living the way we did in Russia before the war, I'd rather be killed."

Because of this attitude among the returning soldiers the Soviet set up "de-intoxicating" centers. I talked to many men who had been through these reorientation courses which attempted to convince the returning soldiers of the old Communist lies about the misery of the workers outside the Soviet. The speakers were usually young Communists, full of zeal, who parroted the Party Line with no sense of the irony of their efforts. They were trying to convince men that the things they had seen did not exist.

Piotr, whom I came to know well after I entered Russia, was one of the listeners at such a lecture.

"I contained myself as long as I could," he told me. "What this Communist speaker was saying was nonsense. Everyone in the room knew better. Finally he asked if there were any questions. I rose and said, 'Comrade, have you been in Europe?'

" 'No,' he said.

" 'Well,' I told him, 'the rest of us here have. We know the *truth* about Europe. You'd better hold your tongue.'

"Everyone laughed. I thought they'd punish me. But there were too many of us who knew the truth. They couldn't send us *all* to slave labor. They hope, I guess, that in time we'll forget how fine life is outside. But we won't forget. Not on your life. And our families won't forget, either, that we are able to bring things back to them that haven't been on sale to any Russians but commissars and government officials for the past twenty years."

The contact with the West gave every intelligent Russian an added series of shocks. The university students had been told that there was no culture worth the name outside of the Communist Party. Their conception of American farm life was formed by Steinbeck's *Grapes of Wrath,* of city life by Upton Sinclair's *The Jungle.*

They learned of France from André Malraux, of England from John Strachey. They believed that the proletarian revolution was imminent in every country of the world.

Now the facts before their eyes contradicted all these prophecies.

Sometimes the more thoughtful Russians pushed under the disturbing surface to the difference in philosophy which made so sharp a division between the Communist and the outside world. Their disenchantment was no less great when these university graduates tried to match their Party-trained wits against those of the young men from the West, the shoddy structure of Marxist-Leninist thinking soon becoming evident.

Yet long philosophical discussions are a pleasure which Russians have relished through all the centuries: Tolstoi's characters and Dostoyevsky's let very few pages pass without some consideration of man's ultimate goal. These Russians of the forties are no different.

I became sharply aware of this soon after our units merged. We were "resting" in an area of devastated villages and scorched fields—resting, but not succumbing to too soft a life even there, deep inside the Russian border. The enemy planes continued their dance of death above our heads, and the sound of shelling was clear whenever the wind blew from the west.

Among our visitors at that time were several correspondents from the Moscow press. We made them at home; after we had told them of the military situation, we spent hours about the campfires examining with them the questions man is never tired of asking: "Why am I here? What is it all about? Where am I going?"

"Uneasy," said St. Augustine, "is the heart until it rests in Thee." The hearts of our Russian newspapermen were very uneasy indeed.

Mischa was the most interesting of the correspondents. He had a quick mind and a restless one, which had received some training in Hegelian philosophy before the war. Tall, well built, with gray-green eyes and a suggestion of the Mongol in his face, he was a personable and successful citizen of the Soviet.

One evening by the campfire Mischa turned to me with an abrupt question: "What is the soul? What? It is a simple myth, really."

I had no intention of admitting to him that I was a Christian, still less a priest. I pursued the line of conversation cautiously.

"Perhaps. And how about your conception of the soul—your belief that it is a myth—is this belief, too, a myth?"

"No, no," he said impatiently. "My thought is a real thing, of course."

"My mind," said Mischa confidently. He seemed to believe that he had furnished the final answer, that the matter of human thinking was well disposed of.

"Your mind is enough to give birth to all your thinking?"

"Of course," said Mischa. Then, to drive the point home, he added: "If your mind became insane, could you think normally?"

"No," I granted him.

"Well, then," he said. "You see!"

"Mischa," I said, "you are going a little too fast. Do you typewrite?"

"Yes," he said.

"If I removed the keys from your typewriter, could you still type?"

"No," he said.

"But you would still *know how* to use a typewriter, even if that one was rendered useless to you?"

"Yes," he said.

"Mischa," I asked him, "do you play the violin?"

"A little. I am not a virtuoso."

"If I cut the strings on your instrument, you could no longer play it?"

"No."

"Yet you would still know *how* to play?"

"Of course."

"Mischa, if I gave the best violin in the world to someone like Sascha, who breaks everything he handles, he couldn't play it, could he? Not without having learned how?"

"No, no."

"And if I give a stringless violin to the best concert artist he cannot play it without strings?"

"No."

"It is that way with our physical brain and our ideas," I went on. "The strings of the violin are necessary for playing, but they do not make the music. The *cause* of the violinist's playing is his knowledge and his talent. The keyboard of your typewriter is a necessary condition of your typing; it is not the cause of your ability to type.

"Our minds are like that: they are necessary for us to think, but the real cause of our thinking must lie outside of our minds. The brain is matter; it has weight, area, color, chemical and physical elements, all of them material things. But the ideas that emerge from our minds go beyond weight, space, color: we are able to create concepts which have no material qualities—yet concepts that are very clear, very precise, very real. And we can also have abstract ideas which we never met in any material thing; yet these general ideas, too, can be very clear, very real. Such as the idea of the state, Mischa. You have never seen or smelt or touched a state, but you know what it is.

"Our ideas, which are of another order than the physical brain, cannot have been caused by the brain; they must trace back to a source which has the same characteristics they have, to a cause which is supermaterial, as they are supermaterial. This cause, which is manifested in all our ideas and in our free will, in our consciousness of being alive, in love and sacrifice and worship—this cause is the original reality. We call it spirit. We call it the soul.

"So you see, Mischa, the soul is not a myth. It is a reality, as real as the ideas that spring from it: ideas of duty, freedom, consciousness and self."

Mischa remained quiet. The distinction I had made, familiar to any student of philosophy in the West, had never entered the manuals of dialectical materialism from which he had been taught. He had never been forced to distinguish between a condition and a cause.

He threw another log on the fire with his great plainsman's arms and sank back on his heels.

"It is evident," he said next, "that man is evolved from the monkey."

"Think so if you wish," I told him. "His body may, indeed, be the end product of evolution. We are not sure. But that is not the problem.

"The problem, Mischa, is this: is there an essential

difference—a difference of kind—between man and the animal? If there is, and if that difference shows itself when man operates on a higher-than-animal plane, then that superiority could not have sprung from an inferior cause. It must have come from some other source. A thing, an animal, a man—none of them can give forth something it does not have within itself. How, then, could man, the superior, have evolved from the monkey, the inferior?"

"That is simple," growled Mischa. "By working."

"Hm," I said. "That seems simple to you? It seems to me to complicate the problem and to avoid the problem, too. For it assumes that the question we are asked to solve has already been solved, and it has not. There are, in Russia and in other countries, plenty of monkeys. They have been 'working,' as you put it, for millennia. Why haven't they evolved into men?"

Mischa gave no answer. Simple as they were, these were objections of a sort the Soviet schools had never posed. I went on.

"But let's take your statement about monkeys working and examine it a little more, Mischa. I do not agree with you that monkeys work. For what does it mean, 'to work'? It means to have a goal before you, to have imagined something which does not yet exist and to seek to bring it into reality. To do that requires intelligence. And intelligence is a thing that animals lack. They have instinctive activity; some of them are capable of imitative activity. But none of them have shown signs of creative activity; they have never shown themselves capable of imagining a goal and making a conscious choice between different ways to realize it.

"That's why, through all time, we see the bees making

perfect octagons in their hives—but never any other cell except the octagonal. That's why monkeys are always imitating us, but never setting us a standard which we accept and try to copy from them.

"The most primitive men do things no animal has ever done. They make tools, build homes, improve their condition, change the face of the earth. The animal has never put fire to his service, and yet the animal has been many times in the presence of fire. The animal never made a hatchet to cut down a tree. Even the very primitive men of Europe drew pictures of bison on the walls of their caves; but no bison ever drew a picture of a man.

"All these things are true because the animal lacks something which is inherent in man; intelligence, which permits man, and only man, to study causes and effects, to discover causes *by* effects, to manipulate matter so that the same cause will, over and over again, produce the same effect. Intelligence belongs to man; without it he could never work. It is the thinking spirit which precedes work, not work which creates intelligence."

Mischa took this little discourse very seriously; he asked me to repeat it. It astonished him by its novelty. He had been led to believe that all the thought of the past was comprised in the little handbooks of Marxist philosophy which he had memorized. Yet here were questions no professor of his had ever raised or answered.

Mischa went away and did not continue the discussion. But the next evening he handed me, with a mournful air, a copy of his students' textbook on philosophy—the official volume issued by the Soviet State. I studied it closely. It was a shocking piece of work. It shamelessly distorted the history of human thought, slandering even such remote masters as Socrates and Aristotle in order to build up the case for Marx. There was here no breath of the spirit of free inquiry, no scientific conscience, no devotion to truths which might be inconvenient to the State. Despotism could go no further. By giving this perverted doctrine to its young men as a foundation to their thinking, it had cynically shackled the minds of Soviet students, preventing them from apprehending truths which did not suit its practical purposes.

The Chinese used to bind the feet of their children; a cruel practice. But the Soviet State has done a far more horrible thing; it has bound the minds of its youth.

CHAPTER 6

Bitterness Among the Reds

FEW of the Red Army soldiers were university men like Mischa. Most of them had obtained their meager knowledge of the outside world from Party lecturers and from the propaganda press. These Soviet newspapers were distributed to us at the front. The front page was usually made up of "voluntary" pledges from industrial plants to exceed their capacity for the next few months. The second page was very similar. The third might carry a boastful and chauvinistic article on the achievements of the Party favorites in some branch of the arts, along with news of Red Army successes at the front. The last page, the one to which everybody turned first, gave a little carefully censored news of foreign events. The more intelligent Russians had learned to interpret this fourth page, to allow for government emphasis, to guess what might have really happened.

With such a background as this, the Red Army soldiers went to pieces in the face of so many contradictions to all they had been taught.

A collective nervous breakdown always occurred when the Russians "liberated" a new area and found new evidence that the cause for which they had sacrificed so much was a gigantic hoax. The first symptom of this breakdown was inevitably drunkenness.

The Red soldiers snatched at alcohol in any form obtainable: first they drank all the vodka, wine and rum in a town; then they drank the medical alcohol, benzine and eau de cologne. Drunken soldiers were soon falling about in the streets. Drunken officers were in no fit state to discipline them.

This drinking was not the simple roistering of the soldier who relaxes after battle; it had a suicidal quality, for the Russian soldiers drank even during battle, when they knew that they were endangering their lives. Near Kosice, in the winegrowing country, the Red Army was never sober from morning to night; on one occasion they stormed the German machine guns with the reckless courage of the drunkard, and forty thousand drunken men were killed. The Battle of Budapest was prolonged for several unnecessary weeks: as soon as the Reds had occupied one section of the town they stopped fighting to exhaust the supplies of liquor which its shops contained.

These Russians did not drink from joy; they drank from despair. I talked about it to some of the most consistently drunken soldiers. They answered me as Andrei did: "I drink, Comrade Doctor, and I shall go on drinking, to avoid having to think why I am alive."

The women soldiers—mostly machine gunners—were sometimes more ruthless and more dissipated than the men. I saw in the swaggering insolence of these girls a fierce determination to compensate for being weaker: they wished to show that they could outswear, outdrink, outmassacre the men. Sometimes they succeeded.

One night I remember well—it was on the plains of eastern Hungary. We reached the town where we were to be billeted after hours of excruciating travel on top of empty gas tanks, piled on trucks which jostled over the rutted, muddy roads. We were exhausted. We threw ourselves down on the floor of the empty warehouse allotted to us and commended ourselves to God. But we had forgotten the lice that clung to our tired bodies; the handfuls of mud, which had to serve us in place of soap in those hard days, had not served to discourage them. We sat up and spent much of the night catching the little beasts, by light of our flickering candles. Finally, we lay down again to rest.

We had not slept long when pistol shots rang out sharply in the night. We sprang to attention, our hands on our guns, ready for a German attack. One of our men tiptoed to the door and carefully pulled back the strip of burlap which hung across it.

Next door we saw a company of Russian women soldiers, staggering in their drunkenness, shouting, laughing, jostling each other at the entrance to the building next to ours. This, it seemed, was a kind of hotel for young workingmen; the girls were forcing them, by means of tommy guns and pistols, to remove their clothes and to have sexual intercourse with them. Those men who attempted to refuse were beaten with the butt ends of the guns until they, too, yielded. All the scenes of rape, horribly reversed, took place before the open, lighted windows of the hotel.

The Red girls had venereal diseases at even a higher rate than that of the Russian Army men. They were forced by their military orders to lead the lives of brutes, and they took their recreation in ways which brutes would have despised. I knew. I had seen them often enough loading huge flour bags and ammunition cases from the Army trucks or plugging along the roads as foot-soldiers, burdened with their heavy guns and packs. After such days, the coarse relief of alcohol and indiscriminate sexual excitement was all they could enjoy.

Although, as a group, such women were as frightening as the Furies, taken as individuals they were touching and tragic girls.

Katrina was one of our women drunkards. I had seen her smash a baby's skull with her rifle butt, while her companions stood by and laughed. I had seen her make evil approaches to the frightened young boys of the Polish villages, and had heard her vile profanity. I had noticed, wryly, that atheist Party members, like herself, retained a kind of inverted reverence; when they wished to smash and kill it was their invariable practice to curse the name of the God who was, they said, a forgotten myth. Of their old religion nothing seemed to have survived except the lust for sacrilege; but that was something. Where there is a passion, even of hatred, there is life from which love may someday grow.

One morning I came upon Katrina, her rifle slung about her shoulders, a canteen full of vodka uptilted to her mouth. She had drunk heavily the night before; her face was bloated, her eyes red and on her twisted lips I saw a look of something like despair.

"Why do you drink so much, Katrina?" I asked her gently.

She spat on the ground and took another fierce swig at the bottle.

"To forget, of course," she said.

"To forget what, my daughter?"

"To forget everything—life, death, my own thoughts. You do not know, Doctor, the things I have seen. They tell us that women are the same as men: it isn't true. There's something terribly wrong with women at a war. You saw me kill that baby last week. I did it because it reminded me of things I can't afford to think about."

"What things?"

"Oh, slushy, silly things. I know better; I've been to the Party schools. I'd be ashamed to tell my comrades any of this, but there must be a streak of bourgeois rottenness left in me."

She looked at me to be sure I was not sneering at her confidences.

"Doctor, don't laugh at me. I'd like to have a baby of my own. A baby I could keep—not one to send to the government orphanages. Sometimes I see the moving pictures showing us the home life of the old, corrupt days before the revolution. We're supposed to laugh at the scenes, at the soft, spoiled women who don't know how to carry heavy sacks of coal or do the things we do. We see them praying on their knees, being deceived by the witchcraft of the priests. We're supposed to laugh at them. I do laugh. But it sometimes looks peaceful and happy and natural, that life.

"I've had too many men. I've drunk too many quarts of vodka. I've killed too many Germans. I could never settle down to a single man and be a mother. Imagine me—Katrina—playing dolls with a child!

"No. I'll go on like this. And one day, on some battle front, a bullet will have my name on it and I'll be ended. Quickly, I hope. But oh, Doctor, why do I feel there might be something more?"

She was crying, partly with the self-pity of the drunkard, partly because she had been able, at last, to pour out these secrets which seemed to her so shameful.

"But, my daughter," I said, "there *is* more. You are unhappy because you are trying to make yourself into an animal. Man is more than that. So is woman. Contentment comes when we admit that we are more.

"Take any of the men you most admire: Marx, Lenin, any of them. Did they do their work by imitating the animals, by fornication and drunkenness? Of course not. They used their human brains. You have a mind, Katrina. You have also a heart. It's your heart that is reproaching you."

"I have only a social conscience," said Katrina. "At least, I guess I have. It should be at peace. I'm doing what the Party wants me to do. I'm fighting; I've killed over forty men. That ought to be enough."

"But you're a woman," I said. "God wishes you to pass on life. . . ."

"Go away!" she screamed. And bitter curses rained on me. "Shut up. Bourgeois! Counterrevolutionary! Trotskyite!"

I said no more. But for a moment I had seen something of the heartache and self-reproach that underlay these brutal assaults for which the women soldiers were notorious. The Party had had its way with them; it had crippled their consciences and misled their minds. But the Party had not been able quite to destroy their deep humanity. It had only made them ashamed of it.

The same disenchantment which led all the men and women to drink made some of them loot and rape on a gigantic scale. The looting had about it the same mad, compulsive quality as the drinking: these soldiers gathered stolen goods in a kind of rage against the

Soviet leaders who had so grossly misled them as to the way of life of the common people in capitalist lands.

What things did the Russian buy and steal? Clothing —any kind of clothing. The Russian populace has been dressed in hand-me-downs since the revolution began: a dress that does not bear a patch is an undreamed-of luxury. Some articles of dress have become such rarities in Russia that no one, any more, remembers their proper use. Russian soldiers stole women's nightgowns and sent them home, where they were worn on the streets at night as evening gowns. I have seen Russian Army female officers proudly wearing cotton nightdresses at official parties.

But the favorite articles of the Red soldiers were the wrist watches. These were bought by the millions and shipped back to Russia; Red soldiers wore as many as eight or ten on their arms at a time. The wrist-watch situation became acutely embarrassing to the Soviet government. An official statement was issued in *Pravda*, saying, "It is not Stalin's fault that the watches of Europe are superior to the Russian make. The commissar in charge of wrist-watch production was a saboteur and traitor. He has been liquidated." The article admitted that only three small factories in all Russia were devoted to the manufacture of watches; it promised that the number would soon be increased.

The Russian attack of nerves did not usually end in such innocent sports as the collection of wrist watches and the emptying of wine bins.

In late 1944 our Partisan unit entered a town in Hungary from which a Russian Army division had recently withdrawn. We wore ragged, faded military uniforms, but we were still recognizably soldiers. The commander of our forces, a Slovakian officer, marched with me a little ahead of the main columns. We went to the first fair-sized house we saw, hoping to find lodgings.

The owner of the house opened the door for us. Behind him we saw his wife, a woman of fifty; at sight of us she paled, gave a low moan and rushed out at the back. We reassured the husband and he brought his wife back, still trembling. What had made her so timid?

A few nights before, the husband said, just before the Russians had withdrawn, some Red soldiers had rounded up all the men of the neighborhood into this very kitchen where we talked. They had posted two guards with machine guns to keep them there. Meanwhile other soldiers brought the village women into a second house and, one after another, methodically raped them. The soldiers had been counted off, in formal "details," for this; company by company they entered the house where the women lay moaning, abused them and then made room for the next group. His own wife had been raped seventeen times that night. She had almost lost her reason. And it was only by a near miracle that they had been able to protect their fifteen-year-old daughter, who had been sent running, in the nick of time, to hide under the straw in the stable. For three days the trembling girl stayed there, fed secretly, until the Russians had moved out of town.

Farther on, in another group of villages, I was asked, as a physician, to examine some of these pitiful victims of the "liberation." One woman of at least sixty-five years lay suffering on a feather bed; she had been raped and had contracted a venereal disease which her advanced age made more severe. In a nearby home I was shown an eight-year-old girl who had been violated three nights earlier and who lay, torn and mutilated, in danger of her life.

Sometimes we who traveled with the Reds were forced to witness such scenes ourselves. I shall not soon forget the town in Hungary where the Reds entered the public air-raid shelter during a raid, turned their flashlights on the frightened women until they found some that satisfied them, dragged them from the shadow into the light near the entrance and committed rape in front of all the civilians. Nor the homes in which the Red soldiers forced the men of the household to the kitchens, under the threat of tommy guns, and locked them in while they violated the women. Nor the commonplace of travel in those frightful days, when no woman dared take a train, knowing she was apt to be dragged to the toilet and maltreated by the Red soldiers.

In Prague itself I saw a company of drunken Russians stop a respectable Czech man and his wife, order the man away at the point of a gun and rape the woman in the middle of the street.

There were other abuses: When the Red Army entered a city its MVD officers always carried a list of anti-Communist citizens, radioed to them from Moscow. The first act of the police agents was to descend on the suspects and torture them. In this work they were assisted by the local Communist Party members. I have seen trucks filled with Communist youths careening drunkenly through the city streets on "liberation day," seeking out anti-Communist civilians so that they might be seized for torture and sure death. I have seen these groups later shoot men and women in front of their homes, while their families were forced to watch.

It was not only the anti-Communists who feared sudden death when the Reds captured a town; any bystander who tried to prevent their atrocities was killed. At the Hungarian town of Gyoer, the Bishop Apony tried to prevent a Russian soldier from raping two women in the air-raid shelter under his palace. He was shot to death.

This lawlessness took other ugly forms: in one town, I came across a Rumanian officer sitting on the steps of the railroad station crying. I went up to him and said, "What is it, my friend?"

He told me that he was the officer in charge of a Rumanian Army train that was headed for the front-line troops of his country, who were fighting the Germans in the mountain snow. It carried desperately needed food and warm clothing for them. A Russian officer had marched up to the train in the station yards and seized a paintbrush, changed the lettering on the side of the train to read USSR and ordered the Rumanians to descend from the locomotive at the point of a machine gun. Then he and his Red associates hijacked the train for the Russian Army.

Soldiers of all ages and nations share a code of their own, a code which makes selfless bravery the supreme virtue and which, by a kind of moral compensation, permits the warrior sexual license, looting, drunkenness and theft. These things we all know. There was nothing new about the conduct of the Russian soldiers except its one utterly shocking distinction: these men had been *urged* by their commissars to commit the crime; no effort was made, by any form of army discipline, to hold their passions in check. Only once before in modern times had such a thing occurred; when the Japanese soldiers captured Nanking their officers made rape official. No people of the West had done so since the pre-Christian days of Goth and Gaul, of Hun and Visigoth.

In scenes of utter horror I was able to prevent an atrocity occasionally. These Russian soldiers who were my gentle comrades in the forest turned into beasts and worse than beasts when they had captured a little village and been given leave to run riot among the unarmed peasants. The commissars encouraged the men—they acted as ringleaders in deeds of diabolic playfulness. Yet their victims were no fat, swollen members of the "capitalist class," no Nazi enemies; they were the poor and trembling villagers of Poland, Hungary, Austria, Slovakia and the eastern part of Jugo-Slavia.

"Scratch a Russian," murmured one of my Croatian friends, "and find a Tartar."

"No," I told him. "Scratch a man deceived for thirty years by lying propagandists and find a man whose rage must find an out."

But the indignation of the betrayed Russians did not always take the form of violence against innocent civilians. Sometimes whole units shot their commissars and bolted to the hills.

My first experience with the Russian soldiers' mass desertion came shortly after our Partisan units were joined to the Red Army. One day a brisk team of MVD officers appeared in our camp and announced that they were going to "screen" the hundreds of civilian refugees whom we were sheltering as camp followers. Our Slovakian officer protested: "You may not question these people about their politics. They were refugees from the Nazis and that is all we care about."

The chief of the new Red mission looked embarrassed.

"We're not looking for civilians, Comrade," he said. "It's Red Army deserters that we're after."

Eighty thousand Russians had deserted in Hungary alone before the end of 1944, and thousands more were disappearing in the areas where we camped. They were young boys, many of them, dazzled by the richness of life outside the USSR and eager to share the "luxuries" they saw in the simple villages of Slovakia and Bohemia. But some of them were bitter, older men who had been plotting for many years how to make their escape from the giant concentration camp that Russia had become; the war, to them, was like the opening of a prison door.

The good-hearted villagers of Slovakia and Hungary often tried to hide such men. Some of the deserters married local girls and hoped to lose themselves in the farms and villages. Others took to the forest, forming small, marauding bands which occasionally swept into the towns on a raiding party and seized provisions from frightened villagers at the point of a gun.

One night, when I was fast asleep in camp, I awoke to find a Christian Partisan shaking me.

"Wake up," he whispered urgently. "Wake up but make no noise."

I rose and started to follow him outside the hut. "Your medicines," he whispered. I went back and got my kit.

We gathered our skis and had made our silent way past the sentry and the sleeping camp before we spoke again.

"What is it?" I asked him.

"A message from Carl," he said. "I don't know what it means. He begged me to bring you to him at rendezvous Number 3."

The woods were narrow here; after a half-hour's walk,

the fields lay bare and open to the moon. We put on our skis and raced across the snow. When we arrived at the appointed spot, Carl, a young Catholic villager who did us secret services, was waiting.

"I didn't dare call the doctor in the town," he said. "The trouble is this: a Russian Army deserter has been hiding in my cousin's home for over a month. He lives above the barn and food is taken to him secretly. You know why. With the town in the hands of the Reds, he'd hardly live a day out of hiding. But tonight he became very ill; we were afraid that he might die. I could not think of anyone but you we dared to trust."

"But Carl," I said, "we cannot arrive, like this, at dawn, with no excuse to give the Red guards. They will surely follow us."

"No, no," he said. "I have arranged all that. My cousin's daughter has a friend who is expecting a baby soon. We took her into the conspiracy. She is now in bed at my cousin's house, ready to groan as if she were in childbirth if the Red soldiers become too inquisitive.

"Your story is that you have come to help her with a premature birth. I'll say that I called you because you are a doctor famous all over the world for cases like hers."

I smiled. Carl was scarcely fifteen; in normal times he would have been reading the novels of Alexandre Dumas, not contriving, on his own, such *Three Musketeers* plots as this.

But it was a successful plan. The Red sentry stopped us as we entered town; we told him Carl's yarn. He let us pass.

When I got to the cousin's house, I was led past a radiantly healthy mother-to-be and into the hayloft where a young man in civilian rags lay suffering the atrocious pains that go with an acute appendix.

It was not an ideal setting for a sterile emergency operation, yet we dared not move the hunted man outside the barn. I sent for boiling water and I spread my little kit of instruments on a clean towel. Then, with the help of the rising sun, I operated on a boy whose name I never knew, whose final fate is still unknown to me.

But he did not die that night or in the following week; so much I know. I was able to save his threatened life from the enemy of infection, which was closer to him at the time than all the Nazis and the Communists.

But not many of the Red deserters escaped. The Benes government of Czecho-Slovakia agreed to repatriate any Russian deserters found in their territory and to let the MVD conduct its own thorough search for them. Many of the Russian deserters walked twenty, even fifty miles inside Slovakia before daring to take a train. When they did, they found that even there the dreaded Russian Secret Police patrolled every train that moved. The Russian deserters had rarely been able to arrange papers that would pass muster with the MVD; they were rounded into concentration camps on the Russian border and shipped as slaves into Siberia. They are there today.

CHAPTER 7

How the Nazis Almost Won Russia

BUT not all the Russians deserted; the Red Army fought valiantly at Stalingrad, as all the world knows. On my own sector the soldiers attacked the enemy with a ferocity and a selflessness worthy of soldiers of any army in the world. Yet these were the same men who hated the conditions of their peacetime life and longed to see the overthrow of their government. Why, then, did any of them fight?

I asked many of the men in our Russian unit what made them so ferocious against the Germans and why, when they were given a chance of assignment to the rear, they insisted on combat service instead. Yascha fought so bitterly because he could not forget the day when his young sister had been carried off by the Germans to serve as one of their Army's forced camp followers. Koli lugged his heavy machine gun up hills with an extra energy because his grandfather, his mother and one of his brothers had been hanged by the Germans when they took his town. Kostia was a frightful fighter, cruel, pitiless and impossible to restrain. Whenever he came near the unarmed German prisoners he killed them.

Why? He was remembering an episode near Kiev. The Storm Troopers had lined up all the Jewish women in his town, completely naked, many of them bearing babies in their arms. They had stood them on the edge of a vast mass grave, shot them in the back and let the weight of their bodies topple them down into the mud below.

Hatred of the Germans was the strongest incentive among the Red soldiers in the combat lines. That there should have been such a feeling among them was proof of an atrocious Nazi blunder which has not been sufficiently understood. For there was a moment when the entire country of Russia lay open before them. There was a chance, which they missed. There was a time when they—or any other invader—would have been welcomed by the masses of the people as liberators from the hated rule of the Soviet.

Among millions of Russians—how many millions we may not know for years—the government of Stalin was and is a desperately hated thing. Soldiers of the Red Army have let the fact be guessed whenever they have been in contact with foreign armies long enough to exchange confidences with them. Ask the American aviators who were in the Aleutians how often they were told by Red Army soldiers: "Tell your government to liberate *us* from tyranny, after you have freed the Chinese and the French."

All of us who have been in battle with the Red Army know.

"We live in fear," the Russians would whisper to us. "We are all prisoners in a gigantic concentration camp within the borders of our country. The MVD has terrorized us. We dare not speak our minds even to the members of our own families when we are at home. The threat of the firing squad or of a slower death in Siberia is always over us. Life at the front is hard, but it is freer than life inside the Soviet."

But weren't these men fighting valiantly *for* the Soviet? No. They were not. They were fighting for their homeland, Russia.

The Communists in power, soon after the Germans had attacked, saw that their only hope of rousing the Russian citizenry was to declare this a holy war, a nationalistic war, a war in which an alien culture was attempting to enslave the noble Slavs. The phrase "rival ideologies" disappeared from the controlled press, as you can see in any library of the world. Instead, *Pravda* and *Izvestia* rallied the people to a national war.

It was only after the victory had been secured that the Communist Party was thrust forward again. Then, in the spring of 1945, the official tone began to change. I saw it in the official Army newspaper, which was issued to our Russian friends. Glowing editorials began to attribute every victory to the "superior dialectics" of the Russians and, in stereotyped phrases, to "the military genius" of Stalin.

But the soldiers were not duped. One day I was sitting in the early spring sunshine with a group of Russian soldiers. All of us were engaged in scraping mud off our boots and uniforms and in cleaning our guns. One of the Party's official propagandists thought that he would make use of this opportunity; he began to quote the stale old phrases about the war. It was the "Communist Party spearhead" which had won, he said. It was the "brilliant strategy of our giant dialecticians against the decadent mentality of the capitalist West."

The Russian soldiers grimly wiped the mud from their equipment. For a while none of them spoke. They ignored his impassioned, gramophone-record speech about the genius of Stalin—until even he lost confidence and his voice began to hesitate.

Then one of the soldiers walked up to the commissar and stared him in the eyes.

"Vassili," he said, "what makes you talk such nonsense? You know better than that and so do we. You, the Communists, have won the war? Don't make me laugh! It's we, the Russians, who are winning it.

"Who made the pact with Hitler which made the whole war possible from the start? You and your clever Communists. Who stayed behind in Moscow at cozy desk jobs while the rest of us were dying in the mountain snow? You and your Communists.

"You've lied to us for nearly thirty years. You told us that the Communist revolution was ready to take place in every country, and that all we had to do was to chase the Germans out of Europe. Then everybody would go Communist and become our friend. That's a lie. None of the people in these countries we've occupied want Communism; when you've managed to get them to accept it, it's been because they are afraid of Stalin. Like us.

"And here's another lie you've told us, Vassili. You've said that the proletariat outside of Russia were treated like dogs—kicked, starved, beaten. Well, we've met this proletariat and what do you think? They wear leather shoes just like commissars at home. They have beds with mattresses, like favored Party members. They eat better than we do, and when they don't like their national leader, they throw him out."

All the other men had dropped their work to listen. They nodded with approval and gathered in a somewhat menacing circle around Vassili. It was no moment for swaggering or threats; these men were heavily armed. He said a weak, "Well . . ." and wandered away.

Vassili did not dare take action then; in a combat area one cannot safely infuriate the soldiers of the line. But I knew that the names of all these boys would be added to the growing black list of the malcontents and I shuddered for them. The first postwar purge, held at the frontier as the troops returned, gathered up the most outspoken of such men and sorted them from the rest. The boys who spoke out that morning are all either dead or in Siberia today.

Such Russian soldiers knew the risks they ran when they contradicted the Communist representatives. Of course they did. But sometimes under the stress of deep emotion, they risked their lives in order to speak out. Danger had become so familiar a companion that even Stalin and the MVD lost their familiar fearfulness.

But it was more often when they were alone with foreigners that the Russians spoke up. And it was not always the private soldiers who expressed their hatred of the Communist government. Sometimes higher ranking officers, men who had been rewarded by the Soviets with high responsibilities, were quite as frank in expressing their distaste.

In the midst of one of our advances through the winter snowdrifts, I ventured close to the line of fire to set up my First Aid station. At the height of the battle, while mortars and shells were raining heavily about our position, I crept with several Russian officers into one of the little underground shelters where warm tea was being made. Colonel Ivan, who was in charge, was too tired to talk; he stretched out on the fir branch couch, his heavy overcoat spread over him. But Commandant Piotr, Commandant Andre and I began to poke at the small fire and to talk. As it happened, both these men had been present a little earlier when the Russian private had "blown his top" to the Party propagandist. The matter was weighing heavily on both their minds.

Commander Piotr was the first to speak. Kneeling down and fumbling through his knapsack for the precious little sacks of tea, he flung out at us, "That boy was right! He will be shot for speaking, but he was right."

He went on bitterly: "I knew this war would be the greatest tragedy in Russia's history. Look at the irony of it—in order to save the country we love, we have had to fight for the Communists. The war saved the Party autocrats and all the little servile, whining bureaucrats who follow them. And *we* won it for them!"

As he waited for the water to boil, he poured out his heart.

"You have been with us a long time, Comrade," he said to me. "You have surely learned by now that the Red Army was disgusted with the Communists long before the German attack. We loved our country, but we hated our politicians. And at first, the war looked like the opportunity we had been waiting for.

"You must understand that never in history has anyone figured out a way by which the people of a country can be liberated in a Police state without the assistance of a foreign war. Never. No matter how many people are against a regime (and surely 90 per cent of the Russians are anti-Stalinist today) it is impossible to launch a successful conspiracy in times of peace. The MVD are everywhere, and they are utterly ruthless. On a mere suspicion of opposition to Stalin, they will massacre an entire village, or send a hundred thousand men to the Siberian wastes. Twenty million men and women may be in those camps today. So long as Stalin has the secret police on his side, even the Army cannot successfully rebel against him."

He spoke coldly, with a fierce understatement that was more impressive than the loftiest oratory.

Andre, who had been silently staring at the flames, interrupted him.

"He will not understand, Piotr," he said tiredly. "You sound like a traitor when you speak that way. No foreigner can understand unless he has lived twenty years under the Terror. Listen, my friend! Our greatest national menace lives within the Kremlin. Stalin is Russia's greatest enemy. He, and his gangsters. They are not even Communists any more. They retain the Marxist tag, but they do nothing to bring about the day when, according to their own Leninism, the State should 'wither away.' Instead of that, every move they make is calculated to strengthen the power of this little group of tyrants who administer it selfishly and for their own perpetuation.

"Our concentration camps are growing larger every year. Our rich Russian earth is being impoverished, so that famine has become the normal thing. Our churches have been dynamited. Our science has become corrupt. Our learning is a wretched, crippled thing; no man may teach a truth which does not accord with the political purposes of these gangsters who have seized our country's throat. We cannot breathe in such an atmosphere of slavery.

"You speak of liberating France, Norway, the countries overrun by the Nazi armies, and it is well; they must be freed. But we, too, want liberation. Oh, my friend, when will the outside world understand that we want liberation, too?"

"We thought that we might get it, early in the war," said Piotr rapidly. He lit his long Russian cigarette and took a deep puff at it. "One of our best marshals, a man with an enormous following, conceived the plan, and the greater part of the Army was eager to follow it. His principle was simple: the first enemy to be crushed is Stalin. The second, Hitler. The plan was that we should permit the Germans to come deep into the country; many of our units agreed to surrender voluntarily to the Germans. The rest would, for the moment, pretend loyalty to Stalin.

"The plot won the acceptance of key men in every division of the Army: its outlines were simple. A secret mission was to establish contact on the very highest levels with the British and American governments. The Allies were to synchronize their military movements with our own. On a chosen day the Army, which had remained in apparent loyalty, would stage a giant rebellion: Stalin and his circle would be seized, the government overthrown. Simultaneously, the Allies were to divert the German strength, so that our imprisoned armies might overthrow the weakened Nazi garrisons left to fight with them. Remember, our divisions of the west were to act, outwardly, as allies of the Germans; they would therefore be armed.

"Then the two sections of the Russian Army were to join forces and, assisted by the British and Americans, attack the Germans from all sides and end the war. A brave plan? Yes, and one to which our shrewdest and most famous generals had agreed."

"We began the first phase of the plan," Andre told me. "No one will ever be able to understand the behavior of the Russian Army in the early weeks of the war unless he knows of the plot.

"You see, we knew the German attack was coming: the best Russian Army Intelligence officers were in on the scheme, and they warned us. That is the reason we were deployed along the western frontiers. That is the reason why, three days before the expected attack, we deliberately ordered trucks, tanks and heavy artillery dismantled and sent off 'for repair.' We wished to be caught *without* the necessary equipment to repulse the Nazi attack.

"And when the Germans did attack, we made things as easy as possible for them. Bridges which should obviously have been destroyed were, under one pretext or another, left intact; this was so that the Nazis could more easily penetrate beyond the frontiers. Jumbled, contradictory orders came to every combat unit. Oh, we arranged things nicely for the Germans—whole Russian armies were surrounded by the enemy on all sides. And these Red armies, following our secret understanding, surrendered as a whole."

"And then what?" I asked in astonishment. "What went wrong?"

The two men joined in a bitter chuckle.

"What went wrong? Just what had been going wrong in Germany for ten years: the Nazi psychology. Listen. If the Germans had behaved in our country as they did in France, if they had been ordered to behave 'correctly' here, too, the plan would have succeeded. But the German generals in command of the east were of another type than those who took Paris. The men Berlin sent us had no conception of winning over the local people. Instead, they launched a brutal campaign of terror. Rosenberg had told them that the Slavs were a decadent and inferior people, that our very name fitted us to be slaves. Very well, the Germans would treat us like slaves. They would literally decimate our race. And that is what they tried to do."

The two men sank their heads deep on their chests as they fed the little fire.

"The massacring of whole populations was beyond description. These Nazi soldiers, who seemed so well-disciplined in France, acted like madmen here. The people were herded about like cattle, shunted off to man the German war factories; gathered up and roped together in the fields, the streets; torn apart, forever, from their families. The relatives left behind began to hate the Germans with a hatred next to which their loathing of Stalin was only a mild distaste. For Stalin's atrocities had affected, perhaps, ten to twenty dissidents in their village. The Nazis slaughtered everyone they saw."

"And the Red armies," broke in Andre. "Do not forget the Red armies. Our soldiers who had surrendered were not left armed to reorganize the revolution against the Comintern. Not at all. Our men were put on trucks and shipped to Poland, sealed in suffocating cattle cars and shunted on to the German work camps. The suffering in transit is indescribable. The sick and the well, the living and the dead were locked in a horrible embrace for weeks of slow travel. No food, no sanitation was permitted in these cars. It was the technique the Germans had worked out earlier for cutting down the size of the

Jewish population within their country. They used it, now, to break the spirit of the captured prisoners of war."

"But you have heard about the battle of Gomel—in Russia," said Piotr, suddenly. "You, Doctor, must have heard of that—the most frightful incident of this campaign."

Yes, I had known men who were at Gomel. It was in the summer of 1941.

A huge encirclement of the Russian Army had taken place by deliberate order of the Russian officers; two hundred thousand Russians surrendered en masse to the Germans. Even the efficient Nazis were embarrassed at having so many prisoners to guard and disarm. The men were allowed to remain in their old camps, disarmed, while they waited for the Germans to dispose of them. Then the ominous sealed cattle cars rolled down the siding: the first units of Russians were jammed into them more tightly than animals going to market, and the train disappeared. For several weeks this ceremony continued; the camps were thinning out. Only twenty-four thousand Russian prisoners remained.

Then orders came from the German rear: the trains were too valuable for this purpose. They would not be back again. Twenty-four thousand Red Army prisoners remained.

My friend was grim when he got to this portion of the story. "At that moment," he said, "a smart staff car arrived; out of it stepped a group of high SS officers. They disappeared for a long conference with the local staff. The results of the discussion were learned soon enough. German machine-gun units surrounded the camps where the prisoners were still billeted. Then they opened fire. I myself heard the cries of agony from those camps, rising high and staccato above the noise of the guns. After half an hour it was all over. The earth was richly soaked with Russian blood.

"Think of it! To the Nazi commanders our lives are of less importance than the wear and tear on a fleet of army trucks!"

Remembering what I knew of this battle all too well, for the scene had haunted my nights, I picked up the thread of what Piotr was saying.

"The Germans forced our people to resist when they committed such horrors. They made themselves so hated that it was impossible even to dream of a temporary collaboration with them. The plundering, the frequent rape, the hangings of villagers—sometimes two hundred at a time in a single bit of woods—was too much for us.

"That was when we of the Red Army decided we must fight. The very men who had hatched the plan changed it—they could not expose their beloved Russia to any more of this, nor allow the Nazis to penetrate into the country at such a cost.

"For the Nazis, we saw, had not come to change the regime. They had come to exterminate the Slavs—to wipe off the face of the globe all men and women of Russian or Ukrainian blood. It was the dreadful Rosenberg race theory in action. We had seen it directed against the Jews before the war. Now it was being applied to our own people. What could we do but fight?"

"I remember," said Andre, "how the word spread from mouth to mouth in those weeks. Orders came to us, secret orders from the marshal and the generals who had been directing the earlier plan, telling us that now we must change: we must fight the Germans and fight them in earnest. But the orders were not needed. Spontaneously the Russian Army had abandoned the game of pretense on which so many hopes were based. We knew that our political freedom would have to wait: Hitler had become the enemy to be vanquished first."

"That's when the resistance started," said Piotr. "It was in 1942. Guerrilla bands of Russians sprang up behind the German lines to harass and murder them. The armies showed the old spirit that had stopped Napoleon on his march to Moscow: descendants of the same despised moujiks emerged with the same scythes and hatchets, torches and antique guns to fight the Nazis. A shudder seemed to run through the Army; soldiers who had been lackadaisical the week before were now cold and merciless men of war.

"The Army came of age. Brilliant young officers rose from the ranks. New strategies were devised. Men who had never courted favor with the Communists were now leading the fight; the Russian authorities did not trust them, but they were glad to use their talents. Generals who despised the Stalinists began to lead the war. Run over the list of the high officers who saved Stalingrad. They are not Party men!"

"So," broke in Andre, "that is why our friend today thought it worthwhile to have his throat cut so that the truth might, for once, issue through it before he died. He and men like him know the score as well as the high-ranking officers; they are as bitter as the generals with medals dangling at their breasts. For our victories were not won by the Communists with their corruption, their favoritism, their self-seeking squabbles and conspiracies.

The victories were won by Russians fighting for Russia."

"The Communists are still a little afraid of the Army," Piotr said, as he poked again at the fire. "That is why, you will notice, the Party propaganda is now playing up the role of the workmen in the war plants, giving *them* the credit for the victory. The Communists are trying to soft-pedal the achievements of the Army. They know that the Army belongs to the people, and that it cannot be trusted to support them."

Piotr rose and stretched. "That's why, my friend," he said, "you see the Party line already speaking out against the British and the Americans. You'll notice every sneaking little commissar around this camp is breathing fire against the countries that have been our allies, warning us that a showdown war with the capitalists' lands is a necessity. Hatred of the Germans saved them once. Hatred of the British and Americans might save them again. That is their hope."

Andre repacked his little parcel and closed the buckle on his knapsack.

"Oh, those British and Americans," he said. "If only they would keep going past Berlin, past Prague and march on into Moscow—march as friends and liberators, not as an enemy! What a welcome would greet them when they stepped on Russian soil! How the Army would embrace them! How the cruel, powerful state would topple, if the people knew that someone was coming in to rescue us from the MVD. You would see such a popular uprising—such mass heroism—as the world has never known in history!

"But I don't suppose they'll come. There were Teheran, Yalta and the pacts signed there."

They were melancholy phrases as he said them.

My friends were accurate in their prediction. Since the end of hostilities, the regime has liquidated its most brilliant military men. During the war, military skill was the first necessity; after the fighting was over, Party hacks were pushed into high military positions and capability was no longer held to be of such great importance as "loyalty" to the Marxist code. The men who won the war against Germany—it will bear being repeated again—were not confirmed Communists.

Who were the real heroes, and where are they? General Vatutin was the man who launched the great offensive of 1944 and whose army first broke through to Poland; his popularity with the Russian people was enormous. He has "died," and few inside Russia believe that this was really "of wounds," as the official report vaguely stated.

Marshal Zhukov held command of all the Soviet troops in Germany; he was worshiped as the savior of the motherland. But he was no Communist. As a result, he was not given the supreme Command in the Eastern theater after V-E Day, as everyone had expected. No military genius was required against the Japanese; the Soviet strategy was to allow the Americans to win our Asia war, to enter it only at the eleventh hour, to reap its spoils. So the honor of commanding the Far Eastern theater was awarded to Marshal Vasilevski, a man "of the regime." Zhukov was sent to the unimportant local command of Odessa; later he disappeared. The list could be made longer—the pattern is the same.

There were other highly placed men whose involvement in the plan is no secret today. General Vlasov was one; he fought against the Red Army, then liberated Prague from the Nazis. After the end of the war he surrendered his divisions to the U.S. Army at Pilsen and was turned over by them to the Russian Communists, who hanged him after court-martial. There was General Zhelnikov, who passed with his armies to the Germans. But men of every rank were involved; the officers who told me of the plan believed that more than a million Red Army men would have surrendered to the Nazis if the program had been carried through, and that another million, in sympathy with them, would have remained apparently loyal to Stalin but ready to turn upon the Communists as soon as the Germans had lost the war.

What armies were involved? There is nothing to be lost by telling now. A Russian Front is a unit made up of several full armies; it numbers from two hundred thousand to half a million men. Involved in the anti-Stalinist plot in 1941 were sections of the First and Second Ukrainian Fronts, the First and Third Baltic Fronts and units of several more.

This is history now—one of the sadder chapters in the history of World War II. In Washington in 1948 I heard the story again from a lieutenant-general of the U.S. Army, who had obtained the same information from a member of the German General Staff while he was waiting trial at Nuremberg.

"The Russians received us like brothers and liberators," said the German. "The Reichwehr had no opposition at all. But then the fools at home sent in the boys of their Military Government: they were under orders from that civilian, Rosenberg: he had now been made Minister for the Ostland. He was burning to turn eastern Europe into one big German colony. He wanted to kill off the native population first.

"He lost the eastern war."

Were the Red Army plotters traitors? I do not think so: they were playing a desperate double game, but their goal and hope was always liberation of their country from a cruel despot. If they are guilty for having accepted evil allies in fulfilling a noble aim, then we all have sinned: for England, the United States and all the Allied governments in exile accepted the help and friendship of Stalin's totalitarian state in 1941. Winston Churchill greeted the Communists as his allies within a few hours of the German attack on Russia. Is it so hard to understand why the non-Communist Russian generals sought the temporary triumph of the German Army to unseat the tyrants who had enslaved their land for many years?

CHAPTER 8

I Learn of the Underground "Plan"

THE RED ARMY was bitterly anti-Communist; even the dullest of us foreigners had discovered that. But it is never enough to know what a man hates; you must also know what he loves. The important fact about the anti-Communist resistance is its positive goal: the leaders who spark the underground movement and keep it alive are not Trotskyites or Social Democrats, capitalists or followers of the Czar. They are religious men and they wish to build a Christian social order.

I am not the only observer to have discovered how faith motivates the Russian heart today. A Latvian colonel whom I knew was captured by a group of Russians during the 1940 war; their officer took him at the point of a gun out of sight of the rest. He said to him, "We shoot our prisoners on this front."

"Very well," said my friend. "Shoot me. I will uncover the target and make it easier for you to aim."

He unbundled his heavy fur-lined trench coat, opened the shirt beneath it and stood, bare-chested, at a short range from the Red officer. He waited. No shot was fired.

"Why don't you shoot?" he asked him wonderingly.

"I cannot fire at *that,*" said the captain. He pointed to the crucifix around the colonel's neck, exposed when he opened his blouse. "Run. I will turn my back. Run and God bless you."

I talked to other men who had had such experiences with the Red Army in towns I never visited. A Polish girl was asked by a Russian lieutenant to find him holy pictures: he offered to pay for them with a diamond ring. A nun in Hungary was offered extra food rations by a Red colonel if she would bring him a book of Russian prayers.

I visited an abbey in the eastern areas of Hungary, where our Red Army divisions were in control. The abbot looked at my uniform and said, "You are a Partisan. Are you also a Communist?"

"No, Father," I said to him. "I am a Catholic."

"I am beginning to believe that one is sometimes both," he said. "Listen to what happened here the day before yesterday."

A Red Army captain had come to him, he said, and had asked to see him alone. The boy was very young, very brash, very conscious of his role as conqueror. When he had been led to a small conference room, and the door was closed, he nodded towards the crucifix that hung on the wall.

"You know that thing is a lie," he said to the abbot. "It's just a piece of trickery you priests use to delude the poor people and make it easier for the rich to keep them ignorant. Come, now. We are alone. Admit to me that you never really believed that Jesus Christ was God."

The abbot smiled. "But, my poor young man, of course I believe it. It is true."

"I won't have you play these tricks on me," said the captain. "This is serious. Don't laugh at me."

He drew out his revolver and held it close to the body of the abbot.

"Unless you admit to me that it is a lie, I'll fire."

"I cannot admit that, for it is not true. Our Lord is really and truly God," said the abbot.

The captain flung his revolver onto the floor and embraced the holy man. Tears sprang to his eyes.

"It is true!" he cried. "It is true! I believe so, too, but I could not be sure men would die for this belief until I found out for myself. Oh, thank you, my Father. You have strengthened my faith. Now I, too, can die for Christ. You have shown me how."

For when the floodgates break at last, and a religious fervor which has been dammed for nearly thirty years breaks forth, there is apt to be a torrent of emotion. The Russians are a passionate people. Their religion is no lukewarm affair of Sunday services and weekday forgetfulness. When once they have decided to take risks for their religion, they may be madly reckless in the chances that they run.

But there is another aspect to the resistance movement: the faith of these men has borne very practical fruit. I learned of this only when the war was drawing to an end.

The news from the west told us of astounding victories as the American and British Armies drove the once insuperable Germans across the fields of France. The Luftwaffe had been destroyed. The buzz bombs showering England had come too late to affect the final victory. On our own front, large units were being moved to Russia for trans-shipment to Manchuria, where another war had still to be won.

The soldiers now openly discussed the coming "march on Moscow." Except among the full-fledged Communists, it was taken for granted that the American and British Armies would push on past the Russian frontier and enter Russia to destroy the Communist regime.

"Churchill and Roosevelt know Stalin must go," the Russians assured each other. "You'll see—as soon as Hitler is out of the way, our time will come."

Most of the soldiers planned only for liberation. They were moved by a longing to see their land released from a tyranny which had caused so much misery and suffering. They did not ask too inquisitively what system of government would replace the Politburo when the Communists had been overthrown by Allied arms.

But some of our campfire conversations now began to turn to the far future, to the day when Russia would again have her own sovereign government, after the British and American Armies had withdrawn. What kind of rule would Russia choose as successor to the Stalin dictatorship?

Vassilyi was a young major who had studied sociology at the University of Leningrad. One winter afternoon as four or five of us sat, still waiting for the Army truck that should have picked us up at dawn, Vassilyi said to me,

"Are you a capitalist?"

I laughed.

"No," I said. "I am no capitalist, Comrade. I have lived in capitalist countries and I know the evils and injustices of the system as well as the Communists do."

"That is good," he said. "For we do not want capitalism in Russia. And the time is coming soon when we shall have to make this clear to our liberators in London and Washington. They may find it difficult to understand."

A young lieutenant chimed in.

"Why worry about that now?" he asked. "Capitalism is better than Communism, anyway. Wouldn't you rather have your children grow up under a system such as they have in Czecho-Slovakia than what we have in Russia?"

"Yes," said Vassilyi. "Capitalism is less cruel than Stalinism. But it still is not good enough. There is a better way. Have you seen this?"

He handed me a tattered mimeographed sheet which said, in Russian, "Plan for Peasant Co-operatives."

"Take it and read it," he said. "You will see that we have not been completely stupefied by these years under the dictatorship. Some of us have gone on thinking. We think ours is a better plan."

This bulletin was the first of many that I was to study with extreme interest—such interest that, when I entered Russia, its author was the man whom I was most eager to meet. Now, in the midst of the war, I became aware of a broad social conspiracy linked with the religious underground of which I already knew.

The Christians are the salt of the Russian earth, but they are only its salt. They are the leaven in the mass,—but they are not the whole mass. I discovered now another section of the anti-Communist resistance movement: the nonsocialist intelligentsia.

In western Europe, just as in America, the beliefs of the intelligentsia have little practical effect: You are pragmatists, men who act first and theorize afterwards. But the Slav is not like that. He begins every act of his life with a doctrine; he cannot separate intellectual conviction from the performance that clothes its logic. Lenin was a true Slav. He read Marx' program and found it intellectually convincing. At once he said, "*Réalisez-le.*" ("Let us bring it about.") It was characteristic of Russians that their thinkers, months before the end of the war, were hammering out the smallest details of the plan for Russia's post-Communist economy. To their way of thinking, the forthcoming revolution was a mere preliminary. The great question was, "What kind of economic system will best fit the needs of modern man?"

Vassilyi and I had many talks. When he found that I had taught sociology he begged me to repeat to him my lectures on the social theories of Jean-Jacques Rousseau and Adam Smith, of Vilfredo Pareto and Ortega y Gasset and any other names of which he had heard. But there was little I could teach him; he had steeped himself in modern social thought as few professors of the West have done.

"Take the problem of machinery," he would say. "You agree with me that it can be made to serve man? You do not wish, like Ghandi, to return to the hand-loom? You are not, like Chesterton, a distributist?"

I admitted that machinery had a future in the world.

"Then," Vassilyi would say, "the problem is one that social thinkers must solve in a new way. Always, until now, the machine has been the property of the few: with us, they are the politicians who control the state; in capitalist countries, they are the rich. Either way is wrong; the machine concentrates too much power in the hands of too few men.

"We believe in personal property. We believe in the individual and his rights against the state. But we believe that some new method of purchase and ownership must be worked out to control the large and expensive pieces of machinery the industrial age requires."

Vassilyi pleaded for co-operatives: the peasants should be given back their land. But the individual peasant could not farm efficiently without a tractor—yet he could not afford to buy a tractor from the profits of a few hectares. Who should give him a tractor?

"The co-operative," Vassilyi would say. "The peasants' co-operative will own the large farm machinery. The industrial workers will own the factory machines. The state will own nothing. It will act as a referee between those citizens or groups who get into disputes. And it will do even this only in accord with written laws, which are difficult to change."

"Suppose," I said to him once, "suppose the individual Russian gets in the way of one of your co-operatives. Will you liquidate him for the good of the whole, as the Communists do?"

"Never," he said. "The rights of the rebel must be preserved. The individual will be sacred with us. There will be no Siberian prison camps. Never. Never again."

Vassilyi put me in touch with other members of the intellectual resistance. In the last period of the war, I rarely missed the monthly mimeographed bulletins in which these theorists of the New Russia exchanged their views.

One of the intellectuals in the movement was a Major Grigori, whom I met at Miskolc.

Sitting in a small, smoky cafe and drinking vodka late one night, I asked him to explain to me how the movement had begun. Grigori looked around him and called over the balalaika player. "Play something noisy," he told him.

Under cover of the music Grigori explained to me how some of the members of the intelligentsia had worked.

"At the time of the revolution," he said, "many of the non-Marxist professors sided with the revolution against the Czars; they saw the need for a change in Russia and they hoped the Leninist group would later moderate its views. These men were allowed to keep their positions, for there were too few dyed-in-the-wool Communists to fill the schools.

"But as time went on and the enormities of the Communist dictatorship grew, many of the professors became enemies of the government. Some of them spoke out and were sent into exile. Others kept silent and organized the intellectual underground.

"My professor of sociology was one of these."

He paused and sang a snatch of chorus with the balalaika. "We must not appear to be too serious here," he said.

Then Grigori went on.

"These men have had to teach Marxism in their classrooms," he said. "There was no other way. But they gathered a few students from every class to whom they taught forbidden theories. Some of their old textbooks were still available in the first years of the Communist rule: these have circulated secretly ever since. Other, newer books on social theory are smuggled in, usually from Finland; they are stripped of their covers and concealed in many harmless-looking packages. Oilcans are a favorite hiding place. Sometimes the important pages are torn from a book and pasted inside the covers of a volume which the Soviet custom guards will pass: books on medicine or physics are often used as a blind.

"So our professors have kept in touch with the outside world. We managed to get Sorokin's book and Hayek's, the writings of Don Sturzo, Haushofer's writings and the American textbook of Berle and Means. We have not been completely cut off from the thinking of the past two decades: good and bad, liberal and despotic, true and false, much of it has found its way to us. Some of the important foreign writings have been translated and secretly mimeographed. There is a secret Russian edition of the Papal Encyclicals *Rerum Novarum* and *Forty Years After*.

"Out of all these years of study and thought some of our leaders in the intellectual resistance have formed their plan."

The "plan"—it seemed at first to have no other name—became a little clearer to me with every such conversation, and a little more impressive. These brave and brilliant men of the intelligentsia have worked side by side with the Christian underground; there has been a valuable exchange of views. The religious group has played a great part in forming the "plan," with its insistence on the sacredness of the individual, its emphasis on the rights of the family against the state.

Reading these bulletins I saw the emergence of a humanist social theory more truly Christian in spirit than any that has ever existed on this earth. The "plan" avoids the error of John Locke, who substituted the divine right of property for the divine right of kings. It avoids the superstition of Adam Smith, who thought that every man's selfishness contributes to the collective good. It admits the necessity for a moral frame of reference in the economic sphere. It brands as evil both avarice and usury (which the capitalist world has never done) but it grants to each man economic and spiritual freedom (as the feudal and corporate states have never done).

The "plan" has reached all groups in the Russian resistance movement while the intellectuals debate its finer points of theory. The trade union leaders within Russia, the nationalist and separatist groups, the Red Army opposition, the disillusioned soldiers returning from the west, these men and women have all some knowledge of the "plan." They circulate it with enthusiasm—it is their own Declaration of Independence from the evils of the past.

I have been handed the mimeographed bulletins by mysterious strangers inside Russia and out: I have been told fantastic stories of the way the sheets are prepared. The same mimeographing outfit is never used twice: the bulletins are run off in factories and newspaper offices, in government offices and Party headquarters; wherever a few members of the conspiracy can gain half an hour's access to a machine. Besides the regular monthly bulletins, special issues are distributed to group leaders and to sections of the movement.

The "plan" is as detailed, today, as was the program of Lenin and Trotsky when they took over the power of government. But it is a better plan than the one they dreamed: it acknowledges the sacredness of man. It does not proclaim such sacredness for the state. It does not accord such sacredness to property.

The discovery of the "plan" heartened me; it gave evidence of a capacity for organization among the men of the resistance of which I had not been certain until then. But an even more inspiring contact came my way in the same early months of 1945. I had the luck to meet and learn to know well a Russian general who had played a hero's part in driving the Germans back—a man whose name I dare not disclose even now, when he is dead, for fear of reprisals against his family.

It was by great good fortune that I came to know this man so well. He was highly intelligent, widely read in whatever books were allowed to circulate in his country, avidly curious about events in the outside world. He had never become involved in politics before the war, nor joined the Party, whose leaders he considered the dregs of Russia. He came from Great Russia and he spoke the beautiful, sonorous speech of that region where, before the war, he had been a specialist in agronomy. Having no Party contacts, he had entered the war as a simple soldier, had been wounded several times and had made his way up through the ranks to his present position of great power by an extraordinary genius for strategy and military organization.

This general met me first in connection with my duties as doctor and sanitation officer. He drew me out, as he did all men who came from the "outside." When he found that I had once been a university professor before the war he said, "We must have many talks. For years I have longed for a chance to speak freely with an intelligent foreigner."

And so I spent many evenings sitting in the ramshackle farmhouse he had requisitioned as his headquarters. It was his habit to dismiss his aide and his servants. He knew that his household included at least one Party spy. Sometimes, for greater security, we set the radio going and spoke under cover of its noise. Once or twice, when the nights were mild, we walked out of doors, exchanging confidences under the crystal stars that stud those northern skies.

"We Russians are a religious people," he repeated to me many times. "The regime has had many failures in the past two decades; none has been more complete than the effort to destroy religion. There are areas near where I live in which a church service has not been held since 1920. But I could take you into homes there where a hidden icon is still brought out nightly for the family prayers.

"I could tell you of couples—young couples—who seek out the old people and beg them to try to remember the words of the Orthodox wedding ceremony, and to say it over them so that the marriage may be sanctified. Parents baptize their babies in Great Russia; there is a vast religious activity binding us all together. It is the one thing we can successfully conceal from the MVD: even they are unable to ferret out the fact that a man has begun his day's work with a silent prayer."

"Did the Communist Party suspect nothing of all this?" I asked him.

"I don't know," he said. "But I'll tell you who *did* know of it: the Gestapo."

My friend had been in several of the most active sectors in the early days of the Russian advance.

"The Nazis—atheists themselves, cynics, hypocrites—still had the wit to see that they would win over people most quickly if they gave them back the right to worship. So when they entered Russia, they opened our closed churches; they allowed Polish and Czech priests to accompany their armies over the borders and to set up altars in town halls of the occupied Russian towns.

Our people flocked gratefully to them. Nazis began making many friends among us by their apparent reverence and love of God.

"The Germans did not follow up this advantage. As you know, their soldiers, acting under contrary orders, were set loose to loot and rape and massacre; the early advantage was quickly lost. But the Communists, in those first weeks, had seen our people crowding to the churches; they were able to gauge the intensity of this religious hunger which had gone unsatisfied for years. And—most shocking to them—they saw that it was the young, as often as the old, who swarmed to Mass and took Communion.

"So the Communists decided that they could turn this strong religious fervor to account. They would tell the people that the old quarrel between State and Church had ended; that the Russian people, in driving out the Nazis, would also be driving out the enemy of Mother Russia, and that they might have back their God as a reward.

"It became a grim and cynical contest, then, between the two most godless governments in the world as to which should most successfully masquerade as the defender of the Russian God."

He spoke bitterly, now.

"I care about my religion," he said. "It was no joy to me to see it prostituted in this way by men who had a deep contempt for it. And yet I knew that the Russian authorities were right: we had to win the war. And they had chosen the only way of rallying the spiritual forces of the people."

He strode up and down his little room and flung himself down on a leather footstool, his leather cavalry boots making him look like some aristocratic figure out of Tolstoi's *War and Peace*.

"You know," he said, "I was quite aware of the duplicity which lay behind the whole move. And yet I have never been more touched, more deeply stirred, than when the proclamation of religious freedom was announced at Moscow, and we were asked to join in public prayers for our dear, desperately menaced land.

"We were on the Caucasian front on the day when the first Mass was said. I visited the nearest town. All the nearby churches had been destroyed many years ago, but there was an old, old priest left behind. That day he chanted the liturgy in a small hut outside the village walls. The fields were crowded with people—children seeing their first Mass, and parents who vaguely remembered the scene from twenty years or more ago, and old people, their eyes brimming as they heard the half-forgotten syllables of the liturgy. Among the crowd were many men in uniform—Red Army soldiers and Partisans and a scattering of higher officers. After Mass, the old priest came out and in a quavering voice he gave his benediction to the kneeling crowd. Tears came to all our eyes.

"And then," he said, "a strange thing occurred. The same impulse swept over all of us—an impulse to get closer to the priest, to get so close that a drop of his holy water might fall on our clothes, on our foreheads, on our souls. We became aware of the spiritual drought of many years.

"Something happened there, when the holy water touched us. We felt strong again; strong enough to go immediately into battle; strong enough to fight and die, without regret, to save our homeland. For she had again become our Holy Russia."

He was silent. Then, sitting upright on the cushion, his finger tips touching, he gazed into the distance and spoke again: "How wonderful that moment was! How wonderful it would have been if the change of heart on the part of our government had been an honest one! If our government officials had become converted in good faith, Russia would have no such trials ahead of her as the postwar period will bring. Good men, men who humbly knelt each week before a gentle Savior, could not keep the concentration camps filled, nor preach a doctrine of violence and hatred for the rest of the world. If the Communists had honestly changed, Russia might rise to very great heights under them. The truly idealistic portion of their program—their professed love of the poor, their pretended desire that all men receive equal opportunities—might then, at last, be more than propaganda promises never sincerely spoken.

"The good in the ideal of Communism cannot be realized until it is separated from the error and falsehoods in which it is embedded. But if the idealistic portion of the Communists' dream were grafted onto Christianity, what a spiritual marriage that would be!"

The general had yielded to the dreamer, the visionary who is not far beneath the surface in every Russian of good will.

"Our Church has become weakened through these years of persecution: she is a frail invalid today. We have had no young priests trained, no scholars developing our doctrine to fit the time. No, the Russian Orthodox

Church cannot rise from her sickbed to save my countrymen.

"That is why we shall need the help of the Catholic Church. The old historical quarrels seem so petty now. Shall we, today, hold apart from millions of fellow Catholics throughout the world because of a 'filioque' in their Creed which some bishops rejected a thousand years ago? No. We Russians, when our day of liberation comes, will happily put ourselves under the protection and tutelage of the Holy Father. Oh, if such an event may come about while I am here to see it!"

"And you think there is a chance of that?" I asked him.

"Of course there is a chance," he said impatiently. "Rid us of the little handful of despots in the Party, and the thing will come about of its own volition. You have seen enough of the Russians to realize that we are hungry for the old religion back. Give us back our churches; our Christianity will overflow into good works, motivated by a revived and passionate love of Christ.

"You have seen in these Catholic countries we have overrun the orphanages, the hospitals, the refuges of the poor. Let the good monks and nuns who run them here teach our young people how to set up such institutions on Russian soil, to care for the suffering who will be left over from this war. They will need the gentle handling that dedicated men and women give. And what a welcome change such hospices would be from the cold and 'rationalistic' places into which our homeless poor are shunted now, heart hungry, fed only on the husks of consolation which 'dialectical materialism' offers them!"

This conversation was not one that I could easily forget. Did the general represent a sizable number of powerful fellow Russians in the Army? Did he and men like him stand in the position of "transmission belts," in Communist language—men through whom a vital Christianity might be spread to the millions of non-Communist Russians who were praying for a change of government?

I began to believe it was true. So many of the Russian officers had come to me with problems which were, at bottom, spiritual; they had come to me, not guessing that I was a priest, but only because they had found that I was not afraid to speak of God. And it was for God that their hearts were hungry. Did I dare withhold from this general the truth about my identity? The risks of telling him were great, but I decided I would take them. One night, while we walked briskly through his garden to keep warm, I said to my friend:

"I can no longer withhold my confidence from you. My friend, I am a Catholic priest."

Startled, he looked at me as if I had gone mad.

"But you are a soldier, a medical officer," he said.

"That is my alias." Then I told him something of the chain of events which had brought me there. He was immensely interested. He begged me to be careful. He poured out a hundred questions of theology. Before we parted on that moonless night he asked me for my blessing.

My general knew, better than I, how dangerous it would have been had my identity been guessed by the commissars who spied upon the camp. They were everywhere. In spite of his high reputation as a soldier, his own life might have been in danger if the authorities had supposed that he was friendly with a Catholic priest. And I knew he would never betray me.

The general did not dare accompany us to our daily Mass or make any sign that he knew of the underground Christianity which flourished in our camp. But he said to me, rather shyly: "My friend, I am soon going back to my country. My military talents are no longer as valuable to the government as they were a year ago. With the war over, we soldiers will be more of a menace than an aid. I may be liquidated. I have not taken the Eucharist in many years. Is there any way that I might secretly receive Communion?"

I thought hard. It would have aroused suspicion among my faithful maquisards if I had failed to celebrate Mass with them on any day when I was in camp. And we are forbidden to celebrate Mass more than once a day. Except—I suddenly remembered—on one day. And that day was drawing near. For on Christmas, the birthday of our Lord, every priest enjoys the privilege of saying three Masses.

"In two weeks," I told the general, "you will receive your first Communion."

It was not easy to arrange. I heard his confession one night underneath the stars. I began to plan the rest.

To say a complete Mass for him still presented innumerable obstacles. He was surrounded by officers and aides. We might stroll up and down without exciting their attention, but for the Liturgy one must kneel and stand and perform many movements which would have attracted attention. A Christmas Mass requires more than half an hour; and I was determined that this Mass should be complete.

But as Christmas drew near the good Lord made it easy

for us. My general became ill—ill with a pleurisy which none of his household could suspect of being assumed. I spent long hours by his bedside, ministering to him as a doctor. On Christmas Eve I found him worse. I sent his weary aides to bed and said, "I will stay with him until he is safely asleep."

The camp became quiet early. By ten o'clock I was fairly sure that everyone was sleeping. At a little before twelve I went down to the kitchen to boil some water and make sure that no insomniac was prowling around the quiet house. Everything was still.

I returned to my patient. His eyes were very bright. Silently I held my watch for him to see; as the hands moved past the hour of twelve and Christmas Day was born, I leaned over him and began, in a low whisper, the Latin words, "*In nomine Patris,*" with which the Mass begins. Then, by his bedside, I celebrated the Mass as it was being celebrated in many thousands of churches at that moment throughout the Christian world. When I leaned over to give him the Host and to promise him eternal life, his eyes were bright with tears. I said a final prayer, turned down the light and slipped off to the other camp where my little congregation was awaiting me for the Dawn Mass, the second of the day.

My friendship with the general was never betrayed. When, later on, our units separated, he asked me, "Would you like to go to Moscow?" I told him I was eager to do so.

"I shall arrange it," he said. "We may become separated by the change of the war but you can always get a message through to me. And if I am still in a position of influence, I shall send you the documents that will bring you through.

"I want you to see Moscow," he said. "I believe that you can do a very great service to my motherland. If you study us at close hand and see how much our people long for liberation, you may be able to touch the hearts of the men in the West. We are dumb, silenced through fear. You shall be our voice."

CHAPTER 9

Secret Believers with the Reds

The Russian resistance movement can never be understood by those who study it solely in terms of the military shifts or the political connivings by which some of its leaders struggle to destroy the Communist control. These methods can fail and the underground will still survive, still live and grow. The resistance is not limited to any rigid program, it does not depend on propaganda or conspiracy alone. It is a spiritual thing. It is indomitable for one reason only—it is profoundly and passionately Christian. We know that "God and one are always a majority."

Not all the groups of the disaffected oppose the Communists on consciously religious grounds; but the whole movement is permeated with the inspiration of men and women who do believe. In the resistance, the Orthodox devout are the clearest thinkers, the bravest leaders, the planners least subject to dissipation or despair. And they are enormously helped by the fact that religion still lives in the hearts of millions of Russians who have never heard of any concrete "plan."

Although I suspected that this was true, I did not

understand its full significance at first. When I met the scattered Soviet troops who joined our forest Partisans in 1944 I moved very warily; I did not know how many of the soldiers had been infected by the antireligious campaign. I did not even dare make plans for an open celebration of Christmas that year; but the problem solved itself and in a curiously revealing way.

The Russian soldiers, who increased in numbers every week, brought with them a number of camp followers, girls who were given various menial jobs about the camp but whose real work with the Army was very often that of the prostitute. These girls were, I thought, much like the same women in a society which professed a rigid morality. They had the same brassy defiance, the same unspoken sense of being outcasts and the same noisy determination that no one should learn how much they minded it.

Sonia was such a girl. She worked in the kitchen, but her true occupation was amusing the Russian officers. And she was tireless in trying to allure the foreign maquis as well. Whenever we visited the soup kitchen, which we did if we had missed a regular meal, Sonia made herself a nuisance with her brazen overtures.

One day early in December I was waiting for the tea water to boil, while Sonia waged her usual campaign of seduction, singing provocative songs and making excuses to press close to us around the fire. I treated her, always, with such deference as only a great lady might have expected. This puzzled her: she had, until then, received kindness from men only as a prelude to lovemaking. Sonia was beginning to think. She said to me, "You ought to make me angry, but you don't," and left me in peace.

Then Sonia fell ill. I tended her and made a point of bringing small gifts each time I made a doctor's call. Now she no longer tried to flirt. One day she said to me, "You people are from a country where religion is open, aren't you?" "Yes, Sonia," I told her. "Well," she said, "that must be what makes the difference." She sighed, turned her face to the wall and I left her to her thoughts.

But a week later she sought me out. "Comrade Doctor," she said to me, "Christmas is drawing near. It will be sad here in the woods if we don't celebrate. You are a Christian: tell me. What can we do?"

"Well," I said to her, "you have a beautiful voice. Do you remember any Christmas songs?"

She thought. "Yes," she said. "I learned two of them when I was a child. I still remember them."

"Splendid!" I said to her. "If you will teach them to our Partisans between now and Christmas, we can have carols on Christmas Eve."

That evening I saw Sonia walking about the camp, very businesslike, with a piece of paper in her hand. She was signing up the men who would attend a rehearsal of Christmas songs. Men who might have laughed at piety from anyone else applauded Sonia's plan. She gathered an interesting group: Russian Communists and French maquis, Slovak Partisans and Red Army boys with no interest in politics—all of them seemed interested in joining Sonia's choir.

Every night from then on the little group met and sang. On Christmas Eve Sonia's carols were a great success: the whole camp toasted her that night. During those weeks Sonia had become transformed. Her lewd singing in the kitchen stopped; her efforts to seduce the maquis came to an end. One January morning on the

Polish plains we woke up to find that Sonia had disappeared; she had taken a little knapsack filled with clothes and simply left. I have an idea that in the village of Poland, where the churches are still open, Sonia is singing the songs of the Russian liturgy today.

No one had laughed at Sonia's hymns, yet I heard the commissars preaching their Party platitudes against the churches week after week in the orientation classes to which all Red Army soldiers had to go. Men from the ranks sometimes made speeches too, reminding the Party members that God, in spite of the official "toleration" of religion, was still their enemy. I wondered what went on inside these Russian minds where official atheism and Christian hymns lived on in seeming amity.

Small events began to educate me.

I remember one occasion when our unit entered a Russian town the assault troops had recaptured a few days earlier. Already the familiar signs of Soviet poverty were there. In the shop windows were no new goods for sale; only a few of them had worn, patched clothing. In a book shop I stopped and idly looked over the titles: Stalin's *Dialectical Materialism* was here, and a Party-approved history of Russia. That was all. On a street corner some soldiers, returned from the west, were bartering bits of trash they had picked up in the capitalist countries for a little local vodka.

A moving-picture theater had opened, with a Soviet propaganda film. This was built about a story of married love, a very sentimental plea for monogamy. Pavel, a Russian soldier who had come into the theater with me, frankly wept as the romance unwound. In its saccharine plot a small boy, hurt to find that other children had a father, while he had none, induced his mother to set out on a long search to find the husband she had abandoned many years before. In the final scene the child joined the hands of the reunited parents and said to them, as if he had been a priest performing a nuptial Mass, "From now on nothing shall separate you ever again."

We left the moving-picture theater and sauntered down the grimy little street. A few claps of thunder startled us; big drops of rain began to fall. Pavel grabbed my arm and said, "Here. Let's go in here for shelter."

It was a small Orthodox church. I looked slantingly at him: Pavel was one of the Militant Atheists in camp, one of the youngsters who let no occasion pass without reminding the Party zealots that the opening of the churches meant nothing to *them*. "Let the weaklings go to kneel and pray," he had told a meeting a few days earlier. "We, the strong, have science to support us and we need no God."

Pavel held the church door open and beckoned me to enter. He shifted his knapsack so that his hands were free, and then he folded them. Slowly, solemnly he walked to the largest icon, crossed himself and stood before it, lost in contemplation. The rain beat down upon the dripping roof. The water leaked through the worn windows and doors. Pavel ignored the storm. He stood and gazed upon the image of his God.

When the rain had ended he turned to smile at me.

"Comrade," he whispered, "how do you like *our* church? Is it as beautiful as yours?"

He was a fraud, that Pavel; when he preached the official blasphemies his tongue was in his cheek.

Other men began to reveal their hearts to me.

One moonless night, as dark as the inside of a chimney,

I was returning to our camp with a Soviet officer. By then, we had been billeted with the Russians for a long time—long enough, in a war, for deep friendships to mature. We knew each other well. We also knew the terrain, so that our feet made their way past every root and stone in our path without the need of any dangerous match flame. We talked in muffled tones. My friend had been a schoolmaster in the Soviet, entrusted with the duty of stamping out from young minds any notion of Divinity which they might have learned from their grandparents of the old, devout regime.

He was telling me of the execution of a soldier that had taken place a few days before, not far from the path we were following. He had seen the mysterious transition; a young man, strong, healthy and filled with life, had been reduced to a little heap of flesh and bones and scattered brains in a pool of scarlet.

"Strange," said my friend, and he lowered his voice, as if he felt the presence of the political commissar who slept a few hundred yards away. "Strange, but I have not been able to believe for many years now that this flesh, these bones, are all that make a man. There is a something else in us which our canny science cannot grasp. There was something else in that young man executed before my eyes—something that does not exist and vanish when a pig is stuck or a cow is slaughtered."

We crunched on through the pools of melting snow.

"I saw that boy's eyes in the moment when life faded in them. It was a terrible thing to watch. For in his eyes I read sorrow, and love for us all, pardon for us—yes, and even prayer. That boy repented. No, Comrade, he was not made only of matter and little, clever filaments of the ready brain. I cannot believe that that is all."

He bent his head to bring his mouth closer to my ear.

"You know," he said, "I have always suspected something of that. And yet I taught the children in our schools the very opposite. I told them that man was only matter, like the animals. I knew it was not true; and yet I taught them that it was."

He pointed towards the barracks where the commissar was sleeping.

"*They* forced us," he whispered. "They controlled us so savagely. They gagged us. They played on our cowardice and made us teach a lie."

He hung his head in a great shame.

"All of us except the martyrs to the truth, who were liquidated long ago, did this dreadful thing. We taught a falsehood which we did not believe. We were forced to do it in order to live. It might have been better if we had not lived."

Life itself was proving the greatest teacher of spiritual realities to such men. Even the deeply indoctrinated Party men discovered in combat areas that there are truths their narrow secularism cannot explain.

One early autumn evening I was returning to headquarters from my "rounds," my visits to the sick and wounded scattered about the forest in their different shelters and huts. It was raining, that drizzling rain that makes life torture in the high mountains, soaking your clothes, soaking the straw on which you sleep, the ground on which you walk.

As I entered the camp, the Russian commandant stopped us. He wore a grave and preoccupied air, as if he were debating something of crucial importance to the war. Drawing me aside, he said to me, "Doctor, you come from a country where many people still believe in

God. You will not laugh at me when I tell you this: my soul is in a state of sin."

I stared at him. He was a man of thirty-five, hung with Army honors, a trusted Party member who should have scoffed at the very use of the word *sin.*

"Yes, my friend?" I asked him gently.

"I have just killed a man," he said. "Killed a man." A few minutes earlier, he said, he had ordered his men to shoot a young peasant over whom there hung some slight suspicion of having acted as a spy. Instead of ordering a fuller investigation, the commandant had cut things short.

"My soul," he repeated, "is in sin."

I could say nothing; I dared not. This man, a few weeks earlier, had been a speaker at a celebration of one of the national holidays. On that occasion, with the smiling commissar standing by, he had delivered one of those routine, stereotyped attacks on religion with which the minds of all young Russians have been sedulously stocked. Sin? Soul? Such words were "bourgeois myths."

I began to watch more closely. I began to wonder whether even the commissars themselves believed this militant irreligion which they preached with so assured and satisfied an air.

But it would have been unsafe to question them. We Christians in the forest hid our devotions from these new Sauls, pending the day when Saul might change to Paul and be our friend. Our daily devotions were still silent and concealed. When we felt an overwhelming need to gather together for common meditations, we sought out a secret place as carefully as if we had been back in Bratislava or Zagreb. We were still surrounded by the secret police who had earlier imprisoned men in

Russia for no more than making the sign of the Cross in a schoolroom, had murdered many others for teaching boys to serve at Mass.

This is why the intrepidity of some of these secret Christians startled me: they were running risks that I should not have dared.

The boldest of the underground believers was a man I met at a time when our units had been given the considerable task of breaking through the German line from the rear to join the main Red Army on the north. The Nazis, foreseeing this strategy, had launched a terrible attack on us in our mountains. The slopes were draped with Russian dead; the fighting was made more terrible by the high crevasses and the treacherous snowdrifts through which our Army moved. We were still accompanied by the pathetic little group of Jewish refugees whom we dared not leave behind.

I was moving in the rear of our advance. It was in the dark of night. In front of me I guided a little Jewish girl of six; behind me came her mother and an old, old man. At one point we had to make a dash, through snow and slippery ice, across a hill against which the Nazi fire was merciless. I took the little girl on my shoulder and told the others to break through as best they could. We made a run for it and broke past the dangerous point just before a louder volley of shots was heard.

Comparatively safe, our little group made its way down the mountain and entered a small village on the Polish side at dawn. We saw a church still standing and next to it a small house, probably the priest's. I decided to take my refugees to him for safety.

I found the Father at home; he promised to provide

some sort of sanctuary for the refugees until the fighting had passed by.

"It will not be wholly safe," he said. I smiled. The mortars were firing less than a mile away and the whine of the shells was still to be heard in the distance.

"No," I agreed. "It will not. But it is better for them here than with the Gestapo."

While we spoke, a knock sounded at the door. The priest opened it to a young Red Army lieutenant, a tall, blond boy. He paid no attention to us: instead he saluted the priest and said to him, "*Batiushka,* will there be a Mass today?"

"Yes," said the priest.

"May I come to it?" he asked. "And will you give me a special blessing afterwards? We are going to attack the Germans today. It will be a big battle. Father, I shall need your blessing."

He was so young, so earnest, so curiously lacking in self-consciousness over what was a most startling request for him to make.

I left the priest's house by his side.

"You are very bold about your Christianity," I said.

"*Nichevo,*" he shrugged. "The Germans have been throwing two or three tons of steel at me in the past few weeks and I am still alive. I can risk a little danger from the Party spies."

He was from Moscow, he told me—a graduate of the University there. That meant that he had been exposed to sixteen years of Communist indoctrination: at grammar school, high school and in his college years. He must have heard the validity of religion denounced at least once a week throughout that period.

"Is your religion new?"

No, he told me. He was one of the Russians whose faith had been given him—at what a risk!—by his parents. His father was a devout Russian Orthodox; his mother a Roman Catholic Pole. Together they had taught him, from his earliest days, to repeat the whispered prayers of the Liturgy and to follow the Church calendar across the whole network of feast and fast days throughout the year. His mother had had a remarkable education. Before the revolution she had studied theology and philosophy with the best scholars at the University of Cracow.

Throughout those school years, he said, she had pointed out to him at night the fallacies of the "dialectical materialism" he was being taught at school by day. He had learned all the Soviet wished him to learn and had repeated it back to them, parrotlike, for his examinations. But he retained, through it all, a deep faith and a reasoned spirituality. When his army unit first set foot on foreign soil, he immediately left his Red companions to seek out a church and see, for the first time, the Mass whose beautiful anthems he already knew.

"The war has not been so bad for me," he said. "I have been able to get to a church almost every Sunday at the front."

"But how?" I asked.

He tapped his heavy soldier's boots.

"On these."

My young friend had walked, that day, six miles, skirting the German lines at a dozen points, before he had seen the church spires that he sought. Now he would have to walk six miles back again.

"They think, at camp, that I am woman-crazy," he

said. "I tell them that once a week I have to have a pretty girl and that I'll go a long distance to find one that suits me. Every Sunday I disappear; when I come back they say, 'Was it a blonde? Was she much better than the women around here?' It's a useful idea for them to have.

"My way takes me off here. Good-by, my friend. God bless you."

And he strode off, across the rutted fields.

This lieutenant had had the advantage of a religious upbringing. But even the men with whom the Party had had its way were slipping away from atheism now.

I remember a train trip to the rear. Our train moved slowly; the ancient locomotive had its work to do, drawing the long chain of flat cars on which we were spread out—soldiers, prisoners of war, camp followers, refugees going home. There was a bitterly cold wind blowing, but the smell of it was sweet, and it was good to see the little sprigs of green showing after the long, white night of winter we had all passed through.

We huddled close for warmth. Mitia, a great hulk of a Russian, a machine gunner, sat by me, his heavy Maxim at his feet. We were old friends, Mitia and I: we had never spoken of the dangerous topic of religion, for I knew that he was an active member of the Communist youth organization. To him, of course, I was merely a foreign doctor, discreet enough to avoid all talk of politics.

Mitia began to tell me some of his memories of the war. He was back in the terrible Stalingrad battles of the winter of 1942–43, when it had looked as if the city had been lost.

"We were running, all right," said Mitia. "My job was to cover the retreat of a group of infantrymen. They were scrambling as fast as they could go over a small embankment that gave them cover. The Germans were aiming right at us with machine guns, mortars, everything they had.

"I was just about to run for the bank myself, when I saw a German crawling towards me. I let him have it. And then another—then a whole swarm of them appeared. I turned my machine gun loose on them and watched their bodies fall. But they wouldn't stop coming. My finger was frozen to the trigger. All I could think of was to keep pressing. Then—you have no idea what a feeling it was—my machine gun ceased to fire. I pressed harder. I almost broke my finger before I realized the truth: my ammunition had run out.

"And the Germans were still coming around that bend."

Mitia lit a cigarette and flicked the match away. It made a slow arc of flame in the darkness.

"You know what I did then?" he asked. "I gave a big cry: '*Gospodi*—Lord, *Gospodi!* Thou alone can help me!' I let my Maxim drop and I made a backward leap into the snow, then another, then a third, praying furiously all the while. The Germans stopped. I got to the other side of the bank, concealed from them, and I began to run. I kept on running, and all the time my mind was saying, 'God! I need you now. I never needed you before, but I need you now. Help me to run to the cover of those woods.'

"Queer, wasn't it? I reached the woods and our own artillery, and I lay gasping for a long, long time. I've always been ashamed to think of it. I, a member of the Comsomol, a leader in the Militant Atheists cell, praying for help!

"But it has happened again, since then. Back at school God seems small and unnecessary—a fairy story that will never bother one. But at the front it's different. At the front, Comrade, one prays!"

In the spring of '45, the Russian Army units into which our international maquis had been absorbed were shifted in eastern Hungary to a section recaptured from the Germans after heavy fighting. Little by little, life was returning to the region. Rubble was being cleared from the village streets. Barbershops, always the first to reopen in a bombed-out town, started up again. The refugee families were trudging back from the caves and forests to seek shelter in these roofless homes, to squat miserably in the churches and schoolhouses while they attempted to build homes which had been hopelessly destroyed.

It was Holy Saturday. The peasants in our Hungarian village carried on the time-honored custom of a procession through the streets. The Russian soldiers stood gawkily by: they had been taught in their schools that religion was the instrument of the ruling classes and the priests, that the proletariat worshiped God only under duress. The piety of the peasants contradicted such a belief.

The processions came to an end at the village church. The crowd scattered. Little groups of Soviet soldiers still stood staring. I entered the church with one of my Slovakian friends. It was quiet, dimly lighted. As we knelt in prayer we saw figures entering and leaving, most of them the kerchiefed women of the countryside.

I heard the sound of girls' feet tiptoeing and two

women of the Russian Army entered, one of them with a military overcoat about her shoulders. They advanced towards the little side chapel dedicated to St. Therese of Lisieux; there stood a charming statue of her, smiling and carrying in her hand those roses she promised she would scatter on earth when she was safe in Heaven. The Russian girls sidled shyly to the Chapel; one of them removed from under her overcoat a large bunch of violets and laid it at the feet of the Saint. They stood silent for a few minutes. Then they went away.

Such little visits were surreptitious, but they became known. The peasants were bewildered. These Red Army women with their swaggering drunkenness frightened them; yet sometimes they behaved like "real women," like devout women.

On the Polish-Slovak-Russian frontier we came upon a mountain village from which all the young and able-bodied citizens had fled. Only a few old women, too weak to make the journey to safety, had stayed behind to die in their own homes. The wretched wooden houses were almost empty; through their deserted rooms these old crones went about their duties of drawing water, puttering at the stoves, waiting resignedly to see what fate they would have to endure. Although all of them were close to eighty, they were not eager to open their doors to the Red soldiers. Word had spread that these men raped women older than they.

They were a devout colony, crossing themselves as they went about their tasks and bowing their heads as they passed the wayside shrines. Most of all they seemed to fear a profanation of their religion. In every home the Virgin's image had been removed from the walls, leaving a little spot of cleanliness to show where the icon had hung since the day the house was built.

Our Army took possession of the village; the scramble for shelter began. It was a matter of first come, first served in such advance units. Into one of the tumble-down houses rushed Marusya, a Red Army captain. She tossed her hat onto the table and addressed the cowering old woman in the tone of one accustomed to giving orders and having them obeyed.

"Hi, old woman;" she said. "I want to sleep here tonight."

"Very well," said the peasant, her eyes suspiciously noticing the skirt: for who had ever heard of *women* soldiers before this?

Marusya carefully inspected the little room. Then she closed the door and walked close to the mountain woman. In a harsh whisper she said to her, "Where is the Mother of God?"

The old woman began to tremble. As she told me the story later, she involuntarily crossed herself with fear. "Mother of God," she was praying silently. "The stories they have told us are all too true. This young devil of a Russian cannot wait to eat or sleep before she wishes to defile your image."

The old woman said evasively, "There is no Mother of God here. You can see it for yourself."

"What!" cried Marusya with contempt. "No Mother of God? Listen, we have been told that you are a Christian people here, that you are devout, that you are allowed to worship openly. And you do not even have an icon on your walls."

She leaned over the old woman, angry with reproach.

"In Russia," she said, "even when it was most dangerous, we always kept an icon hidden in our home. Always. Have you so little courage here that a few Communist Party hacks on the outskirts of the village made you destroy the Mother of God?"

The old woman was ashamed. She went to the deep goosefeather bed and drew from it the hidden icon to reassure this astonishing visitor.

"That's better," growled Captain Marusya. "Put her back where she belongs. *I* shall protect the Mother of God, I with my tommy gun."

The old woman restored the icon to its place. Then the captain unslung her rifle and stripped the heavy gloves from her hands. She pulled her uniform straight and ran her hands over her hair. Thus prepared to make a proper obeisance, she walked up to the Virgin, stretched her arms in the form of a cross and recited the traditional prayer believing Russians have said many millions of times to the Mother of God *"Pod tvoin milost . . . spasi nac."*

And I remember another woman.

It was during one of our halts in Hungary at a great military hospital for the Red Army, one set up in a convent. The Sisters still retained the use of one of the wings. Olga, a Soviet woman surgeon of exceptional ability, was stationed here. I spoke to her often as we went about our work among the wounded. One day I asked her if she would care to meet the Mother Superior, a keen, intelligent woman and a doctor, too. Olga hesitated a moment and then agreed. After that, the two women met often; there was no political commissar in the hospital and encounters were easily arranged. Day by day I watched a real and strong friendship develop between the two women whose backgrounds were so strangely different.

One morning we were told that we must move and that the medical staff would go first to the next position, some hundreds of miles away. Olga came to say good-by to the Mother Superior. While I stood waiting to take her to our ambulance, I heard her farewell speech.

"The war is nearing its end. Soon everyone will return to his peacetime work. I have been so happy with you here. I have loved the sort of life your Sisters lead. When the demobilization is over, may I come back to you? Will you teach me your religion? Will you let me join you here as one of your nuns?"

The Mother Superior, much affected, embraced the Soviet woman and made the sign of the Cross over her. There was an impatient honking from the driver of our ambulance. Olga and I must go. That night she was dropped at a hospital nearer to the front and I returned to the forest. I never saw her again but I often prayed that she was able to return to the life she had learned to love. . . .

Not all the Russian women were able to adjust so happily to the discovery that there was another, kindlier way of life than the one they had been taught. Some of them found the sight of Christian wedding ceremonies more than they could bear.

In Poland the churches were open: the Russian policy of religious toleration was for the moment in full swing. The beautiful ceremonies of the Polish Church held a great fascination for our Russian soldiers. And whenever a wedding was to be held the Reds, men and women, gathered at the church, wide-eyed to see this fuss being made over what, to them, was a mere matter of signing papers in the gloomy office of a Soviet registry. The women soldiers stood entranced by this new pageantry —the lighted candles, the old chants of the choir, the crown of flowers on the head of the white-robed bride. It was their first glimpse of marriage as a sacrament.

Young Natasha, a Red lieutenant, attended one such marriage ceremony with me. She was a very intelligent young woman, with a fine, high forehead above those dark, paintbrush eyebrows which distinguish some Russian women's faces. During the ritual she was intent on every detail; when the priest gave his blessing to the kneeling couple and the procession started up the aisle she stirred and said, "Come on." I followed her.

Outside the church, Natasha mingled with the crowds of peasants who were kissing the bride. A village photographer was there; he posed the young couple in the stiff and self-conscious attitude usual to such groups. Natasha watched this, too.

Then she walked up to the bride and said to the surprised young woman, "Will you let me have a photograph of your wedding? I would value it very much."

"Gladly, gladly," said the peasant girl.

That evening Natasha sent one of her soldiers to the bride's home and obtained a crude little wedding photograph, printed on a postcard. On the back of it she wrote the address of her mother, in a central Russian town. Then, in a trembling hand, she wrote this message, which I copied down: "Dear Mama. This is how the people get married here. In the church, before a priest, and for always—not, as in our country, like dogs who see each other and couple right away. I can't bear that any more. Farewell, dear Mama."

I copied that message with a heavy heart; for the card was found next morning on the table next to the lieutenant's dead body. Her service revolver had fallen from her hand as she fired into her heart.

Such tragedies were inevitable: when the Communist youth saw something of life outside of Russia, they were bound to discover that much of what they had been taught in their schools and by the Party propaganda was a lie. The awakening took many forms.

The Russian men did not enjoy seeing the women soldiers rape and loot and swagger. Many of the young men said to me, "These girls! I shall never marry one of *them*. They are like prostitutes. They belong to any man who asks them. Me, I want a wife who will be all mine."

Such a viewpoint, fifteen years ago, would have been branded as "counterrevolutionary." But not today. It is interesting to note that the Soviet authorities have rediscovered the family, as a psychological necessity, at a period when many so-called Christian countries are still encouraging easier divorce and smaller families and a casual attitude towards the marriage vows. Western leaders might usefully study the events in Russia, where a complete abandonment of Christian principles has been tried, and rejected—even by the atheists of the Soviet.

For at one time the Party thought it had exterminated the family; the Thirteenth Bolshevik Congress described it as the "formidable stronghold of all the evils of the old regime."

"What was it like during the easy days of divorce?" I asked some of the young soldiers of the Red Army.

"My older sister," said Aliosha, "had a marriage in the mid-thirties, with a member of the Party. One day she came home from work and her husband opened the door.

"'What do you want here?' he asked her.

"'Well,' said my sister, 'I have just come home.'

"'This isn't your home any more,' he told her. 'Here are your bags. This morning I went down to the bureau and registered our divorce.'

"That happened to hundreds, thousands of women and to a fair number of husbands, too."

"Didn't the husband have to pay anything?"

He shrugged his shoulders.

"Sometimes, if he could be caught. But often the husbands left town and married some other woman in another part of Russia. It might take months to track him down. And then, if he had married four or five or eight women, the allowance he paid to any one of them could not amount to much. My sister got nothing."

She had been a victim of the early laws.

Now all that was changed; the Communists themselves discovered that sexual license was no foundation for the state. In 1935 the divorce fee was raised from three to three hundred rubles. Men who changed wives frequently were threatened with punishment for rape. Abortion became a crime punishable by death within the Soviet; doctors and midwives dared no longer perform the operations. But millions of women, trained to regard human life lightly by the Marxist principles, ruined their lives by performing abortions on themselves.

Many of the Russian women soldiers I met had such tragedies behind them.

It was in the Carpathian Mountains that I first encountered the curious, half-guilty, half-defiant attitude with which the Communist women regard such things. A woman soldier came to me, knowing that I still had a few tubes of the precious sulfa drugs, which no Russian Army doctor owned.

"What's wrong?" I asked her.

"My hair is falling out," she said.

"Well," I told her, "that's nothing serious."

But her eyes were wide with pain and worry. I saw that there was something bothering her of which she was afraid to speak.

"Have you ever had an abortion?"

"Yes, Comrade Doctor," she said, lowering her eyes. Then she raised them up and stared defiantly at me. "Altogether, I've had eleven."

I tried to explain to her the dangers of such things—the shock to the nervous system, the psychological conflict involved. Tears ran down her face.

"Why did no one tell me?" she asked. "They only said abortions were against the Party ideal. I thought it was propaganda to make us work harder for the state."

On another occasion one of the high-ranking Russian officers approached me. He was shy, embarrassed, showing the confusion one expects of a naughty child, not of a tough member of the Soviet combat forces.

"Comrade Doctor," he said. "You know that I sleep with Comrade Katrina. Well, something very unfortunate has happened; she's pregnant. Now, Comrade Doctor, I know abortions are forbidden to good Communists like us, but you're a foreigner. Maybe you can help us out."

"Why do you want her to have an abortion?" I asked him.

"Ah," he said, "I have a wife and children back in Russia. I can't care for her when the war is ended. An operation is the only way out."

"Don't worry," I told him. "I'll talk to Katrina. We'll find some way out of this difficulty."

I saw the young Partisan woman the next day, moping about the outskirts of the camp, and called to her.

"Katrina," I said. "Please come here."

She was blushing. She knew her lover had confided her secret. "How long have you been pregnant?" I asked her.

"Three months," she said. "Are you going to—?"

I broke in on her unfinished speech.

"I am going to congratulate you," I said firmly. "It is a great privilege to be a mother, to give life to a new human being. One of the finest things in life is the dignity of motherhood. And you will be a mother, Katrina."

"But I'm a soldier," she said.

"Yes," I told her. "I know that. And I know that you might find it difficult to care for this young life, which has been confided to you. But Katrina, you must have the baby. Then you and I will arrange that he shall have a chance to live and grow up among people who will care for him."

She stammered and finally said, "All right. If you can arrange a home for the child, it won't be so bad."

I cared for Katrina during those months. She shed her sense of shame when she found that even one man accorded her a greater respect because of the child. The officer who would be the father also treated Katerina with great tenderness. She had a normal delivery there in the woods in my little surgical hut.

I took the baby from her, as she wished, and gave him for adoption to a kind-hearted Polish Catholic couple who had lost their own baby the year before. When we left that section Katrina went to pay a farewell visit to her son; she came back to thank me, with tears in her eyes.

As I got to know these women of the Russian Army well, I realized that their swashbuckling cruelties were the fruit of a frantic effort to escape from guilt; the corruption was only skin deep. Both men and women, when they came to me to ask for medicines to cure their venereal diseases, cast their eyes at the ground and shifted their feet. "Something" told them that these maladies were different and more reprehensible than the chilblains and fevers which they contracted through no fault of their own.

Some of the women soldiers had gone further; they devised a strict code of chastity, in defiance of all they had been taught. I have seen Red Army girls reject the advances of soldiers with as much indignation as any woman brought up in a strait-laced community, and in the same terms.

"Do you take me for a prostitute?" such girls would say. And the men, rebuffed, looked their shame. No, I decided. The sense of right and wrong had not died in these tough men and women from the Soviet; it was only narcotized. It would awake, and soon.

CHAPTER 10

I Enter Russia in Disguise

THE new and dangerous plan of entering Russia under the general's protection had top priority in all my movements in the last spring of the war. My identity, I knew, would have to be a good one; the Russian authorities already knew of me and of my interest in their shifting policies. I had been the man sought out by the Soviet minister, long ago, in that summer garden when the USSR was seeking (honestly, perhaps?) to discover on what terms it might secure peace with the Catholic Church.

I believed that the policy in Moscow had changed since then; in February of 1945 the Russian Orthodox Patriarch violently attacked the Holy Father's Christmas message of two months before. The Patriarch was all too apt to be reflecting the opinion of the Party leaders when he spoke. With the victory over the Nazis very near, the Politburo no longer had to make concessions to the conscience of the Christian world. The men in Moscow already knew, if we in the forest did not, that they were safely in power: the British and U.S. Allies would not demand a change of government in Russia. The Communist despotism would stay; soon it might safely revert to the frank atheism of the early days.

But the political hierarchy was not the only Russia; there were the Russian people themselves to be reckoned with. In order to learn more about their hopes and beliefs, I decided to enter Russia.

For this, I must travel to the west: my general himself had been moved to the rear and I must find him to secure my proper pass. I wished also to visit Debrecen and Kosice, make contact with the French and U.S. missions in these cities and help my friends. An American aviator from Boston had made a spectacular appearance among our Partisans when his plane, flying out of Bari, Italy, had been forced down into Slovakia. I had promised this boy I would help him reach the American authorities. And our French Partisans, too, wished to be put in touch with their own countrymen; it was not safe, at that moment, for these non-Communist foreigners to be stranded among the Reds with the war coming to an end. We set out together, a group of eleven men.

Our little party found it easy enough to travel to the rear: with knapsacks on our backs we jolted over the abominable roads in a series of jeeps and weapon carriers. Ours was not a formal war; hitchhikers were welcome.

Our first objective behind the front was Army Headquarters in a Slovakian village; here I asked the officer in charge if he had news of my general. He did not, but he suggested that I interview Valerian Zorin, a Russian civilian whose office was nearby and who, he said, had "good political contacts."

"He is apt to know the movements of these big shots

better than any of us in uniform," he said, with a trace of bitterness.

I did not know about Zorin then: I sought out the office to which I had been directed and was greeted by his secretary, a typical young Russian, kindly, laughing, what the Spaniards call "simpatico." I remember this man well because of the sharp contrast between his personality and that of his employer.

For Zorin was the sort of man who scowls in his sleep —a man of dark skin, dark hair, dark menace in the eyes. In our opening conversation I saw that he picked his words carefully, although the matter was a casual one. I believed that this was a man the Party would assign to a job of spider-web intrigue.

And my instincts about Zorin were right. For as I look at the tattered map of eastern Europe today I see that Zorin then, in February of 1945, had already begun the Czecho-Slovak Communist *coup d'etat* which burst on an astonished world, in its finality, in February of 1948. Zorin's job in Czecho-Slovakia was to organize the Communist Party, to gain control of the "commanding heights" of power within the country and to give orders to Gottwald and the other local Communists. At the moment when I met him, he was setting up the network of Communist-backed "Partisans" who were to run the villages and cities as secret police. Our poor, ragged Slovak Partisans had never numbered more than 30,000; in the hardest times their ranks had shrunk to few more than 1,000 men. Now, under Zorin's prodding, 136,000 "Partisans" were named and given jobs in the new secret police. These men were not all Party sympathizers; some of them were racketeers who had peddled food and fuel and newspapers, at black-market prices, to the Partisans of the forests in the early days of the war.

Zorin was not a man to be taken lightly. After a few harmless words of sparring, I decided not to mention to him the name of the general whom I was seeking. Instead, I mentioned my political friends; I asked after the Soviet minister who had first approached me. I told him (what he surely knew already) that there were rumors that his government would like to establish relations with the Catholic Church.

He shrugged. "The Patriarch is all the church we need," he said. His expression suggested that even this might be too much.

Zorin is one of the intransigent Party members whose hatred of religion is more unrelenting than their hatred of capitalism itself.

"He is a good weather vane to watch," I told myself as I rejoined my little international group and headed towards the West in another convoy. "If Zorin's power increases, it will mean that the crusade against God within the Soviet will start again."

Zorin's power has never waned. After the war he was the Soviet Ambassador in Prague and acted as the real master of Russian policy there. Back in Moscow as Vice-Secretary of Foreign Affairs, Zorin visited the United States in 1947 as a delegate to the United Nations. He returned to Prague in time for the Communist coup which resulted in the death of Masaryk.

So long as men like Zorin are in favor, religious toleration in Russia will remain a mockery.

In Budapest, at last, I found the clue that led me to my general. There I also had an interview with another Soviet diplomat whose name was to make history.

Gregoriev, when I visited him, was already the top man in the behind-the-scenes drama of Hungarian politics. He was a small man with a heavy, peasant's frame. His Hungarian was excellent—too excellent to have been learned in Russia. He has played, in Hungary, much the same role as Zorin in Czecho-Slovakia. When I saw him in the Soviet headquarters offices, I said, "There is a Christian Party here which is really radical. Its plans for land reform are sweeping; both the Catholic and Protestant leaders are behind it. Now that the Communists in Russia have made their peace with the churches there, will your government approve such a party in Hungary?"

"Approve it? No!" he said to me. "The Small Holders' Party is religious enough for anybody: why, one of its leaders, Father Balog, is a Catholic priest."

This, lamentably enough, was true. Father Balog was one of the dupes of the Communists. The MVD agents used his presence in the one large political party to prevent the formation of some other which might have put forth a program of real reform. Then in 1947, with Gregoriev pulling the puppet strings, Father Balog drew his following from the Small Holders' Party and helped the Communists to take complete control of the state.

Such conspiracies have come to maturity only now, two or three years after the surrender of the Germans. I saw the web being spun, the plans being laid on that trip when the military victory was still unwon.

But my purpose at that moment was not to study local politics; it was to enter Russia and see the secret religious life. For this reason, my general was then the most interesting man in Europe to me.

When I finally found him, it was at the officers' rest camp of Zakopane in South Poland. He pressed my hands warmly.

"I am glad that you have come," he said. "I have not forgotten my promise. Come back tomorrow, and I shall have a plan for you."

When I entered his office on the following day, I was introduced to a graying man with warm, kindly eyes, who was to become my friend. This was Colonel T.

"I have talked to the colonel," the general said to me. "He is returning to Russia soon with a convoy of troops for Manchuria; the USSR plans to declare war on Japan. The colonel is one of us. He will be very happy to have you travel with him as far inside Russia as you care to go. He will always provide you with transportation and with passes, if you wish to go for trips alone. Trust him. He is your friend."

It was decided that I should not join the colonel's party here; Zakopane was too well provided with Party spies and I had been in contact with a number of political figures in recent weeks. Instead, I would hitchhike alone to Novi Targ and, at the Soviet Army headquarters there, present the order which my general wrote out for me.

"This will assure you of a car and escort to the frontier of Russia," he said. "There you can meet with Colonel T. anytime within the next three weeks. It will be safer so."

I made my way to Novi Targ and presented the magic pass. I was given as escort a close-mouthed Russian major who bore all the hidden insignia of the secret police. We set off in an official car through Poland to the Russian border on the first of May.

I had an immense curiosity as to the condition of the

Church in Poland: no adequate information had reached me nor, I suspected, had reached the outside world. I believed that five minutes with a Catholic spokesman in Poland would be worth a gamble.

I appraised the major as we rode through the devastated countryside. He was a typical member of the secret police; a plodding, conscientious man, the sort whose reports would be a dreary compendium of unnecessary details. I knew the type. In an unexpected situation he would be incapable of action, until his slow wits had referred back to the rule book and chosen some directive under which the circumstance should fall.

I decided to give him a very unexpected circumstance indeed.

"I see by the map," I said, "that we shall have to take badly shelled roads if we drive directly for the border. It is a pity to submit your splendid Lend-Lease automobile to such a strain."

"Yes," he said. "A pity."

"Had it occurred to you," I asked him, "that we might detour by way of Cracow? It is, of course, a magnificent town and one of the oldest in Europe. But that is secondary. What really matters is the condition of the roads. Perhaps your driver has heard something about the two routes?"

He spoke up, as I knew he must.

"The roads via Cracow," he assured us, "are in excellent condition. As for the direct route, I cannot answer."

The major was a little uneasy over the change of plan. But after a ten-minute period of thought he brightened. He had now mentally drafted the paragraph of his report in which he would explain the detour in terms of Party loyalty. "In order to preserve the property of the

Red Army, I ordered the driver to avoid the badly damaged roads."

When we reached Cracow I kept him interested with the sights. I pointed out to him the second oldest university in Europe. There was the Wawel Cathedral, with the Tomb of St. Stanislaw: since the fourteenth century this Church had never been closed until the Nazis slammed its doors. Down there was the dreadful Ghetto where the Nazis had murdered a whole community of men. As the car came to a stop at a busy corner in the center of the town, I reached for the door and said to the major, "Wait here, please. I have to see a friend. It will take less than half an hour."

Before he could gather his wits about him, before he could speak, I slipped from the car, darted around a corner and lost myself in the crowd.

I had not much time. I did not know my way about the city in its wartime state. I did not dare inquire my way of the police. Then my heart gave a leap: coming towards me I saw two nuns.

I approached them and in a low voice spoke to them in Polish, "I am a Catholic priest in disguise. How do I find the parish of Father X?"

The Sisters stared at my Partisan officer's uniform—but they had lived in the center of a war too long to be surprised at anything.

One of them murmured directions for reaching the Franciscan Church, a block or so away. Here I quickly found a priest and addressed him in Latin. He told me how to reach the rectory I wished. Within six minutes of my abrupt departure from the car I was closeted with the curate, for the priest I sought was out of town.

"I do not know how long I shall be in Russia," I said,

"but it is possible that I may stay only a little while. If I do, what word do you wish me to deliver to the Christian world of the West?"

It was the first link with the outside Christian world the poor Polish Church had had since the German attack in 1939. The curate told me of the great toll of priests who had been seized and tortured by the Nazi armies; of how the authorities had suppressed the trade union movement; of how the Christian youth organizations had been driven underground.

We spoke rapidly. I memorized the facts as he gave them to me in Latin and hastened back to the corner where I had left the Red Army car. Climbing into it, as if it were the most natural thing in the world, I said to the major, "I'm sorry to have delayed you. My friend was not at home. This is an interesting old city, isn't it? Do you wish to take time for shopping or shall we push on?"

My behavior was, from the MVD standpoint, so outrageous that the major had no answer to give. Nothing in his rulebook had prepared him for a situation in which a prisoner of the MVD should take advantage of the pretty fiction which pretends that he is a guest, free to move in a military area as he may please.

"The Polish people are kind," I said to the major later in the day. "If we stop at any of these houses, they will heat water for our tea, to warm us."

The major was shivering in the mountain cold. He nodded.

"When we come to the next house, we'll stop," he said.

We entered a farmer's house which had once been prosperous but was now in the dilapidated, paintless condition of half the homes of Europe, with broken panes at the windows stuffed with rags, and a cold stove in the kitchen. But on the wall I saw a crucifix.

The major brusquely asked for tea.

"I'll help you make it," I told the peasant woman. I saw her glance uneasily from the crucifix to our uniforms and I knew what was passing through her poor frightened mind: We were the enemies of her Lord, for we were Soviet soldiers.

When I was alone with her in the kitchen I said to her, in an undertone, "You are a devout woman. Pray for the conversion of Russia."

She was startled. I quickly made the sign of the Cross over her and rejoined the major in the other room. I had bewildered the poor peasant woman—but bewilderment is a more comfortable state of mind than groveling fear.

We passed through dozens of such small, hopeless villages. Men and women walked with rags bound about their feet. The stillness of devastation lay over the towns. In one railroadworker's hut, where I had stopped for a midday meal, the talk lagged. The faces of these poor people were gaunt with hunger and misery. As we gathered about the table for our pooled luncheon—my Army rations, their frozen potatoes and tea—the Angelus rang out from the nearby church and the old peasant woman crossed herself. She looked at me defiantly, believing that all who traveled with the Reds were probably enemies of her Church.

"It's all that's left to us now," she said. "We've lost everything else. But while the church bells ring, we still have God.

Then, in embarrassment, she bustled into the kitchen.

Throughout Poland the churches were open all day, every day, and they were filled with praying figures. We stopped for the night at a village close to a Carmelite monastery. Two girls lived alone in the house where I was billeted. Their father had been killed in the war, their mother had died of hunger and cold.

"You still are believers here?" I asked the older girl, nodding towards the monastery. She was evasive. Then, as if taking a great chance (which, indeed, she was) she said: "I've been studying in the Communist high school. Some of our teachers try to make us atheists."

Then, as she took up the kerosene lamp to guide me to the room where I was to sleep, she murmured: "They don't succeed."

These Poles stand today where the devout people of Russia stood in 1919: their religion is very dear to them and they cannot grasp the fact that the regime forbids it.

We reached a Polish bordertown on the seventh of May at midnight. Starting towards the barracks to go to sleep, I walked into a group of howling madmen in the yard outside.

News had just come over the Moscow radio that Germany had surrendered.

It was no night for rest. It was a night, as all the victorious armies around the world decided, from London to Kunming, for drinking the last drop of whatever was at hand. I abandoned myself to the hour: the MVD dropped their usual stiffness and produced a captured radio by which we could get the news from London, if someone knew the language. I did. As the Russians crowded around me, I gave out rough translations of the English broadcasts. The soldiers, like all the soldiers of all the armies on the winning side, were stunned. It was almost impossible for them to believe that the goal towards which they had strained every fibre for the past years had been reached. There was no need, now, for them to fight for victory. But any other kind of living seemed impossible!

And then over each man separately dawned the very personal realization "It's over and I haven't been killed, after all. I'm one of the lucky ones who came through." And then a wave of shame at the memory of the other men—the better men—who had not come through.

The next day we set forth to drive through a deliriously happy countryside. The civilian population, at least, had no complex emotions to trouble them; the war was won and they were filled with joy. In every village where we stopped, the people crowded around the staff car. Women of all ages wished to kiss us. Every soldier was a hero that first week. Householders begged the privilege of having us as their guests; farm wives brought out treasures of fruit and vegetables. Children threw spring flowers into the car. My first impressions of the Russian town where I was to meet Colonel T. were unique among visitors to that dreary area: I thought it the gayest city I had ever seen. For it was a gala town.

There was a delay of five or six days while I waited for Colonel T. and his party to arrive. It was a breathing space in which to make my plans, in which to review the stories I had heard from earlier visitors to Russia. . . .

Like everyone else, I had known many travelers who went to prewar Russia on officially conducted Intourist trips. I, at least, would be free of Intourist chaperones.

But I had also known a very different sort of visitor to Russia. Wandering about the Maytime hills, I reminded myself of the time when a Roman Catholic priest of whom I knew had secretly entered the Russia I was about to visit.

It was in 1926. The Jesuit Father D'Herbigny was at that time director of the Oriental Institute at Rome. On one memorable evening he was asked by Cardinal Sinsero to go into St. Peter's Cathedral to pray with him at the tomb of the earliest Pope of all, St. Peter, who was crucified for the Faith.

As they knelt by his tomb, the cardinal said to the young priest, "Father, I have brought you here to deliver a message which may mean your martyrdom. The Holy Father, as you know, is gravely troubled over the persecution of the Church in Russia. The Soviets have killed or exiled every Catholic bishop. This means that no new priests can be ordained and, in time, it will spell the death of the Church within the country.

"The Holy Father wishes that you be secretly consecrated as a bishop, so that you may enter Russia. You will then lay your hands upon a few priests there, consecrating them in the greatest secrecy, and giving them the right of ordination."

Father D'Herbigny went to Berlin, where Cardinal Eugenio Pacelli (who is now the Holy Father) secretly consecrated him. The new bishop entered Russia and secretly consecrated six Russian Catholic priests as bishops. Now they, in turn, could confirm young Catholics and ordain young men as priests.

All of these men were apprehended by the Russian secret police. All of them but one were murdered. The sixth—Bishop Sloskan—was of Latvian birth; when he was imprisoned, a few years after his consecration, word of the tragedy reached Latvia and aroused the interest of influential officials there. So he was exchanged with a Soviet prisoner.

I had met Bishop Sloskan in Belgium before the war. Although he was only in his thirties, he looked seventy or eighty and was a broken man. He himself told me how the GPU came to his house in his absence, searched his desk and went away. The next day they returned, demanded the right to search his papers and triumphantly produced, from among them, a military map which he had never seen before.

"What is this?" asked one of the secret police, in mock horror.

The bishop looked at it.

"This," he said, "is the evidence you planted here yesterday in order to find an excuse for making an arrest."

In jail, he had been tortured cruelly. His cell was surrounded with steam radiators which were turned on full, so that the temperature rose to over 125 degrees. After an hour of this, the windows were thrown open and the heat turned off; the stinging winter winds of the steppes blew on him in his scanty clothing. After an hour of twenty below zero cold, he was given another hour of intense heat. When this had gone on for six hours, his examination began.

On another occasion he was placed in a cell painted a glittering white, with brilliant lights beating down on him from all sides and reflectors in the ceiling. Dazzled, blinded, maddened after seven hours of this, he was again led away for questioning. His answers were faltering, confused.

On the basis of these examinations the bishop was condemned to four years in Siberia, followed by three years of imprisonment at Solovki, on the White Sea. He suffered great agonies, with all the prisoners. But in both these places he had managed to say his daily Mass. "How?" I asked him. He told me how the word that there was a bishop in the concentration camp had spread through the entire Ukraine. Whenever a new political prisoner was sent to his jail, he managed to carry with him an innocuous-looking hunk of rye bread. Inside this were concealed whole grapes. The bishop was given the bread and from the hidden grapes he himself made the wine necessary for the Mass, which he said nightly, crouched under the rafters above the prison barracks. He distributed the consecrated Hosts on his way to work in the morning; hidden in a bit of clean cloth they were concealed round the roots of a tree to which the Communicants came during the day.

This bishop gave Communion to over one thousand Catholics in the Siberian camp before he was most marvelously saved to tell the story.

We have a saying in the Church: "Saints are to be admired, not imitated." I had no desire to emulate the heroism of Bishop Sloskan. So I was glad when the waiting time was over and I had no more opportunity for gloomy thoughts. The signal to move was given me abruptly: one night, when I returned to my barracks, a notice on my door told me that at five o'clock the following morning our convoy would take off. The next night I should sleep inside the USSR.

CHAPTER 11

God's Underground in Russia

ONCE inside the Polish border of the USSR I began the six-months' adventure that has left me with a deep and loving admiration for the Russian people. The risks they run for God and for Russia have become routine to them: they are not sustained, as I was, by the thrill of dangerous novelty. To live on the side of a volcano for a night may be an exciting escapade; to be forced, by duty, to make your home and to keep your family there is apt to be a matter for daily, painful mortification.

As we jogged along the rutted roads in our lone convoy of army vehicles, I had time to consider my situation. I was clothed in a Partisan officer's uniform, and since there were many Russian members of such Partisan units, no one need know from my dress that I was a foreigner. My spoken Russian is fluent—and if I occasionally stumble over an unfamiliar word, so do the Georgians, the Ukrainians and many other subjects of the Soviet State.

I had many other assets: I carried the rank of major, with all the privileges this entailed. I had a countersigned pass from the general; a single document guaranteeing that I was a priest and giving my true name was well hidden in my shoe, under the heel, which had been nailed back into place by a reliable shoemaker. I carried no other documents and no firearms. It seemed to me I had no reason to feel uneasy.

Our first destination was the city of Orlov. There I had been told to contact Gorky, a trade-union leader and a member of the underground. He would pass me on to other friends in other cities.

I had memorized his name and the address of his home and information on how to reach an alternate contact, in case he should not be available.

"Never write a name inside of Russia," I had been warned by Grisha, the clever little Armenian-Russian who had briefed me for the trip. I had met him in the Polish bordertown, when my friend the colonel brought us together at his headquarters and had suggested that we take a walk.

Grisha led me through the quiet town square and past the rubble of a dozen bombings to the bridge, still standing across the moonlit river. As we leaned on its rails, he talked to me about the Russian resistance movement, of which he had been a member for all the years of his grown-up life.

"You are more interested in the Christian cells, the colonel tells me," he said. "That is all right; we all work together. I will start you off with contacts in several of the towns in western Russia, for the plans for your convoy may be changed and we cannot be sure that you will get to Orlov first. But if you do, there is a man by the name of Gorky (memorize carefully what I will tell you now) who will receive you when you have given him the password. He will pass you on to others, in the cities you plan to visit. If you tell him that you wish to meet religious families, that is easily arranged."

Grisha told me of the methods by which the giant conspiracy is kept alive. They are simple devices; the American OSS, the British Group 240 would learn little from the Russian underground.

Strangers are received by a resistance member only if they give the correct code message. My first contact was to be made by bringing Gorky a gift made up of exactly these articles: one quarter-pound of tea, five large potatoes, a handful of raisins. These were to be placed on the table of his home in a certain pattern, and I was to say, as I laid them down, "Your friend Sasha asked me to pay you my respects and to thank you for your kindness to his mother."

Gorky would reply, "We had heard that Sasha had been killed. His mother will be overjoyed to hear your news of him."

"The words must be exact," Grisha had told me. "If there is any slight discrepancy, we suspect that the stranger comes from the secret police. Sometimes, under torture, members of the underground have revealed a portion of the code."

The codes are changed frequently. Whenever any member of the resistance is arrested, the whole system of passwords is revised. Whenever anyone in the conspiracy believes that he is under observation, the code is changed. And as a matter of routine, it is revised every month: that is why it is possible to make use of vegetables and fruits in season for the coded gifts.

Nothing is more dangerous in the Russian resistance movement than to use a discarded code; everyone you approach then assumes you to be a member of the NKVD (now known by the newer name of MVD, or Ministerstvo Vnutornith Diel). Once such a catastrophe did occur; two young boys, afraid they would forget a new vegetable and fruit code, wrote it down for easier memorizing. That afternoon they were seized, the papers found. The police attempted to contact every family in the village by means of the code; but fortunately, word of the boys' arrest spread quickly, the code was discarded and no one else was caught.

"You will be put in touch with members of the underground in every city of Russia," Grisha said. "It is quite possible, in the confused conditions of the ending of the war, that other members of the resistance may approach you, even without an introduction. Everyone is expecting the American and British Armies to enter Russia and to liberate them soon; some people are becoming careless. Be very chary of those who speak to you without a proper introduction. It is probable that they are honestly anti-Communist, but they have not been tested for reliability. These strangers may not know how to keep a secret. Tell them none."

Grisha's instructions were my sole passport to the underground. But they were sufficient. In another section of the convoy I knew that a staff car was traveling and that it carried my good friend, the Colonel T., a man alerted by my friendly general to look after me.

In Orlov I went straight to the poverty-stricken neighborhood where Gorky lived, following the simple diagram of the city which Grisha had impressed on my brain. I knocked. A large, broadly smiling young Russian opened and said, "Good day."

My heart began to thump: this was the opening performance of the little drama of the groceries which I had mentally rehearsed a dozen times. I found myself tongue-tied with stage fright.

"Come in, come in," said Gorky, warmly.

Murmuring my thanks, I made for the worn and rickety table in the center of the room. I produced my little range of articles and laid them neatly on the table top: the potatoes here, the tea in the center of an oval, the raisins to the left. I spoke the words that I had memorized.

Gorky fluently gave the correct answer. Then he smiled at me and pressed my hand.

"Come into the other room," he said. "We shall have many things to talk about."

Gorky's home was at the extreme end of the underground; through his capable hands passed the resistance members from the war. To newcomers, like me, he gave detailed instructions on how to avoid suspicion.

"You are traveling with the Army? Good. You have papers enabling you to leave the convoy for a day—a week—from time to time? Very good; but do not overdo this privilege. Your greatest protection, my friend, lies in your presence with a regular unit of the Army."

Gorky told me his own story. He was the son of a prerevolutionary Bolshevik who had been jailed under the Czars. The son had grown up believing that Heaven itself would come if the working classes were once given political power. ("I still think so," he told me. "The *people*, the common people of Russia, are good. No one has yet tried letting them rule themselves. I want to destroy the Communist clique so that they can have that chance.")

The father of Gorky had helped the revolution and

had tried to retain his faith in the Party after it took over. He had felt that the early excesses of the regime were its growing pains. He had believed that this experiment *must* work—that it was the sole hope of a suffering humanity. He had felt many twinges at the early liquidation of the kulaks, for he was a kindly man. But he said nothing, did nothing to jeopardize the new state. His children were brought up to be faithful members of the Comsomol.

Then came the purges: Gorky's father was summarily placed under arrest and put on trial as a "traitor" and a "counterrevolutionary." Charges of Nazi affiliation were produced, and this in spite of the fact that Gorky's beloved mother was a Jew. The hideous injustice of the event, the absurdity of the charges, the irrationality of the whole procedure had shocked Gorky into realization of the evils of the regime.

"One night," he said to me, "a frightened neighbor came to my door and said, 'Hide me. The police are seeking me.' That was the moment of decision. A year before, when my father was alive, I should not have hesitated to refuse this man. I'd have turned him in as an enemy. Now, I said, without hesitation, 'Come in. I will hide you and help you.' From that day on I have been an active member of the underground."

Gorky was not a religious man. When I asked him about the Christians in the resistance movement, he said, "They are the bravest. They are the most cheerful. I wish that I could share their secret. Maybe someday I will—but not yet, my friend. I am not ready for that. But see here. Here is something prepared for one of your Christian friends."

He showed me a pile of melons in the corner. They

looked identical until he pointed out a tiny marking on one.

"This melon has been opened and fitted together again," he said. "Inside it now is a tiny bottle of sacramental wine. An old, old woman will stop here tomorrow; she will gather up these melons and hawk them through the town. At a certain tree she will sell this particular melon to a laborer who is sitting on the ground, whittling a stick. He will be a secret priest."

This was the first mention I had heard of secret priests still moving cautiously inside a Russia which had declared a policy of "religious freedom" to the world.

"But don't the Christians go openly to church these days?"

Gorky smiled.

"Some do, yes," he said. "Those Christians who are hopelessly compromised with the regime and have nothing to lose, do patronize the legal churches. But the real religious life of Russia is still underground; there are far more confessions heard, more Communions given by the secret priests than by those in the State-tolerated churches. You will see."

When I left Gorky that night, I quietly rejoined my Red Army group in the temporary barracks where we were billeted. The next day we set out for Briansk. As our overloaded trucks jounced across the Russian countryside I murmured to myself the name and address of the man to whom he had referred me. I was now a full-fledged traveler on the underground railway that criss-crossed the Soviet.

As I traveled it in the following months, I talked to many people every day, drawing them out, listening to their stories. I came into contact with elements of all the major groups: the secret police, the Comsomols, the peasants, the industrial workers; the old people and children and young married couples; the intellectuals and people who could not read or write; the priests who said Mass openly and a priest who lived the life of a fugitive from the MVD. I talked with hundreds, thousands of the Orthodox faithful and to Roman Catholics, as well as to Protestants, Jews, Moslems.

Listening was my work. Perhaps another visitor on the same mission as mine would not have found so many people eager to pour out their full hearts. I do not know. But I know that the people whom I met were pitifully eager to unburden themselves of their doubts and miseries to a listener from the outside world.

As we talked, bits of the pattern of the religious underground began to emerge. I began to see by what manifold devices the Christian faith in Russia had been kept alive. In a village near Kiev I picked up one brightly colored incident; it fitted neatly into another anecdote that was thrust on my attention in Smolensk. The jigsaw puzzle took shape. The marvelous design became clear. I began to understand not only *why* the atheist campaign had failed, but *how*. God's underground became an intelligible whole which I could look upon and admire.

There are large gaps in the picture still. There are many groups of ardent believers inside Russia whose path never crossed mine. There are so many stories of heroism and sanctity which have never reached my ears.

But here is the first, incomplete picture of the religious underground as it unrolled before my eyes during those months when I, who hid the fact that I am a priest, found a deep and eloquent belief in God about me everywhere. . . .

It was in a small village not far from Orsha. I was staying in the home of a young carpenter and his wife, to whom I had been certified by the Christian underground. On the first evening of my arrival the young man said to me, "There will be a traveling singer in the town tonight. It will be worth your while to hear him."

I was delighted at the chance. These troubadours who wander from village to village in Russia are growing scarce today, for the Soviet state makes no provision for their support and they depend on the kopeks of the peasants for their living.

On the outskirts of the village, by the side of a lake, a great bonfire had been built. The villagers gathered about, squatting on the ground. The minstrel was already playing his accordion when we joined the group and the audience was singing with him—one of the deeply melancholy songs of old Russia.

The minstrel was an aging man with a serene and beautiful face. He had a fine sense of drama; he interwove the songs that everyone could sing with long narrative chants. It was by such troubadours that the *Odyssey* was sung in ancient Greece and the *Chanson de Roland* in the medieval West.

"Listen," whispered my host to me as one of the long chants began. "Listen carefully to this."

It was a chronicle of the days before the revolution which he was singing now—a simple love story. But was it? To my astonishment I realized that the minstrel's voice was leading in a Russian Easter hymn, "*Christos voskrese . . . Christos voskrese.*" On the outskirts of the crowd an old man's voice was raised. Soon half the swaying crowd was singing with him. Then the minstrel's voice went on, alone. After a while he sang another church hymn; again the people joined in.

When the last "Amen" was sung, we started home.

"Explain it to me," I asked Aliosha, as we walked down the lane towards his home.

"These minstrels keep the old religious songs alive," he said. "I learned them, years ago, from listening to men like this. They are clever. They weave the hymns into the story, so that they can say to anyone who questions them, 'We're just telling a tale from the old, dead days.' But they are religious men and they are making life better for us all."

Aliosha and his wife might themselves have formed the heart of a troubadour's tale. They had been married for seven years when I knew them, and their home was a small oasis of devotion in the town. They said grace before meals, and evening prayers.

"How wonderful," I said to them, "that you have built a real Christian marriage under the very eyes of the Militant Atheists. It must have taken great courage."

They laughed.

"Courage?" said Aliosha. "We were frightened of our shadow in the early days. No, my friend, we didn't start out to have a Christian marriage. God and God alone saw to that."

Aliosha and Marya had married during one of the periods of particularly severe persecution of the Church. Aliosha was always devout, he said. His mother had taught him his prayers and his catechism. He did not know Marya was a believer, too; this was not a secret one lightly shared in days like those. And both of them were under eighteen during their courtship: if they had admitted to anyone that they had ever been taught to pray, the consequences might have been very serious for their families.

So Aliosha and Marya were married in the Soviet Government bureau. They lived together in a home with no icon in sight. They never breathed to one another what was in their hearts. Every night in bed Aliosha closed his eyes, forced himself to breathe regularly and, in silence, said his prayers. Lying next to him, Marya waited until she thought he was asleep, slipped out of bed to the other room, knelt down and said her prayers. This duplicity went on between them for over a year.

"Then little Ivan was born," Marya told me. "I decided I had to have him baptized by the priest. Oh, what plotting I did so that Aliosha should never know. For I thought he was a thoroughgoing atheist. I thought he would be shocked if I suggested such an old-fashioned idea as a christening."

When Aliosha was away from home, in a neighboring village, Marya took the baby and walked the fifteen miles necessary to reach the nearest priest. Here she had the baby properly baptized and walked home, with a light heart: Aliosha need never know.

"And I," said Aliosha, "I was grieving over the fact that I dare not ask Marya to take the baby to a church. She would have laughed at me—I was sure of that! When she fell ill I decided the good God had given her a little sickness so that I might have an excuse to take the child away from home. I said, 'I'll take the baby to my mother for a few weeks until you're well.' My mother was devout. When I got to her home I said to her, 'Take the baby to the priest. Have him baptized.' "

Aliosha laughed.

"He must have been surprised, that man," he said. "My mother told him the baby's name and gave him the name of our village.

" 'Will you baptize Ivan for me, Father?' she asked.

" 'No,' he said. 'I will not.'

"She was astounded.

" 'But why not, Father?' she asked him. 'Why, why not?'

" 'Because I baptized this baby last week when its mother brought it on to me.'

"Imagine! When my mother came back to the house and told me this, I was numb with astonishment. I walked all the way home in a daze, carrying the baby, trying to think things out. All these months, when I had been so careful to conceal my faith, my dear Marya had been playing the same game with me.

"I was so happy. Suddenly, there on the country road, it came to me how very happy I was. For Marya and I need not pretend to one another any more. The one thing that had been a barrier between us was removed.

"I was passing a place where, many years ago, there used to be a little wooden wayside shrine. It had been torn down when I was still a child, but I remembered the Cross that used to stand there. I knelt down by the side of the road with the baby in my arms and said my prayers.

"Then I came back to Marya. She was surprised to see me so soon. 'Here's your little Christian son,' I said to her." . . .

Sometimes even greater difficulties stand in the way of arranging to have a Russian baby baptized by a priest. When Piotr told me his story, it reminded me of the long train of pilgrims carrying their children for baptism to the Slovakian priest on the Russian border. I had found this Piotr in the small café where he worked, giving him the password from the previous town.

"We are post-office Christians in this section," he told me gravely, as he took my valise against my protests and guided me through the narrow streets.

"Post-office Christians?" I asked him.

"Look about you," he said. "You can walk through every street in this town and you will not see a church: after the revolution nearly all of them were burned, along with the mosques, and there has not been a priest in residence here for many years.

"But we are good Christians, some of us, just the same. And we bring up our children in the Faith and take our chances that we may be betrayed. A man has to die sometime, doesn't he?"

"But this post-office Christianity?" I asked him. "What is that?"

"It began first when my grandfather died," Piotr said, as we made our way through a maze of narrow alleys and steep stone steps. "Religious funerals were forbidden, and anyway, there was no priest here to perform one. My grandmother was heartbroken: she said, 'You have to find a way to get his grave blessed.'

"Well, I thought about it. Then I said to her, 'Who do you know in old Samara who is a believer and can be trusted?' She told me of an old lady like herself.

" 'Write to her,' I said, 'and enclose a little of the earth from Grandfather's grave and ask her to have her priest bless it and send it back to you. Then you can scatter the consecrated earth over him.'

"She wept, she was so happy. Then I had a bad time,

wondering whether it would work. I didn't know what the Church rules might be; maybe the priest would refuse.

"But he didn't. He blessed the earth, and it came back safely, and after a while many of the other people in the town began doing the same thing. Whenever there was a funeral, they sent earth from the grave to Kuibishev to be blessed."

We had reached the old stone house in whose ground floor rear Piotr lived. His wife, Katya, greeted us warmly.

"Katya," said Piotr, "show him your ring."

She proudly held up a little loop of gold on her wedding-ring finger. Piotr wore one like it.

"That's post-office business, too," Piotr explained. "When we got married we wanted a religious ceremony. So I sent the two rings to the priest and he said the Nuptial Mass over them. When the baby was born, we had holy water sent to us for the baptism, which we performed ourselves.

"Yes, this is a town with Christian husbands, wives and babies, and Christian dead in the cemetery. But it's all done by post-office ritual." . . .

Many of the underground Christians had stories of last-minute rescues and extraordinary coincidences which they took as signs of God's special intercession in answer to their prayers.

Mitia was a factory worker, a fine gray-haired man to whom I was passed on by a Christian in the previous town. When I entered his home I saw an icon on the wall, with a little votive lamp burning boldly before it. I looked my surprise.

"It would be no use for *me* to hide my religion," he chuckled. "My name has been down on the suspect lists since before the GPU became the MVD. I was a church sponsor in the early days."

"Oh," I said, "you've had a church where you could worship all these years?"

"No," he said. "Not by any means. But at one period a pretence of legality was built up around this closing of the churches. It was announced that twenty signatures of parishioners would be enough to keep a church open. I signed my name. So did nineteen others. Then—the Communists would say it was the sheerest coincidence—one of the twenty was arrested by the secret police in the middle of the night, on charges that were never disclosed. Her name was Danzas; she was a professor at the university and she was sent to a concentration camp. That left only nineteen sponsors on the list. The next day the church was closed for 'lack of parishioners.' We were not, of course, allowed time to find a substitute.

"This device was used in the closing of hundreds of churches. Any one of the twenty sponsors might be seized on trumped-up charges, in order that the church could be 'legally' taken over. Later, of course, the officials were less finicky; they simply requisitioned the churches for warehouses or dance halls. But these are sad matters. Let me show you something that will make you happy."

He motioned me to come closer to the icon: it was a lovely thing, a representation of Our Lord seated in the central panel, with His Mother standing on the left, St. John the Evangelist on the right. The background was the color of burnished gold. The paints were as bright as if it had been finished yesterday.

"That is an old icon," he said. "And it has been exposed to dampness, cold, heat and friction during the periods when even I had to wrap and hide it. In the old days it would have needed repairs five or six times in the twenty-odd years it has been hanging on that wall. We used to send our icons to a special colony of workmen in Nijni-Novgorod, who brightened them up and replaced the chipped paint. Since the revolution that has been impossible. But look carefully. Do you see any signs of wear?"

"No," I said. "None."

"That is the little miracle of Russia," he told me. "It has happened in thousands of cases: our icons are restored in ways that we do not understand."

In many other parts of Russia I heard the story of the icons that were mysteriously restored. The legend has grown and it has brought happiness and faith to those in the Russian catacombs.

CHAPTER 12

One-third of a Nation

OUR convoy reached Tula on the outskirts of Moscow, and then the great capital itself. We were dead tired; we had been traveling since dawn that day and what we longed for most was sleep.

In Moscow, at least, we did not have to beat up our own lodgings. A Red Army captain sought me out and said, "Follow me, Comrade. I will take you to the place where you are billeted."

It was a large barracks, darkened for the night. He led me to the cubicle where I was to sleep and left me. I blew out the candle and gratefully flung myself onto the narrow bed. I was not in a mood to criticize my lodgings.

The next day, however, I discovered the disconcerting fact that as an honored Partisan officer, a guest of the Red Army, I had been assigned to one of the best billets that the capital could provide. That meant that I was housed in a building set aside for the members of the dreaded secret police.

"And this," I thought, "is too much of a good thing."

The problem of celebrating Mass each day would be

made much more dangerous by the presence up and down these corridors of trained watchers of the MVD. The only time when I could count on privacy was after everybody was asleep, and Russians are notorious for going to bed late. I still carried the precious wine for the Mass concealed in an iodine bottle and the Hosts of unleavened bread were mixed with my aspirins. For greater safety I had not brought my Missal into Russia with me; I celebrated my Mass from memory, reciting whatever Epistles and Gospels I was able to recall.

My room was a small one, just large enough for a table and a single bed. I learned to spread out two copies of *Pravda* on the bed, while I prepared the materials for the Mass; in case of interruption I could cover everything with one of the newspapers and lean protectively above them with my body stretched along the end of the bed. It was well that I had devised this system for an emergency.

One night, just as I was ready to begin the "Introibo," my door burst open and a woman MVD captain walked in. She looked surprised when she saw that I was clothed and that I had a lighted lamp by my bed: she herself was dressed for the night. I knew her; her husband, another MVD officer, had gone away on a few days' leave. She sat down, quite without embarrassment, on the far end of my bed and began to talk.

"My husband is away," she said. "And I don't like to sleep alone. I thought maybe you were lonely, too."

I ignored the hint and cast about quickly for some subject that might interest her.

"Tell me about your childhood," I said rapidly. There are very few people who are not glad to talk on this topic. "Where are your mother, your father?"

She glanced at me, ready to take offense because I was not beginning a flirtation.

"My father is dead," she said sharply.

"What did he do?" I persisted. I had somehow to steer the conversation into safe and friendly channels.

"He was a doctor," she said sullenly.

"Where?"

"Oh, here in Moscow. For a few years in Leningrad. And once, when I was small . . ."

The device had worked. Her own memories began to interest her. Soon she was telling me all that she remembered about her father. He had been such a kind man, she said. So good to her mother and to the children, so willing to get up at any hour of the night to go and help the sick.

As she spoke, her mood softened. The tender Russian heart began to show. She said to me: "You know, Comrade, I cannot believe that such a kind man, such a wise man, could just disappear when he died and leave no trace, nothing to survive of all that he had made himself. Sometimes it seems impossible that such a man should simply cease to be. Death has utterly destroyed someone I loved so much."

"But, Comrade," I said to her, "your father did not utterly die. Man is not annihilated at death. Our spirits survive."

The captain stared at me.

"How wonderful it would be if that were true," she said.

"It is true," I told her.

For two hours we discussed the source of man's spirituality. The Red captain put many questions to me, and they were intelligent ones. She had been puzzled by a dozen problems which the materialism of her schoolmasters had never answered. They came tumbling out; and as I outlined the basis for religious belief, she nodded. This, she said, was what she had been seeking.

At four o'clock in the morning we ended our discussion and the captain left. I proceeded to celebrate my Mass, saying a special prayer for her and for her husband.

The next night, as I was again preparing my Mass, she broke in on me. She had scarcely got inside the door before she said, "Comrade, tell me more about God."

So, for a second night I talked to her about religion. As she was leaving she said, "My husband will be home tomorrow. He has never met anyone who spoke of these things, I know. May I bring him to you?"

"Of course," I said.

During the next month I gave instruction to this couple. After ten days or so, they brought in two other women members of the MVD, and a man who was engaged to one of them. Then, every night, I held my convert class of men and women who sat cross-legged on the floor of my tiny cubicle, drinking in the glorious news that God exists and that He is kind. They asked me many questions; they passed through the difficult inner struggle of every convert who has to abandon familiar conceptions in order to make room for the new. Before I left the city I had baptized seven members of the MVD, heard their confessions and given them their first Communion in my little room in the very center of the Soviet secret police!

One of my own doubts had been answered. The religious hunger of the Russian young people was real—it was not the child of any battle-born hysteria. Not only were the combat soldiers looking for God; even the officers who had never seen battle were groping toward belief.

Had I been able to stay in Moscow, I told myself, I could have had three years' work instructing and converting members of the secret police alone!

In Moscow I arranged, through a contact Gorky had given me, to meet one of the daring "traveling priests" of whom I had heard so much.

We met in the cellar storeroom of a large apartment-house: he, of all men, did not wish to risk being seen with a foreigner. We sat on upturned packing boxes, our gloomy corner lit by a little wick burning in a saucerful of oil.

"Tell me, Father," I said to him, "why you are still so distrustful. Can't you appear on the streets in your cassock, as some priests do?"

"Oh, yes," he said. "I might do that. And for a little while I might be safe and happy. I should like to be above ground. Dodging secret police officers is no pleasure to me. But suppose I revealed myself as a priest and were left unmolested today? Do you know what would happen? Well, I do. And I will tell you.

"In one year, or two, or five, the Party line will change. The Communists cannot afford to let God into the hearts of the Russian people, for God crowds Marx and Lenin out. The authorities will remember this someday. Every open church is a threat to them. *Every* church. Even if the present Patriarch co-operates as enthusiastically as any Comsomol, he cannot drop all mention of God from the ceremonies of the Church. He cannot utterly obscure the Christian conception of the universe. The contradiction between Communism and religion cannot be concealed for long. This new, renovated Orthodox Church of Alexei will be closed down, as the 'Living Church' of the twenties was."

He spoke without bitterness, this old man with the transparent eyes of the very good. He seemed quite relaxed: fear for his personal security was, I guessed, an emotion from which he had detached himself many years ago.

"What will happen when the Communists crack down on the puppet church again? Eh? What will happen then?" he asked me. "I will tell you, my foreign friend, what will happen. The priests who are so happy in their tolerated churches today will be put on trial, poor boys. Some of them will be sent to Siberia on some charge or other. Others will become outcasts—beggars—again. And all of them will be watched, as priests, pastors, rabbis have been watched since 1919. If they try to leave their town, the police will know it before they have traveled half a *verst.* And the poor people whose priests have been taken away will be left alone again, with no one to baptize the babies or shrive the souls or make the marriages holy. Do you see?

"Some of us must remain underground for that. And another thing—only the secret priests can shake off government spies. I have traveled around for many years now. I know the places where the need is greatest. I know how to disguise my Mass kit, how to wrap my stole so that it fits into a peasant's hat. I'm an old hand at this work. And I must keep out of sight now so that I can continue the work later, when the registered priests are put away."

Above us the church bells were ringing for Sunday Mass. Men and women were walking through the streets, heading for the churches as if Christianity were no more endangered here than in Paris, in New York. It was true, of course, that the orders to the Party men still held: they must not admit to a religion if they wished to advance in their careers. But fewer than 3 per cent of the Russians are Party members; on the surface it appeared as if the USSR had decided to allow the other 97 per cent to worship as they chose.

"Can you be sure of the Communists' bad faith?" I asked him. "Especially now that they have allowed the Patriarch to open a seminary again?"

He smiled a sad and gentle smile.

"Do you know how students are selected for that seminary?" he asked. "They must first have passed through the State University, and they are sent to be priests only if the University authorities recommend them for the seminary. I wonder how much a priestly vocation is considered by the Soviet Committee that judges these cases? And how much 'political reliability' is weighed? Oh, my friend, do not be misled. It is not by such concessions as these that the sincerity of the Soviet is judged. I will tell you how to judge it.

"When the Communist government releases from its prisons the surviving bishops and priests and rabbis and ministers who are there on purely religious charges: then I will say, 'They are seriously considering a change.' When the Communist-dominated governments of Jugo-Slavia and Hungary cease persecuting the clergy in those countries, I will say, 'Now, they have really begun to change.'

"When the Stalinists allow missionaries from other countries to come in and preach the word of God, I will believe that their hearts have softened. When these people in the government act in accordance with the moral law of the universe, throw open the concentration camps where they have secured twenty million slaves, I will say, 'They are on the way.' But I will never believe that the persecution of religion is finally ended until the Marxist textbooks are withdrawn from the schools and the propaganda for materialism has ceased.

"Never mind whether the churches are open or closed, if you are trying to study the Communists' future policy towards our God. The Nazi persecution of religion was one of the worst in history, but the churches never closed. No. So long as the men in power here continue to persecute a single Russian citizen unjustly, and to deny him his God-given rights, they are persecuting Christ."

A knock—three short, two long—came at the door. The old man opened it. He greeted a young workman and said to me, "I asked Father Josef to come to meet you."

"You too are a priest!" I exclaimed. "But you are so young."

Father Josef smiled. "I am a graduate of the underground seminary."

He described to me then what was the most audacious of all the bold gestures of defiance thrown in the face of the Bolshevik state: the Moscow Orthodox Theological Seminary. Young men attracted to the religious life had studied here for years, until the place was detected and closed in 1938. Under Archbishop Barthelmy they were given secret instruction in the evening hours; during the day most of the seminarians attended the Soviet university.

"We had a secret church," he said, "concealed in a warehouse. The registered churches were far too closely watched for us to dare make use of them."

After his ordination my friend had taken up the dangerous work of the "traveling priest"; disguised as a carpenter, he traveled about, visiting the villages which had no churches left in them and administering the sacraments to secret believers.

When the policy of toleration was announced, after the German attack, his superiors had chosen this very village for him to work in; it was surrounded by an enormous area which had lacked a church for twenty years.

"Did you ever work among the unconverted?" I asked him.

"Oh, yes," he said. "Of course. Working with the youth to undo their atheist schooling has been one of our most important tasks.

"That's one reason why young priests were needed. It was easier for us to build up friendship with boys and girls. Often, on my travels, I'd stay in a town a few days and organize an athletic team. I'd teach them soccer and football and make friends with them. On my next trip to that town, I'd have a little cell of athletes waiting for me. It was easy enough, talking to these boys and girls, to lead them on to other things. We'd start a singing group: after they'd learned half a dozen patriotic airs, I'd teach them a hymn or two. Or we'd get together and read the Russian classics: it wasn't so hard to transfer their interest from Tolstoi or Dostoievesky to the New Testament. Always, in every group, there would be a few whose hearts were drawn by the religious teaching. I'd gather them into a secret cell, and teach them how to pray.

"I've made converts of young people whose mothers and fathers were ardent, icon-burning atheists. So have many of the other priests. A whole group of such cells of

Young Christians exists all over Russia. Some of them have a name for themselves: 'Christsomol,' to distinguish them from 'Comsomol.' But they are apt to be reckless, these brave young ones. I am afraid for them when the inevitable religious pogroms come again."

But I was eager to meet some of the Moscow people who were not members of the underground; for this reason I had taken letters of introduction from Russian front-line friends "in case" I ever found myself inside their country.

One day I visited a woman whose address had been given to me by her brother, one of the comrades at the front. He was not a Christian and neither, I supposed, was she. He said to me, "If you get to Moscow, look up Olga. She has plenty of friends among the Party big shots. She can tell you their gossip before it's taken place."

Olga sounded worth a call. I found she had a telephone—a sure sign of prosperity—and arranged to call on her late one summer afternoon. Her apartment was one of the most prosperous I had seen: the tea was served on fine French china. We sat on well-cushioned, prettily upholstered chairs. Several good etchings hung on the walls.

Olga was a widow. While she was arranging the tea in the kitchen, her ten-year-old daughter began to chat with me. We were quite alone in the apartment. The little girl noticed a military medal I wore because I had found it carried a certain prestige value within Russia. It was from one of the Balkan armies; it happened to be in the shape of a Greek cross.

The child looked at it gravely and then said, to my amazement, "Christos."

"What do you know of Christos?" I asked her.

The mother returned as I was speaking. She set down the tea things and looked at me with sorrowful eyes.

"Oh, Doctor," she said. "It is so hard to know what to do in Russia today. My child may suffer because I have made her a Christian. Yes. But I have spared her the alternative—life in a bleak and godless universe."

Olga then told me the story of her conversion. She had never received any Christian teaching from her parents. It was a curious tale.

When Olga was a student at the university she was President of the Comsomol. She was utterly loyal to the Party and loyal, as well, to logic and the pursuit of truth. She had not guessed that these two creeds could ever come into conflict.

But there were things that began to trouble her, in her second student year. "*Nichevo.*" The Party leaders could straighten them out. She arranged an appointment with one of the secretaries, so that she could learn the explanation of these things she did not fully understand.

"Comrade Secretary," she said to him. "You tell us that material comfort for the masses is the goal of our state. Yet we are surrounded by nothing but misery, poverty, famine and filth. How is that? And you tell us that the Soviet exists for the contentment of the workers. Yet the workers are never safe: any one of them is apt to disappear without warning, in the middle of the night. Yet these people who have offended the regime are neither capitalists nor landowners. They are simple workers like ourselves. How can you pretend that they are counterrevolutionists?

"We are asked to sacrifice ourselves to the ideal of world revolution. We are asked it every week. But you tell us, Comrade Secretary, that man is incapable of acting selflessly. So how can we sacrifice ourselves? Tell me, Comrade Secretary. I am puzzled and I want to know."

The secretary she had chosen was not one of the "philosophers" of the movement. He found her questions embarrassing and too dangerous to be discussed. He said to her, "Forget these things for the moment, Olga. We will talk of them another time."

Olga saw that this man was not going to help her. So she sought out one of her university professors. He was one of those men who have sold a good brain into bondage; one of the pitiful cynics whose "scholarly" treatises are made sickening by the hypocritical pretense that Stalin has been the great innovator in his field—whether in astronomy or medicine, literature or history. From this man Olga received nothing but the suggestion that she devote herself to her books and leave these questions for older heads to decide.

But Olga was too logical, too persistent, too loyal to truth for that. Still convinced that there must be a way of explaining her doubts away, she discussed them with a man who had left the university a few years ahead of her and who had once been active in the Comsomol. He was sympathetic, a little evasive, but he said, "Keep on thinking, Olga. You are on the track of something big. Speak of this to no one else, but come and talk to me from time to time."

The more Olga thought, the more she observed, the graver grew her doubts of the whole body of Marxist premises. When she had reached this treasonable conclusion she took it to her friend.

"I, too, have seen the fallacies," he said. "And now,

Olga, let me help you. The things we have been taught were false: you have discovered that. But do not despair: a far more wonderful philosophy exists, and it is true."

This friend introduced her to the study of Christianity. Since she was now over eighteen, he dared to introduce her to a priest who lent her many books. She became a Christian. But she still kept up her friendship with the Party leaders.

"Some of them will see the falsity of this doctrine we have been taught," she said. "I want them to have someone there to help them when they do. That is why I have so rarely gone to church—why I have no underground connections. If I were known to be a believer, I should lose my friendships with the people I most wish to help."

Olga was one of the first to lead me to believe that the number of Christians within Russia is far greater than those on the outside suppose. "One-third of us believe in Christ," a Red Army friend had told me at the front, and it had startled me. Now I began to think that even this estimate might be too low.

I decided to spend more of my time in contact with Russians who had not been certified to me by any member of the underground, in order to form my own judgment of how many Olga's there might be, working alone, outside any organization, in the religious war.

So, I laid careful plans to escape from the Red Army escort and to travel by train. Even armed with my general's pass, this method of getting about might be slow, uncertain. But it would give me my chance to talk to many men.

CHAPTER 13

I Travel on My Own

RIDING "hard" (third-class) on one of the slow trains across Russia I fell into conversation with an official of a kolkhoz, or collective farm. Was he a Party member, I asked?

"Oh, yes," he told me. "But there are not many of us where I live. It's a thankless job trying to get some sense and revolutionary spirit into these backward kulaks. Would you believe it? Only last week I discovered that one of my best fieldworkers was a *priest!* And that he had been spreading his hocus-pocus under my nose for years."

"Amazing!" I said to him. "How was it done?"

"Oh," he told me, "there have been other cases. They're sly, these priests. I can't spend all my time nosing around the barracks when the people are supposed to be in bed, and it seems that half the population of the farm have been coming to him for midnight Mass. He admits he has baptized and married the citizens for years.

"We might never have caught him, except for an accident in the field. A man got caught in a threshing machine and everyone could see he was going to die. What does this priest do but cross the field, big as life, and kneel down next to the dying man and make the sign of the Cross over him?

"I yelled, 'What do you think you're doing?' He didn't even answer me till the man had died—went on muttering there in the wheat. Then he stood up and said, 'Ivan was a Christian. He wanted to make his peace with God.'

"I turned him over to the police in short order, you can be sure. But how many are there like him whom we haven't caught?"

The man was shocked and shattered. He went on: "I talked to some of the other Party members about it. They tell me even worse things have been discovered. A man with a responsible hospital official's job in Tashkent died and was given a religious funeral, against all the rules. When the authorities investigated, they found that he had been an *archbishop* in disguise!

"Oh, they're sly," he said. "Take their ration cards away, send them to Siberia, kill them off, nothing you can do seems to discourage them.

"From their zeal," he said, slowly, "you'd almost think they believed their religion themselves. What a waste, Comrade, to have these men working so hard and selflessly on the wrong side. If they were only enlightened, educated men, what Communists they would make!"

I felt a real pity for this man: the battle he was fighting was already lost.

At my very next stop I had another proof of this.

It was in a city where a few Orthodox Churches were open. I attended Mass on Sunday, and afterwards, decided to risk an open visit to the priest. I would, of course, be observed by the spies who always haunt the churches, but I could risk boldness in this city. I knew my baggage had not been searched—the secret pattern of my packing was undisturbed. I was reasonably sure I had not been shadowed; by now, I was fairly expert at determining such things. If I were picked up by a police spy at the church, I knew at least six methods of losing him in a city of this size.

In the vestry I saw, to my amazement, a Russian boy of nine or ten years. Knowing the harsh penalties that await anyone who speaks of religion to the children of Russia, I said to him: "What are *you* doing here?"

"Waiting for the Father," he said calmly.

"Who told you about religion?" I asked him.

"My comrade."

"And who told him?"

"Another comrade."

The priest had joined us now. After we had exchanged greetings, and the little boy saw that I was well received, he said, "Shall I tell him, Father?"

The priest nodded. "Well," said the child, "we do it this way."

He held up his left hand, fingers outspread. "I have five friends. I know my catechism from my comrade, who learned it from his grandmother. I have to teach it to my five friends. When they have learned it, I give them an examination. Then if they pass, they become teachers. Each of them has to pass it on to five other friends. That's the way it spreads."

"But aren't you afraid of the police?" I asked.

The little boy shrugged the usual "*Nichevo.*"

"Wouldn't the police arrest you if they knew?"

"Oh, yes," he said. "*Nichevo.*"

"Mightn't they even kill you?"

"*Nichevo.*" Then he became serious. Very gravely he said: "They can kill me," and he put his hand on his heart with a gesture of unconscious drama, "but they can never kill Christ in me."

This candid child had formed his own "underground" in the shadow of a tolerated church. Such free-lance believers seemed to meet me everywhere.

There was, for instance, Maria. I met her quite by accident. Wandering around a strange town one day, gazing into the shop windows and studying their pitiful array of shoddy merchandise, I lost my way. It was a quiet section; no one seemed to be in the streets. I heard the sound of violin playing coming from one of the apartment houses and decided to ask the musician if he could tell me how to find my barracks.

I knocked. The door was opened for me by a handsome girl of seventeen, her violin bow still in her hand. While I was asking her my way, I heard a voice from the next room, a man's voice, crying, "Maria. Maria. Who is it?"

"An army officer, Papa," she cried. Then she smiled at me. "My father is an invalid. He has very little to interest him. Would you like to come in and share a glass of tea with him? He would be very glad to talk to someone back from the war."

I said I would be delighted. The father was a man of about fifty—worn, ill, haggard. The room was furnished with the usual rickety table and broken chair. The plaster was peeling from the walls. I sat down by the bed and Maria went to get us our tea.

"You are from Slovakia?" he said, when I told him

where I had been fighting. "Once, I attended boarding school there, very long ago." He began speaking to me in Slovakian, haltingly, searching for the words but taking a great pleasure in the display of this talent which had rusted so long unused.

"What school did you attend?" I asked.

He looked embarrassed. Then he mentioned the name of a Catholic school for boys.

"I, too, was taught by the monks," I said quietly. "But such schools are not allowed to teach in that country since the war."

He looked at me appraisingly.

"Do you remember this?" He quoted one of the familiar prayers in Slovakian.

"Of course," I said, joining him in repeating the final words. Then I took a chance: "It is very beautiful," I said.

Daring a little more with every remark, we had soon reached the point where we trusted one another. He told me his sad story. He had been a young teacher before the revolution and had stayed on at his post through all the changes. He passed several times through the hands of the MVD; his illness was the result of a severe beating at their hands, a few years back.

"Those secret-police raids," he groaned. "You cannot know the terror under which we live. It is night. We hear a car groan to a stop in the street before the house. Armed men get out. Everyone in the neighborhood is awake; every heart is trembling; everyone is saying to himself, 'Who will be the victim this time? Have they come for me?'

"Then a skirmish, somewhere. A slammed door. A woman crying. Footsteps. The motor starts up and another Russian has been taken away to death or the living death of the concentration camps.

"In the worst periods, when the purges are on, we sleep every night with a few bits of food and toilet articles under our pillows, in case we should be taken. And when once a man has disappeared, his family mourn for him as dead. No one ever returns from these midnight disappearances."

We were speaking in Slovakian. Maria returned with the tea. Her father said to me, "Do not be afraid to continue in Russian. She is a good religious girl, no Communist."

"But that is wonderful, Maria," I said. "Have you ever been in a church?"

"Many times," she said.

"But how? You are so young?"

She smiled. "There was only one church left in the town where I grew up," she said. "It was very far away, in a cemetery on the edge of the town. A shack, in fact, where an old priest said Mass every Sunday at six o'clock in the morning.

"You know, of course, that no child under eighteen was allowed to go to church. But my mother would not hear of leaving me behind her. From the time I was twelve years old she always took me. She used to dress me up in an old woman's clothing, with a shawl and a stick. She taught me to lean down on it and hobble and to keep the shawl over my face. Every Sunday we made the trip that way until I was old enough to go into the churches openly."

Traveling alone by rail, with no set destination, I had the bad luck to stop in a town through which the soldiers were returning in vast numbers from the front. It was impossible to move; the station was crowded with civilians sitting patiently on their piled-up belongings, brewing tea on the floor, sleeping stretched out in the waiting room. Many of them had been there eight, ten days hoping for a train to take them back to their homes in the former combat area.

Every day I visited the station. Every day I saw the trains returning from the front, swarming with soldiers. Men piled on the roofs, hung out of the windows, held themselves by a perilous grasp of the hands to the ledges of the doors.

The town was overflowing with refugees. With the greatest difficulty I found a place to stay: a poor little home on the outskirts of the town, with its roof caved in so that rain water fell upon my bed. The stove had been destroyed. The nearest thing to plumbing was an open WC in the yard. Yet I passed several days of great contentment there. It was summer, now, and there was a fine round moon on display. Every evening I sat in the little yard behind my lodging, in the area where half the neighborhood met to laugh and sing the melancholy songs of Russia. There was little talk of politics or war. It was a good time.

I had established contact on the first day with Vova, a young man who worked for Gorky's underground. One day I asked him to tell me how he had become so ardent and active a member of the Christian resistance. He said, "Come out of doors. We can walk down by the river."

As we walked by the deserted riverbank, this is what Vova told me:

"I was a member of the Comsomol when I was

younger: everyone belonged to it. It was the thing to do, if you wanted to have holidays and special privileges. I also joined the cell of Militant Atheists: why not? It seemed to please the Party big shots and the activities appealed to us. We were taught a severe, priggish little lecture to be delivered to any older person who hinted that he might believe in God. And when we passed a church we were to call out a few jeering words at anyone going in. We were also given little tracts on atheism to distribute.

"I was a model example of Soviet youth. I was active in Party work. I studied hard at dialectical materialism. I believed that when the whole world had become Communist, man's problems would be solved."

Vova kicked a pebble and thrust his hands angrily into the pockets of his shabby coat.

"That was until the age of about sixteen. Then I began to question—oh, a lot of things. Especially love. We had been told at first that everyone ought to be promiscuous; that was in the early days during the post-card divorces. Later the Party line changed and lifelong marriage became the new ideal.

"That switch made me wonder. If the Party heads could have made a mistake on a thing like *that,* they might be wrong on other things. If they had had to come around to the old-fashioned ideas of my grandparents in the matter of sex, they might some day find the old people had been right about—well, for instance—God."

We turned and started back along the river path. The day was brilliantly alive with the lights and scents of spring. The sun danced on the water and the cool air spanked our cheeks. It was very good to be alive.

Vova paused. "With some of my friends I debated

these matters. We began keeping a sharp nose out for the old books, and we discovered quite a lot of them tucked away in forgotten corners. Once or twice we even found, by a miracle, some new books printed abroad and brought into the country by visiting foreigners. The bellboys in the hotels where foreigners stay were our best source for these.

"Anyway we started reading everything we could find on religion, philosophy, economics, sociology. We did not understand all we read, but we were startled to find that men could write so logically without using any of the ideas we had been given at school. A secret traveling library became the most exciting thing in our lives; those worn-out, ragged pages opened prison doors to our minds and let light in."

Vova stopped, looked about us to be sure we were out of earshot of any casual passerby and said, "We had better stand here while I tell you the rest of it.

"One night a friend of mine, a member of the same Comsomol as mine and another Militant Atheist, gave me a bunch of papers written out in longhand. He said, 'Pass it along to those we can trust.' I placed the papers inside a torn place in the lining of my coat and did not take them out until I was alone, the door safely locked behind me.

"Then I looked at the writing. I read it all through, from end to end, without a pause. It was an amazing story. I did not know who had written it, but it touched my heart. It was the Gospel according to St. Luke."

He was whispering now, very fast, with the words tumbling out so that he could tell me all before the inevitable interruption should arrive.

"That night was the turning point of my life. Up to

then we had heard of Christ, of course, but as a convenient myth used by the capitalists during many centuries to exploit the working class. In St. Luke I studied Christ. I saw that he had been a poor man and the friend of poor men. I memorized the words His Mother said: 'He hath put down the mighty from their seats and hath exalted the humble. He hath filled the hungry with good things and the rich He hath sent empty away.' I said, 'They have lied to us about this Christ.' I said, 'I think His way is better than the way we have been taught. I want to follow it.' "

Vova's eyes were very earnest. He spoke simply, without self-consciousness or any sanctimony. His approach to Christianity was as fresh, as simple as that of the fishermen of Galilee.

"I passed the pages on to other comrades. And they, some of them, felt as I did. Inside our Militant Atheist cell we organized a secret inner group; an elite who secretly studied the forbidden teaching.

"We had, at first, no other Christian writing than the Gospel. We copied this by hand, so that every member could keep a hidden copy for himself. But then God was good to us; an old man, a lodger in our home, died and among his possessions I found a torn and tattered medieval history, written before the revolution. It told about the monasteries, and how they had kept the Faith alive during centuries of war and confusion. It gave the Rule of St. Vassil. We studied it, and we said, 'So that is the way to be a Christian.'

"All this, remember, was clandestine, for we had even more to fear than older believers would have had. We had been given positions of Party trust and we would have been called traitors. So we read these books only in bed, under the blankets, by flashlight. We discussed Christianity only after we had made elaborate arrangements to be alone and safe—and only in the open air."

A cart came down the road, drawn by a worn and scraggly mule. Vova lit a cigarette, burst into a Russian song and waited until the driver was well out of earshot. Then he went on.

"We finally decided to do a very rash and reckless thing. We could not escape from Russia to join other Christians, but we could, perhaps, escape the surveillance of the Communists inside our country.

"At that time a great campaign had been launched to induce young people to organize *kolkhoz,* or collective farms. We were young and strong and considered politically reliable. Our application was granted; we took over a good piece of land to work."

Vova leaned close to me and he dropped his voice.

"That *kolkhoz* was a monastery."

He laughed at the astonishment in my eyes.

"Yes," he said. "We did the best we could. We could not chant the psalms and other holy verses mentioned in the rule in old Slavonic, for we did not know how. We said a few prayers we had been able to learn. We had obtained a complete Bible now and we studied that.

"This lasted for two years," he said. "Then somehow, we never knew how, the MVD became suspicious. They raided the monastery and found our Bible. Together with two comrades, I had managed to hide in the fields. We made our escape by night. The rest were carried off to prison.

"The war divided me from those two friends. I do not know what has become of them. But someday, somehow, we will get together. And then, in an even more distant section, we will establish our monastery again."

There have been other secret monasteries within the Soviet: most of them were peopled by men who had been monks before the revolution and who continued their community life in secret, taking factory jobs as a cover and carrying on their devotions after dark. The Militant Atheists League in 1938 announced the discovery of two underground monasteries, one of them in Kiev.

Were there underground convents in the Soviet, as well? I never knowingly encountered a nun in my travels. But when the whole chronicle of God's underground is told, I suspect we shall find that there have been secret communities of women religious, too.

I might, perhaps, have learned of a Russian convent, or found some other missing bit of the jigsaw I was filling in, had I not suffered serious mishap. It was in a town where I had the home address of a Christian trade-union official active in the underground.

It turned out to be a shabby little house, with a scrawny tree growing out of the parched earth before the door. I knocked and waited. Soon a woman opened to me, smiled broadly, beckoned me to enter. Her husband looked up inquiringly from the table where he had scattered before him the pieces of a broken alarm clock, brought back in some soldier's knapsack from the west. He was trying, poor man, to repair it.

No explanation of my presence was necessary; officers entered anyone's home those days in search of lodgings, of food, of information. My smile told these good people that I meant them no harm.

"I have word from Ivan," I said, repeating the password. "He is well and will be returning to Russia soon. Meanwhile, I bring you a little gift."

I spread out on the table the prearranged articles; one apple, three pears, a head of lettuce, a small packet of tea. And I waited. I waited in growing fear.

The response to my greeting should have been instantaneous: one of them ought to have said, "The pears are very fine this year." Instead, they gaped at me. The man said, "But, my friend, you are kind, indeed. Sit down and have a bite with us."

Something had gone wrong. I watched my hosts carefully; there was no such exchange of glances as I half expected, no suggestion that I might have fallen into a trap.

"Grushenka," the man called out suddenly. "Come here."

From the other room came a girl of fifteen or so. She smiled.

"Grushenka," said her father. "Run to the home of Nicholay. Tell him we have a visitor. Ask him to excuse me if I do not come to the meeting."

Grushenka smiled and left. My heart sank. It seemed all too obvious where she had gone.

There was nothing for me to do but to sit there making amiable conversation, sipping the scalding glass of tea that was brought to me, waiting for the blow to fall. At any moment the door might open; Grushenka would be in the background, preceded by the police agents she had been sent to fetch.

"Yes, yes, the war with Japan will go on for months," I was saying. "So much seems clear." But my mind was busily reconstructing all my movements of the past few days: had I made a slip anywhere along the route? Could the last underground contact in Kharkov have been a spy, sending me to my death? Had I anything in my knapsack that could possibly implicate any of the underground conspirators? Would the colonel be able to square things with the MVD?

The door was flung open without a knock. In came a great burly man with bright, shrewd eyes and very black and curly hair.

"Our neighbor," murmured my host. "We share the house together. You understand that we have never enough housing here."

The new arrival stared briefly at the little pile of groceries still lying on the table in the proper pattern for the code.

He shook my hand and called for tea. His eyes exchanged a warning glance with mine.

And then I saw what had happened. Through bad luck I had made a contact with a member of this household who was outside the movement: no one had warned me that it was a two-family home, and it would be dangerous to retrieve the mistake. I must pass on to the next city and the next contact without attempting to learn whatever this friend might have said to me.

As soon as I could, I murmured my excuses and began to leave. As I turned to the door the newcomer idly lifted up one of the pears I had set out.

"The pears are very fine this year," he said. "It is too bad you were not able to stay and sample them with us."

"Yes," I said. "It is too bad. But I shall be in Russia for some time. I can enjoy the pears in other cities."

He nodded. I left the house where I had passed my most uncomfortable half hour of the whole war. . . .

It was on this same memorable trip that I made a careless gesture which might once have landed me in Siberia, in the prewar days of open persecution. Instead, it won me the confidence of Vanya and his wife, and provided my first contact with the Protestant branch of the secret religious movement.

Vanya was the barber in a Volga town. I had been directed to his home when I got off the train and asked where I might find lodgings. A few nights later, as I sat in the dingy little parlor waiting for dinner, I was quickly making the sign of the Cross when I caught sight of Vanya's face in a little mirror hanging on the wall just over my head. I had thought myself alone. Vanya had seen me but he smiled and said, "We, too."

Vanya and his wife Elka were Baptists. They told me their story and described the risks run by the faithful during the thirty years the Soviets have waged war against the churches in Russia. In the early Bolshevik days there had still been a traffic in smuggled prayer books and Bibles across the Polish border. Vanya and Elka were members of the network of agents who distributed them. One night they had to go to a town where the Communists had burned all the churches, and jailed or killed all the known ministers and priests.

"We had to deliver the books to Ivan, a pastor who had come to the town disguised as a tailor," Vanya said. "We reached his city late at night. There were no street lights and we were uncertain of our way. As we stumbled through the mud, carrying the heavy suitcase filled with books, an MVD agent stopped us.

" 'What are you doing here?' he asked.

"We told him we were seeking Ivan's home, bringing him tailor's materials. He escorted us, silent and suspicious, and as we arrived at the dark little house he said to me, 'That suitcase. Open it.'

" 'Comrade,' I told him. 'I will gladly open it when we get into the light. But Ivan has a dangerous dog. Best let me go first and see that he is tied. He knows me.'

"The agent watched sullenly. I slipped to the door, gave the signal knock and waited in fear. When Ivan opened it I pushed inside hurriedly, emptied the suitcase, hid the prayer books under a pile of lumber in the kitchen and stuffed the suitcase with lengths of cloth. Then we let my wife and the agent come in. The delay had angered him.

" 'The suitcase,' he said sternly. We were ready for him. Its contents were innocent, but he was still suspicious.

" 'And where is that dangerous dog?' he said.

"My heart was in my mouth. So far as I knew, Ivan had never owned a pet.

" 'The dog?' said Ivan. 'Why, he is tied up for the night!'

"He led the way to the yard, where an ugly mastiff was chained. The dog had been a gift sent to him only the day before. That dog saved our lives."

Now that they were certain of my sympathy, Vanya and Elka told me many things. They repeated the sharp warning I had received from others:

"The greatest danger to you," they told me, "may be in the present policy of toleration of the churches by the authorities. Do not be misled; this is a wartime measure. So long as the Communists are in control no true priest may safely admit that he is a priest in Russia.

"Treat every man who calls himself a priest and does not flee from Communist detection as a quisling and a spy. The churches in Russia are open today. Yes. But they will be closed again tomorrow if the Communist clique remains in power. Above all, avoid the followers of Acting Patriarch Sergius, the man who has called Stalin 'our leader under God.' He betrayed his church to the Communists once before in the twenties. This 'toleration' is a hoax."

It was a needed warning, even now.

In spite of all I had been told there were still times when I wondered whether I might not be unnecessarily suspicious, especially on Sunday mornings when in some town I dared visit one of the Orthodox Churches and hear Mass.

The congregations were of all ages, all types, standing or devoutly prostrating themselves. An occasional Red Army uniform appeared among the younger men; the others had the shabby, tattered clothes most Russians wear. The priests no longer wore the heavily embroidered vestments of the prerevolutionary days. Most of the fine icons had been stripped from the walls; their gold leaf had caught the eye of some marauder twenty years before. But the ceremony was the same, and it was very beautiful as the voices of the choir rose in the richness of the Eastern liturgy. A great many people seemed to feel free to assist at Mass with no fear of the secret police. Could this toleration, after all, be real?

But one day, in the home of a family with whom I was lodging, I picked up a copy of *Comsomolskaja Pravda,* the official paper of the Comsomols. It was dated September 16, 1944, and it contained an article by the Party Secretary Susloff of Stravropol Rajkom. It read:

"Some teachers have been recently reported, who show a great tolerance towards religion. The number of teachers who are actually observing religious practices has also increased.

"The attitude of our Party towards religion is well known. It remains unalterable. Our Party fights religious superstition, because it defends science."

Soon after that I saw reprinted in the Party literature Article 122 of the Soviet Criminal Code, which was evidently felt to be a needed warning to those naïve Communists who believed that the government had actually made a truce with God, as Patriarch Alexei and his group were assuring foreigners.

The Article runs: "Teaching children or minors the principles of religious faith in public or private schools and in violation of the binding rules will be punished by correctional compulsory labor up to one year." Article 126 was also republished: "The penalty for practicing religious rites in State or social institutions or enterprises, as well as the placing of religious pictures in said institutions or enterprises, will be correctional compulsory labor up to three months or a fine."

These reminders were meant to warn the Party members not to take seriously the "tactical retreat" towards toleration of religion which the authorities had made.

Later, when I had left Russia, I uncovered further, ample evidence of the duplicity of the "toleration." I obtained records of Communist Party closed meetings in both Paris and Prague, at which the members were warned not to take the "toleration" seriously: it was tactical and temporary, they were told. Atheism remains the long-range Party line, as the Communists make very clear today to those who can read *Pravda.*

The postwar rules for fighting religion were printed in July, 1947, in the form of a brochure issued by the central executive committee of the Comsomol. They make the issues very plain:

1. Never forget that the clergy are the bitterest foes of the Communist State.
2. Try to win your friends over to Communism and remember that Stalin, who has given a new constitution to the Russian people, is the head of the "Godless," not only in the Soviet Union, but all over the world.
3. Prevail upon your friends to avoid contacts with priests.
4. Beware of spies and tell the police about saboteurs.
5. See to it that atheist publications are widely distributed among the people.
6. A good Communist must also be a militant atheist. He must know how to use his weapons and be experienced in the art of war.
7. Wherever you can, fight religious elements and forestall any influence they might bring to bear upon your comrades.
8. A true "Godless" must also be a good policeman. It is the duty of every "Godless" to protect the security of the state.
9. Support the "Godless" movement with money which is needed particularly for our propaganda abroad, since under present circumstances it can only be carried on underground.
10. If you are not a convinced "Godless" you cannot be a good Communist and true Soviet citizen. Atheism is insolubly tied in with Communism. Both ideals are the foundation of Soviet power.

Only the very credulous can believe today, in the face of mounting similar evidence, that the church of Alexei is anything but a Soviet stooge, a puppet-church.

CHAPTER 14

The Non-Christian Resistance

Back with my Red Army group in Moscow, I spent several social evenings with the Soviet upper classes; with men and women who enjoyed a sort of Horatio Alger success under the "classless" regime. The colonel had arranged the introductions for me: I knew from him that some of them belonged to the resistance but that this was never discussed in social gatherings.

At one such home not far from Lubianka I looked about the drawing room, where glasses of vodka and champagne were being passed by a butler in livery. I thought, "It is a scene from Tolstoi's time. In a moment Prince Andrey will come in."

The pale-faced young man who sat at the piano was playing Tschaikovsky's *Pathétique*. Beside me on the velvet-upholstered sofa, sat my hostess in a gown from one of the great Paris dressmaking houses; her hands were ringed with diamonds, brought back from the war. On the floor was a fine Aubusson rug re-looted from Germany, to which it had been shipped from Paris by some Nazi officer. The whole room was furnished with other expensive articles similarly "liberated," as the soldiers say. There was an antique cabinet and a set of spidery gilt chairs. Paintings of the French Impressionist school hung on the walls. At the window's were curtains of heavy gold damask. And, out of courtesy to a few foreigners among the guests, the conversation was in French!

Parties like this are extremely dangerous to men involved in such vital secrets as ours: for the Russians pride themselves on their capacity to drink. Champagne, Hungarian and Slovak wines, brandy, vodka are passed in quick succession. After dinner there is frequently champagne punch.

I worked out a whole series of devices to protect myself from the effects of drinking, without seeming to refuse. I found that if you eat a bit of pickled cucumber, the drink has less effect. With discretion, you can pour water into your vodka and brandy glasses without being seen. Sometimes it is possible to pour water into the vodka glass and drink every toast in water.

And there are other tricks familiar to all the men and women throughout the world who have something to fear from having their real business known. Early in the war I learned to pack my bags in a careful pattern, with the angle of the sleeve folded in a certain way; the boots so placed that, seen from a certain viewpoint, their toes form a parallel line. In Russia I never went out without such preparations. Very often when I returned to my room, I saw that my baggage had been searched.

More disturbing than this, by far, was the constant possibility, indoors, of a secret microphone. Many of the homes I visited belonged to men quite well aware of the danger. When secret conversation was about to begin, someone would seize a balalaika and play it very loud, to drown out our talk from any hidden instrument. Or two or three men would sing while the others spoke in whispers. But the safest way of avoiding trouble was always to confer ouside the city, in the open air.

Once during my month in Moscow I wished to meet all twenty or thirty members of a young men's trade-union cell. The conference was arranged as a mushroom-picking party. We walked to the Park of Culture and, as we squatted close to the earth in groups of twos or threes, we were able to discuss the forbidden topic of the post-Communist plans.

But the most exciting event of that period was my meeting with a professor who had written many of the bulletins on the "plan" to which most of the resistance groups are pledged.

Professor R. was now a colonel in the Army, scheduled to return to the West after a mission in Russia. I had heard, through members of the intellectual resistance, that he might be found in a suburban town near Moscow on a certain day. I bribed a sergeant, with two quarts of vodka, to drive me for a "sight-seeing" tour of the countryside.

Arrived in the professor's village, I established contact with the local leader to whom I had been referred. The code here was a simple one: I approached his home. When he came to the door, I said, "I have messages from the front. I have been asked to bring news of Natasa and Vanya, of Vladimir and Josef. And I wonder, my friend, if you have any milk?" The names had to be pronounced in an exact order: I waited until the coded answer came.

"Milk is scarce with us, but we have always a glass for friends."

I entered and explained my purpose: I was eager to meet and talk to the professor, and this would be my only night in town. Could it be done? Before I left, a meeting had been arranged. I was to go, at moonrise, to a certain field beyond the town. I was to approach a certain tree, drop down into the uncut hay and wait for him there.

The arrangements worked out well. That night in the field, when I was quite sure that no one from the road was watching me, I dropped down to my stomach and lay quietly. In a minute or two there was a rustling. A smiling face appeared at my side.

"Good evening," the professor said to me.

For several hours we lay there and talked of the future in the sweet-smelling hay. From this man I learned many technical points of the "plan" which had been hazy to me before. I learned, particularly, the story of its origins in the world of thought.

"Marxism was never Russian, you understand," the professor said to me. "Marx was, of course, a German. His ideas are a hodge-podge of Hegel and Feuerbach. Nothing could be more distant from the Russian genius than this German materialistic philosophy which has been imposed on us. Russia has never become Communist; we have been the victims of a group of gangsters who used Communist catchwords to keep themselves in power. Even the leaders are not honest Communists today.

"The years of the Stalinist terror have prepared Russia for a great destiny, however. These decades of horror have completely swept away the debris of the past, so that we begin on a clean sheet to write a new chapter in world history. We are preparing the 'plan' for Russia, first. But the 'plan' will, in the end, be Russia's gift to the whole modern world.

"The 'plan' is Russian through and through: its spiritual father was Vladimir Soloviev, the nineteenth-century philosopher whom the Czars sent into exile. Soloviev's books are the most precious treasures of the resistance library. Read them if you would understand what is happening in Russia today."

I knew the writings of Soloviev, an extraordinary thinker who had become a revolutionary, and for a time, a follower of Marx. Then he began to have philosophical doubts; he realized that materialism is too narrow an approach to social problems. He became an ardent Christian. While an exile in Croatia, he wrote a magnificent book, *Russia and the Universal Church.* In this he pointed out the necessity for realizing Christianity in every phase of life. He was a forerunner of the movement "to take Christ into the market place." He was a prophet of the "plan." He saw that if God is left out, no code of laws can last, nor can any economic planning establish true justice.

The professor, murmuring close to my ear, said this: "In the West they call us Russians mystics. But few of us are that. What they mean is that we are very simple people, too simple to accept the hypocrisy of the modern West. We do not know how to pay lip service to an ideal and act against it. With us, a theory and a belief must flower into life itself.

"I am not a very devout man. But I believe that Christianity is the greatest creative force in history, and that very few good things in the relations between man and man have come about without its energizing power. Believing that, I cannot disregard religion.

"Russia will give the world the first sociology it has ever had which is capable of bringing peace and plenty to all men. And it will be a profoundly Christian sociology."

The "plan" has not been written down in any definitive volume. Its theory and details are published in scrappy, mimeographed sheets which no one dares to save. It only exists as a detailed scheme in the brains of men like the professor with whom I had my hayfield conference.

But the system they are preparing might be described as the "human social order." It has three fundamental premises:

First, that the human being is of overwhelming importance in himself and that any control over him exerted by others must be held at a minimum. No man's conscience is to be forced in post-Communist Russia. The *integral* human person must be safeguarded; man must be held inviolable, not only to protect his body, but also to safeguard his soul.

Secondly, the "plan" recognizes the fact that man does not live or grow in isolation; his development is to a large extent determined by his human environment. It is the duty of a social system to see that the conditions of the citizen's life are propitious for his greatest growth. This requires a far greater consideration of the family as a social unit than any system, capitalist or socialist, has so far given it. According to the "plan," one of the four lawmaking and law-administering bodies of the state will be representative of citizens voting as family groups.

Thirdly, even the family is not self-sufficient: it is subject to the pressures of the country's economy. An economic system should serve the purposes of family living, rather than demanding their subjection as all the older economies have done. Specifically, it should demand that the workers participate as co-owners in industry and farming.

Fourthly, the state is a necessity, but it has no value *in itself;* it is not a Moloch to whom the citizens should be surrendered. The job of the state is to co-ordinate, to make laws which will facilitate the normal development of the individual, the family, the social group; to act as a referee to prevent any individual, or family, or group of workers or peasants from infringing on the rights of others.

To keep the state from becoming dangerously strong, there must be several legislative bodies with the power to administer and enforce their laws. Besides the two congresses elected by individual voters and by family units, there will be a third, chosen on a basis of working cells: the men who belong to a factory, say, will elect a representative from among themselves, as trade-union groups already do. There will also be a fourth representative body chosen by citizens according to their cultural and religious groupings. The Roman Catholic, Orthodox and Protestant churches and the synagogues will choose their representatives.

The "plan" is democratic, in the sense that the power of government flows from below, that the citizens' representation is based on the plebiscite. But this program avoids the error which has permitted modern dictators to assume control of the state by reference to the polls; both Mussolini and Hitler, you remember, observed the letter of the democratic law. They destroyed the freedom of their peoples in apparent response to an overwhelming ballot-box demand.

To safeguard against such a betrayal of the democratic

process, the "plan" admits limitations on the rights of suffrage. The "plan" protects minorities from the occasional mass-madness which might make the majority endanger its rights. The "plan" recognizes the possibility of error in the judgment of the people; gives full rights to the natural moral law, recognized by every philosopher from Plato's time to ours.

Enthusiasts of the "plan" include leaders of the major resistance groups within the country. I found myself in touch with most of them; although their motivations varied widely, there was always a small, hard core of disciplined believers whose religious zeal inspired the rest.

The single exception to this rule consists of the Trotskyites, who are more ardently atheist than the Communists themselves, and more intransigent in their refusal to co-operate with any Christians. These men and women are an important factor among the intellectuals. They are the doctrinaire Marxists who believe that Stalin and his clique have sold out their revolution; they wish to have another try at making Communism "work." Their hatred of the capitalistic world is relentless: for any American or western European to work with them, even as a matter of temporary tactics, would be extremely dangerous. Fanaticism of their type is fearless, and they have had the experience of outwitting the secret police of Stalin's state for years.

The other anti-government groups, however, are eager to co-operate with any liberators who may reach them from the outside world, provided they are treated as free men, building a sovereign state along the lines which seem the best to them. The anti-Communist Russians are proud and they wear their years of suffering like wound stripes: they will not take kindly to any patronizing efforts by outside politicians to coach them on the way to run a state.

Who are the members of these groups? Prominent among them are the young ex-Communists who have become disillusioned. Some of these have exchanged their Marxist ideology for a belief in Christianity; but there are others still searching for a philosophy to replace the one they have lost. Many of them are impressed by what they have seen in the countries to the west which they visited as soldiers during the war. But very few are attracted by the theory of capitalism. What this group admires outside Russia is the freedom from police-state control. Their leaders are deeply attached to the "plan" and would not support another system.

Perhaps the largest of all groups of dissidents now consists of the Red Army deserters and the civilians who are in contact with them. In the forests around Briansk a quarter of a million men refused to put down their arms at the war's end; they included complete army units with their officers. Large concentrations of such men still existed around Lwow, Kiev and Stanislawow in 1946; some are there today. Sympathetic villagers help them to conceal themselves and carry food and supplies to them.

There are also the nationalist groups: some of these have had a desire for independence since Czarist days. The Ukrainians have never taken kindly to the Communist regime; they abhorred the collective farm system and resented the whole philosophy of the police state.

Besides the Ukrainians there are other groups who resent the Soviet government on grounds of national sentiment. All the Baltic peoples, the Lithuanians, Latvians, Esthonians, clamor for freedom. So do the Ruthenians, who were only attached to Russia at the end of the war. From an earlier period dates the nationalism of the Finns, the Georgians, the Armenians, the Turkestan Moslems, all of whom are also demanding freedom.

That these "nationalist" groups are also motivated by a moral purpose is evident to anyone who has met their leaders and heard the stories of their martyrs. A proclamation circulated by the Lithuanian Underground Resistance, reads:

> Supreme Committee of Joint Democratic Action, to All Active Partisans and Province Leaders:
>
> We are fighting not only for our own freedom and existence; but for ideas common to the whole world. These ideas represent democratic ideals held by the Western democracies which led them to destroy German tyranny at the cost of the best lives in Britain, America and other nations.
>
> The Russians have infiltrated all branches of our life. We do not want to live as the Russians do, where man is an enemy to man. We are fighting, therefore, not to become a man who lives like an animal and will kill for the bread of another man. We do not want to become robots like most of the Russian people. We are fighting because we want to keep our moral life, which is based on Christianity, from which developed all Western civilization.
>
> Our fight is but one small part of the world-wide fight between humanity and tyranny. We are alone in this terrible fight and we are suffering, but we hope that we are contributing to the common world-wide fight to

restore human rights and freedom. We are fighting because God ordered us to fight the devil; we are fighting and we will fight until our goal is attained.

Among the Russians themselves there are numerous crosscurrents of resistance. The police state inevitably breeds its own destruction; every time the MVD arrests a rebel against Communism, it makes enemies of his relatives and closest friends. A vast network of opposition has sprung up after every purge.

Then there are the millions inside the concentration camps, men and women who have a better reason to hate the present state than any others. Such prisoners have close contact with the resistance movement through the arrival of the newly arrested; most of them are aware of at least some phases of the "plan." The deportees in Siberia and western Asia include many Balts and Finns and Poles who lived outside of Russia until recently. Unlike the Russians, they have been unaffected by any Communist teaching; the entire socialist theory is detestable to them because it has brought terror to their countries and themselves.

The political prisoners of all groups stretch in a vast curtain across the north. In the spring of 1948 political prisoners were being moved in locked trains to Kamchatka and Sakhalin, day after day, night after night. In Shanghai in April of this year, I spoke to eye-witnesses who had seen the chained men and women at work on Sakhalin roads; since the end of the war four to five million such prisoners have been moved across Russia from the west. These include Hungarians and Croats, Poles and Slovaks, Czechs and Austrians, as well as citizens of countries invaded and attached to Russia.

Immediately after the war, a coup d'état in Russia might have succeeded and with very little shedding of blood. If the Allies had worked with the anti-Communist leaders in the Red Army, if they had insisted that Russia must clean house in order to join the community of nations, if they had demanded the end of the dictatorship and the elimination of the concentration camp form of government, the country might be free today. Marshals sympathetic to the plan were still alive and in command of troops. Large units of anti-Stalinist Russian troops were concentrated on the borders and were engaged in actual fighting against the regime. The Crimea and the Ukraine were in an uproar. If the Allies had then supported the Russian underground, as they earlier supported the French maquis, world Communism today might have no more vitality or adherents than Nazism. But this chance was lost.

Today the chances are less bright. The Politburo has weeded out from positions of military authority many of the men who do not belong to the Party clique. It has tightened its controls. Unless vast rivers of materials are shipped into the country, the Russian resistance can not overthrow the authorities by a coup d'état.

For one of the tragedies of history is this: it is easy enough to begin a dictatorship. It is very difficult to end one, difficult even for the men in power. Today there are three kinds of men at the head of the Soviet: there are the convinced Communists, who really believe that their system will sweep the world and make it a better place for men to live. They have become a dwindling minority, even among the Party authorities. Second, there are the government officials with a passion for power who must maintain the present system to retain it. And lastly, there are the opportunists, men so deeply committed that they can never go back. These are the officials who have killed so many Russians, betrayed so many friends, ordered so many thousands of victims to the concentration camps that their lives would be very short if the protection of the MVD were once withdrawn.

Altogether they number a small group of men, but they have all the power, and terror is their daily weapon. They have prolonged the tactics of an emergency for over thirty years. They have made normal, everyday routine of martial law. No one has yet discovered how such a police state can be stripped of its powers without foreign aid.

The Russians are the helpless victims of a few evil men as surely as the people of any country the Nazis occupied. The Russians are as much our friends, as eager for our aid, as the DeGaullistes were in France in 1942. The resistance in Russia cuts across all lines of class and race and education. Listen to what Ivan said to me in Moscow, to what a score of other Ivans told me in different cities and at different times:

"We had a factory that was producing well: we were cited several times in the Party press. Wages were good, as wages go. The morale of the factory was high. Our chief was a young and very clever engineer who made things hum.

"And then, Comrade, what happened? The engineer was ordered to give the overseer's jobs to the active Communists. He tried them out. Some of them were stupid, others were brutal and incompetent. Well, he wanted production. He thought he was there to get results. So he demoted the Party men and chose his overseers for efficiency.

"Our engineer was 'relieved' on grounds of political unreliability and sent away for trial. God only knows what happened to him. But I can tell you what happened to *us*. We were given a Party hack who didn't know how to run a factory. Materials never arrived on time. Machines were not repaired. Production dropped and our wages went down with it.

"Do you think we like a system that can do that to us? Do you believe that any of us have security, when our livelihood depends on another man's ability to please the secret police?"

Like the industrial rank and file, the trade union officials are with the West. During the war, many of these men talked to the union leaders in Hungary and Poland, in Rumania and Czecho-Slovakia. They discovered what could be done for union members when the union was allowed freedom from political control by the state.

The Russian peasants have never been reconciled to the regime. The purges of Old Bolsheviks angered and antagonized thousands within Russia; but the liquidation of peasants turned millions into stubborn, silent enemies of the state.

All these groups are loosely in touch with one another; their leaders include many types of men. The Old Bolsheviks were theorists: most of them had been professional revolutionaries all their lives. The new Russian revolutionists have their theorists, yes. But they also have supporters in every phase of the nation's life. Through the whole enormous conspiracy moves the activating force of Christian love; this is the factor which makes it the strongest underground the world has seen since the martyrs of the catacombs toppled the Roman Empire with the weapons of self-discipline and faith. For Russia has a resistance movement whose leaders refuse to do evil that good may come. They are a force no police state can withstand. Their victory is as certain as the rising of tomorrow's sun.

And what of the other religious groups? Under the "plan" they will be given full freedom. Under the Communists their history is essentially the same as that of the Christians—a brutal and unrelenting persecution punctuated by seizure of their houses of worship, imprisonment and torture of their clergy. Since the Revolution the Moslems have never been allowed to have muezzins calling the people to prayer, even in the cities where this had been the practice since the time of Mahomet. Their mosques were closed; their mullahs shared the same campaign of vilification as the Christian priests. For a devout Mohammedan to ask for a permit to go to Mecca would have been madness during the period from 1919 to 1942.

But the Moslems, too, profited by the "toleration" policy, and by the Soviet political wish to win friends among the Arab states outside its borders. In 1944 it was suddenly decreed that Moslems might make the Mecca pilgrimage and that transportation would be arranged for them by the government.

I mentioned the fact to one of the leaders of the Christian underground.

"That privilege," I said, "is a greater concession than the Soviets have made to any Christian group."

"Perhaps," he smiled. "But *timeo Communistes et dona ferentes.* The privilege of traveling outside the Soviet

Union has been very carefully restricted, during the past twenty-five years, to the most highly certified of Party zealots. It is hardly likely that anti-Soviet Moslems will be suddenly allowed to spread stories throughout the Middle East of the atrocities their mullahs have suffered.

"I should look very carefully at these 'Moslems' who go to Mecca, if I were a Mohammedan from the outside world. An Orthodox priest who goes abroad to represent the Patriarch Alexei is not necessarily a sincere believer in Christ, as we know he may be an MVD agent in masquerade."

As for the Jews, anti-Semitism in Russia is an unhappy current which was artificially increased in 1939. During the period of the pact with Hitler, the Nazis refused to have dealings with Soviet Jewish officials; as a courtesy to German sensibilities the number of Jewish officials in the Commissariat of Foreign Affairs was reduced from 60 per cent to 15 per cent. In other bureaus, too, men and women were dismissed at this time out of race prejudice alone.

The religious Jews have suffered, during the Soviet years, the same miserable persecution as the Christians. The possession of a prayer book has led the simple Jewish worshiper to exile in Siberia, along with nearly all his rabbis. Whenever Jews have attempted to meet for their religious holidays, the police have broken up the "illegal meetings" and all those present have been discharged from their jobs. Synagogues have been seized for theaters and warehouses.

It appears that the position of the religious Jews, today, is even worse than that of the other devout groups; I found no sign in Russia of reopened synagogues in any town. Organized boycotts against the Jews in the Kirghiz Republic have gone unpunished since the war. The Soviet Extraordinary Commission which sat on German war crimes committed in Russian territory listed no Jews among the victims, although many thousands were killed in the Ukraine and in the Baltic states. In the Ukraine, anti-Jewish riots have occurred and only the *victims* have been put in jail.

I had found many traces of anti-Semitism among the Red Army soldiers in the forest. I found more in Russia itself, and among Party members. But it was a racial prejudice, and not a religious one. For it is impossible in Russia today to hate a Jew because of his religion, because that religion, wherever it exists, is a better-kept secret than catacomb Christianity.

CHAPTER 15

Resistance in the Ukraine

I DECIDED to leave Russia and to carry back to the outside world the precious fact which my visit had confirmed: that the Christian Fifth Column within the country is a reality, that the Russian people must not be identified with their tyrannical rulers, and that we of the West have an obligation to liberate them from the oppressive despots whom they hate.

"Leave Russia? But certainly, Comrade," said the colonel who had helped in many of my plans. "We have a group of army trucks going through the Ukraine next week. If you travel with them, you can be assured of safety."

I must have looked puzzled for he added: "Some of the western districts are still a little disturbed, you know."

I did not know. How should I know? For six months my only source of news had been the Soviet press and radio, from which all unfavorable news is carefully deleted. But I had learned that it is not wise to ask too many questions.

"The Ukraine will be fine for me," I said. My papers

were stamped. I was told to report on a certain day at a Moscow barracks from which our caravan would start out.

It was an interesting and illuminating experience, that trip: it taught me something that has been very carefully concealed from the outside world. And that is that there were, in November, 1945, enormous bands of anti-Stalin Russian soldiers who had refused to be immobilized and who were still fighting in the forests and mountains a year and a half after the end of the European war.

Our caravan consisted of over two hundred trucks armed with machine guns, tommy guns and artillery.

When we came to our first large town it was only about four o'clock in the afternoon; nonetheless orders went out, "We will spend the night here."

"Why?" I asked an officer with whom I had struck up a conversation during the day, as we rode on a pile of mail sacks in one of the trucks.

"Bandits," he whispered. "Traitors. Russian Partisans. Whatever you want to call them. In this country we're entering, it isn't safe for the Red Army to stay anywhere except in the biggest and best-lighted towns. Even there, we don't go on the streets after ten o'clock at night. You'll see."

I did, indeed. The next morning two of our men, badly hurt, were carried on stretchers onto the trucks. They had been ambushed by snipers on the edge of the town the night before.

And so, gradually, I learned the truth about the anti-Stalinist maquis. Red Army officers on the trip told me that this Resistance numbered about one and one half million men; they were deployed from the mountains of

Subcarpathian Russia to Kiev—and even beyond the Dnieper to the east; others were in the Briansk forest, south of Moscow. One of their leaders there was Stefan Bandera, a Ukrainian nationalist for whose head the USSR would have paid a very pretty price. His followers, called "Banderovci," had hoped, at the beginning of the war, to use the presence of the German soldiers as a pretext for cutting loose from Russia and setting up an independent Ukrainian nation of forty-five millions. They were involved in the large anti-Communist plot within the Red Army of which I already knew. On closer acquaintance with the Germans, they—like the other Resistance leaders—were forced to abandon this hope: it was clear that Hitler had no intention of letting the Ukraine remain free. His victory would have meant that the province became a slave colony of the Reich, as it is now a slave of the USSR. In this frying-pan-versus-fire situation the Ukrainian nationalists reluctantly decided to fight for Stalin to help him defeat the even more drastic tyranny of Hitler. Bandera became a prisoner of war under the Nazis for a while.

But after V-E Day, when the Germans had withdrawn, Bandera and his followers, now free, resumed their old hope of a Free Ukraine. His soldiers refused to turn in their arms to the Soviet; they took command of whole large areas of the country and refused to let Red officials return to them. Since many MVD units had joined them, they were aware of the secret police activities by means of which Stalin usually liquidates such groups. When the danger became too acute in the towns, these Free Ukrainian bands dissolved into the woods.

They are fine guerrilla soldiers, as our little party discovered to its cost. In spite of all our precautions, scarcely a night passed which did not cost us one or more victims of raids by the outlaws.

One morning, in a town of some one hundred and sixty thousand, the officer in charge of our caravan asked me to go with him to the headquarters of the Red Army garrison. There we met a Soviet commissar in a state of great excitement. He told us his story. In a little village, only five miles out of town, the Banderovci had struck the night before. They had kidnaped the president and secretary of the local Party and nineteen MVD agents. They had plundered the post office, and seized the grain gathered into the Soviet government warehouses. Then they disappeared into the forest.

The commissar who told us these things had barely escaped with his life. He had come rushing to the nearest Army headquarters for help. But the Red Army officers refused to move from their garrison; they knew they were no match for the forest-maquis.

More than once since the war's end, the Soviet government had tried to subdue these areas. Big stretches of forest had been burned to get them out. Full-dress offensives had been launched against their supposed positions. More recently, vast numbers of Ukrainian civilians had been deported to the northern wastes to deprive the Banderovci of the support of their countrymen, who hid and fed them.

But the maquis were growing stronger. New desertions from the Army swelled their ranks. Even today thousands of these men survive in small groups and fight the regime.

This Partisan group, too, should be numbered among our friends within the Soviet. Even those of them who have surrendered or been captured by the Communists are still an insurgent element inside the Soviet concentration camps.

That trip through the Ukraine had other incidents.

I remember entering a town so tortured and torn by enemy bombs that no single roof was still intact. We parked our Army trucks and our Studebaker staff cars around the town square. We tried to sleep, our feet curled under us, our heads in one another's laps, in whatever cramped positions an automobile affords to half a dozen men who turn a sedan into a Pullman.

When the first streaks of dawn pierced the sky, I got up and stretched myself. The sun was rising above the great plain. I stood still, loving the beauty of the day. And then I noticed that I was not alone. Circling our staff car at a respectful distance was a little scarecrow of a man—barefooted, clothed in rags, bent by age and misery to so grotesque a shape that his head was on a level with his knees. He carried a dirty kerchief knotted into a bag; into this he poked such articles as his sharp eyes detected on the ground.

"Good morning, Comrade," I said to him. "What are you doing out so early?"

He took a backward step in fright. His eyes moved rapidly about our little camp, as if looking for an excuse. Then he saw that I was smiling. He sighed.

"Ah, Comrade," he said. "Do not be harsh with me. I am searching for scraps of garbage to feed my children. My seven hungry children."

I looked at him with astonishment. The town where we were encamped was in the center of the wheat-growing Ukraine, "the breadbox of Europe."

"You have no bread?" I asked.

It was his turn to look astonished. He peered at me with the shrewd and calculating look of one who suspects a trap.

"Don't you know that we have no food?" he asked. "You, an officer?"

"No," I told him. "I have been in Russia proper for half a year. I have heard no news from the Ukraine."

The man lowered his voice and threw a glance of apprehension towards the caravan, with its red flags flying at the radiator caps.

"They haven't told you," he said. "But the population here is in a pitiful state. We are starving, and it is not because the crops have failed. Our starvation is a punishment, a deliberate punishment because of the revolt. We are considered traitors here. The MVD says that those who can't be trusted shan't eat."

I believed him. He was emaciated, obviously ill. His face showed the deep lines that hunger etches. He shivered in his scanty rags.

"Comrade," I asked him, "do you have a job?"

"Yes," he told me. "In that factory." And he pointed to the stacks that showed behind a line of houses on our left. "I have just come off my night shift. I work, but our wages are not much good to us when they cannot be exchanged for food. The bread ration has been set so low; once a week we are allowed to buy a quantity of food that would not feed us properly for two days.

"My children are growing: they need to eat. So whenever the soldiers have passed along this route I come here, looking for whatever scraps they have thrown away. Garbage is not to be disdained in times like these, my friend."

His moustache trembled. I saw that he was on the verge of tears.

"Wait," I said to him.

I walked to the staff car and fumbled in my knapsack for my day's supply of bread. I took the ration from the musette bag of the sleeping Vanya—a good friend who would also wish to help this hungry man. I handed both rations to the stranger.

There was a sound of marching feet on the pavement. The MVD morning patrol was approaching. I turned back towards our car. No need to draw the guards' attention to the poor wretch.

But the Red officer in charge of the detail had seen him shrinking back against the row of desolate and unpainted shacks. He stopped his men and shouted: "Get out of here. You have no business coming close to the area. Get out!"

Curious heads were raised in the trucks and staff cars. The MVD officer turned and addressed them sharply:

"None of you is to mix with these local people. Understand? And above all, no one is to give them anything to eat. They are beggars. Let them starve!"

The Ukraine I remember as one vast dust cloud. Jolting over these impossible roads, we breathed dust from the wheels that jounced in front of us until our hair, our clothes, our bags, our guns were penetrated by the suffocating cloud.

The fields were ripe, the crops were fat. But the lack of men to work them was apparent even from the roads. Everywhere we saw women. They were dressed in long linen dresses, white before the dust had blended them into the monochrome of dun. These clothes they made themselves, on home weaving machines, from linen grown on the collective farms nearby. They were barefooted, these women, and their legs were swollen from overwork. Their big red hands were those of the laborers who loaded and unloaded sacks of grain, steered the crude hand-plow, led the scrawny horses and belted them when they lay down between the shafts. Their skins were tough, their faces taut, their eyes glazed with tiredness and despair.

These women did not welcome us when we drew up by the side of their fields for a noonday rest; they stared at us with cold hostility. We were the hated Reds, they thought. We had robbed them of their God, then of their men, and now we were taking away their daily bread.

But some of their men would be returned to them, those who had not been killed in the fighting or sentenced to slave labor for political activity. Our caravan encountered one of the returning troop trains at the border point where the soldiers must pass inspection before being allowed to reenter their country.

All along the railroad track for the last ten miles before the Russian frontier, the sidings were surrounded on both sides by piles of papers. No letter, no document, no book or newspaper could be brought back into the country. The wise soldiers tossed overboard every printed or written thing they had.

At the frontier town, women engineers were busy uncoupling the cars and piling fuel for the engine. The soldiers stood in little groups, trying to joke with them.

"Aren't you glad we liberated you from the Germans?" said one of them.

The Ukrainian women stared sullenly.

Finally one of them muttered, "We were better off as

we were. The Germans had reopened our churches, though they murdered and starved us. Now the Reds have closed the churches again, and they murder and starve us, too."

An older woman straightened and looked defiantly at the poor young soldier as if he, personally, had brought all the trouble into her life.

"Yes. The Nazis burned our homes," she said. "But we can live without a roof. What do you people do to us? You take our food away. That's worse."

She turned away before he could answer, and hid her bitterness by bending low to examine the locomotive parts. The boy, chagrined, walked back to his companions.

The returning soldiers at the frontier were separated into three groups of men; they stood or squatted in the sun, holding their identity cards in their hands, waiting for their names to be called.

"What is this for?" I asked one of the Russian officers.

"We're checking them against the commissar's reports," he said. "All the army units who were disloyal at the beginning of the war are going over there."

He waved towards a road down which a detail of men were shuffling under heavy guard.

"They may be shot."

"And the other groups?" I asked.

"There are whole units that grumbled and showed counterrevolutionary symptoms during the war. That's category two." He pointed to a row of rough barracks, on a distant hill.

"They wait there to be sent to the north. Siberia."

"The others?" I asked.

"The others *may* be all right. We check each name

against the commissar's report from the front. Yes, some of these men in Group Three will be allowed to go home."

I looked at the three groups of men. Those who stood together in Category Three were fidgety and frightened; theirs was the nervousness of hope. The other two groups had passed beyond the stage of cruel suspense; a few were angry, but most of them wore the slight, sardonic smiles of those who know that they are doomed. They showed the curious cheerfulness of condemned men, who relish each passing moment with a miser's greed.

The Ukrainian peasants could not be trusted: so much was known to even the dullest moujik in our company. When we came to a town in the Ukraine, the people now spoke in the Great Russian language.

"It's the population exchange," they said, and nodded knowingly. "The Russians from the Volga area are being settled here."

Whole trainloads of Ukrainians were being evacuated from this section to the north. We passed them, traveling on flatcars with no shelter against the cruel sun, sad huddles of humanity being jerked and jostled to the north as a political precaution. They were the villagers who had shown too much sympathy for the anti-Stalinist outlaws. They were being replaced by Russians shunted south from their homes on the returning trips of the same cattle cars. Now these peasants were being forced to settle in the Ukraine, where they did not speak the language of the dissident maquis and where, it was hoped, their sense of strangeness would prevent further resistance.

"How many peasants have been carried north?" I

asked a Red engineer on one of these exchange trains.

"Hundreds of thousands," he told me. "Hundreds of thousands to date. And there will be more."

How deeply the Soviet system is hated by the Ukrainians! How completely the Bolshevik propaganda over the past twenty-seven years has failed to win them to a loyal support of the regime!

I got to know something of the the feelings of these people, thanks to my friendship with Kolia, a Ukrainian soldier who was traveling with us as an interpreter. Kolia was not, himself, a trustworthy Communist, but he was shrewd enough to hide his feelings and competent enough to make himself valuable to the commissars. We had long subversive talks during our travels in the staff car; we spoke in French, which none of the other officers could understand, and I had come to look on him as a trusted friend.

In a Ukrainian village on the plains, we piled down from our crowded, dust-encumbered cars and stretched ourselves. A draught of warm, rationed water from our tin canteens rolled on our tongues as if it had been Napoleon brandy. We shook the dust from our caps, ran combs through our matted hair and straightened our crumpled uniforms.

"Now," said Kolia to me in French, "let's go calling."

We circled behind two rows of houses so as to avoid the eye of our companions.

"The commissars would not like us to be sociable," he said. "But I know one of the head men from this area and no informer will betray me. It will be interesting for you to meet some of our people. Come. Here's a fair-sized house. We'll visit here."

We walked into one of the low peasant *isbas* and

knocked on a door behind which voices were heard. There was sudden silence, then whispering and a few quick, guarded movements behind the door.

"They're hiding the crucifixes and the black-market food," said Kolia. He called out a few words in Ukrainian. The door was opened by a young woman in an embroidered peasant blouse.

Kolia spoke to her rapidly and she beckoned us to come inside. In a matter of seconds, we had been accepted into the circle of peasants seated on the floor: there were no chairs left in this home. Every foot of space seemed to me to be filled with very young or very old faces; in this single narrow room two families lived—the mothers, their parents, their three little girls and two little boys. Both husbands were away with the army.

We were made welcome. Kolia mentioned the names of relatives; he brought news of soldiers who had left, years before, for the front. We had brought bottles of vodka from our knapsacks, and small bags of tea. The hostesses bustled about, heating water and polishing glasses for us. Katia, the woman who seemed to be in charge, produced some cucumbers. We dug deeper into our pockets and discovered bags of tobacco and some shreds of old newspapers in which to roll our cigarettes. It was a little feast.

Katia and one of the older men began to talk politics. They spoke in Russian of the war, the peace, the probable fate of the returning army. Then the old man glanced sharply towards the door and towards the tightly closed window. Assured that we were not being spied upon, he said to us:

"They've started again. They've begun to persecute our God.

"One hour from here," the old man whispered, "the MVD descended on all the village families last week and told them they must abandon our 'batiushka uniate,' our traditional church. They ordered us to pass over at once to the Russian Orthodox communion.

"Imagine that! These devils only stopped the old persecution against all religion when they had to, to win the war. At that time they were willing enough to let our own churches open again. They promised us that the toleration of religion would continue forever if we'd help them fight the Nazis.

"Now, already, they're beginning the persecution again, but on new lines. This time we are to be allowed to worship, so long as we worship the Orthodox way. It is a mad business."

Kolia turned to me: "They do not know, these MVD Moscovites, how to deal with the people of our Ukraine. Bribery and threats won't make us change our ways; our people become hard, silent, hostile when an outsider tries to frighten us. Is it not so, my friend?"

The old man nodded.

"Only two families in the whole district have betrayed their faith," he said.

"But what a scandal that was!" broke in one of the younger women. "Imagine! The traitors helped the MVD to go to the church and take the keys away from our *Batiushka*—take the keys of his church away from the good old priest who had been there all through the persecution!"

"Yes," said the old man. "Vassil, our friend, saw it all. The two apostate families came to the church with the MVD agents and said to the priest, 'Give over the keys and get along with you. Your flock has changed: they wish to join the Russian Orthodox Church under the Patriarch Alexei.' They turned him out of doors in the middle of the night."

"But the Ukrainian soldiers would not stand for it," one of the women broke in. "As soon as some of our fighting men returned to our village from the front, they marched to the church with sticks and stones and demanded that the new Russian Orthodox priest return the keys. They hustled him out of doors and sent word to the old Catholic priest that he might safely return from hiding. They will protect him now.

"The ex-soldiers have been taking turns there ever since, standing guard day and night to see that the Catholic priest is allowed to remain and celebrate his Mass undisturbed."

We stayed with this good family overnight, Kolia and I. We stretched out on the bare floor, our heads almost touching in the narrow room, and waited for the dawn. From time to time we heard a sharp volley of machine-gun fire: the maquis on the fringes of the town were exchanging shots with the Red Army sentries on patrol.

"How devilish this new persecution is," Kolia said to me, as we rejoined our caravan in the hour after dawn. "If the Communists continued to fight against *all* worship (as they used to do before the war) we know that our peasants would defy them and worship secretly (as they did before the war). But by this new persecution, the Reds hope to canalize religion, to force the people to worship at an altar whose priests can be controlled and regulated by the Russian authorities. It is a trap.

"And aren't they clever people, my Ukrainians, to understand the ruse so quickly? The temptation to worship openly and without fear of the secret police must be a strong one. But they have not been deluded—you yourself saw that last night. They know that if they yielded now, if they made this one concession and bent the knee to the Orthodox instead of the Catholic God, they would be the spiritual prisoners of the Reds. They see that the quisling church is a real threat to them.

"I am proud of my people: they won't compromise. They would rather suffer persecution and continue to worship secretly, as they have done for many years, than accept the gift of religious 'freedom' from men who hope to corrupt and undermine their faith."

It is important for us to understand, along with these wise and pious peasants, the sinister significance of the Soviet move to substitute the Russian Orthodox for the Catholic worship. For the pattern is being repeated in every country where Communist influence is strong.

We of the Roman Church have no quarrel with our brothers who worship in the Orthodox churches—the Greek, the Serbian, the Armenian, the Syrian, the Abyssinian and the rest. We recognize their good faith and we consider them as truly members of the Mystical Body of Christ as those of us who look for guidance to the Holy Father. We recognize the validity of their sacraments: a Roman Catholic, in the absence of a priest of his own church, may accept the last rites from an Orthodox priest. It is not bigotry nor a desire to see the Roman congregation grow at the expense of the Eastern Churches which makes us so determined that this Russian campaign of apostasy shall fail.

But the USSR'S campaign to win communicants to the church of their choice is a political move, aimed at the eventual destruction of all honest religion. The hope of the Communists is to make Moscow a "third Rome," a religious center whose Patriarch will be the prisoner of the Bolsheviks, subject to their threats and commands.

In the western Ukraine—known as Ruthenia before the war, when it formed part of Czecho-Slovakia—the postwar persecution of the Catholics is now as severe as it was in Russia itself in 1922. But this time the Communist efforts are not applied to the killing off of all religious belief; instead, they are attempting to drive the believers into the Orthodox Church, since Patriarch Alexei is still their prisoner. To impose this change on the populations they are determined to go to any necessary lengths: in Lwow in July, 1945, three hundred Ukrainian Catholic priests assembled to warn the faithful against the Communist propaganda and to plead with them not to join the church of the puppet-Patriarch. Less than a dozen of the priests escaped; twenty of them were shot, and the rest sent to a concentration camp.

Monsignor Roza of Uzhorod, Ruthenia, was seized as a prisoner of the Russian authorities because he warned his faithful against the false Russian Orthodox Church. So was Monsignor Chomysyzyn, the eighty-year-old Bishop of Stanislawow, until he died in a Communist prison cell. By 1947 the Communists had jailed every Roman Catholic bishop in the now-Sovietized territories of Poland and Ruthenia. Priests, monks, sisters have been deported to Siberia in work gangs, on such a scale that Cardinal Ernest Van Roey stated in a pastoral letter that "the Ruthenian Greek-Catholic Church has ceased to exist as a religious organization."

The distrust with which we Roman Catholics view the present-day Moscow Patriarch is echoed by Orthodox believers.

From 1917 to 1941 the Russian Orthodox churches

throughout the world had no contact with the persecuted church inside Russia. In some countries their communicants were largely made up of White Russians who had fled the country at the time of the Communist revolution. But in other places, such as Manchuria, there were older congregations of the Russian faithful. They had taken orders from the Moscow Patriarch for years before the Communists came to power. These churches found themselves autonomous after 1917 because of the impossibility of communicating with their spiritual head.

But when the 1941 policy of "toleration" was declared inside of Russia most of the "outside" churches gladly re-established contact with Moscow; throughout the war they gave full allegiance to the Patriarchs Sergius and Alexei.

It was only when the war had ended that these Russian congregations abroad awoke to the fact that the "toleration" policy was a mere matter of Communist tactics, that the church in Russia was being used as a quisling and a "front" for the same atheist regime. Then there was a world-wide severing of the ties that bound these churches to the Moscow Patriarch. By 1948 the largest Russian congregations—in China, France, Germany and the United States—had repudiated Alexei's authority.

The refusal to accept Moscow's leadership was inevitable on grounds of principle. It has also been a practical necessity. For the Orthodox bishops who have come from Russia as emissaries to visit outside congregations have often brought along Party spies. In Prague in 1946 I recognized an MVD agent whom I had known in Russia; when I inquired about him, I learned he was the secretary of the Russian Orthodox bishop there.

It is not pleasant to have to doubt the good faith of

men who come from Russia or its satellite countries wearing clerical garb. Yet it would be naïve to ignore the fact that some of them are agents. In 1947 two Hungarian "priests" traveled across the United States, lecturing in favor of a greater collaboration of the West with Russia. It was only when the suspicions of a Wisconsin bishop had been aroused that the truth came out: they were Communist agents, never ordained, using the passports of two authentic priests who had died in a Russian concentration camp.

Not all the priests of the Orthodox churches in Bulgaria and Serbia have accepted the Moscow yoke. Those who have remained faithful in those countries are suffering a persecution similar to that undergone by Russian priests in the twenties; and it is unlikely that any of these good and holy men would be traveling abroad today. Passports from eastern Europe are granted only to friends of the atheist regimes.

It is not only the Roman and Orthodox Catholics who protest against this campaign of the Soviet to make the Church its political prisoner. Traveling through the Ukraine, Kolia and I visited several members of another sect, half-Protestant and half-Orthodox, who were equally unwilling to compromise.

I remember one Sunday morning when we picked our way through the narrow, muddy streets among the goats towards the bulbous spire of a church. We had expected to find either a Roman Catholic service of the Eastern rite or a Russian Orthodox ceremony; instead, we found a small congregation worshiping according to a liturgy strange to me.

Kolia whispered: "This is something interesting for you. After the service we will talk to the minister."

In the little sanctuary we sought him out: he told us that his Protestant sect was a very large and very ancient one in Russia, that some six million worshipers belong to it. Most of them are scattered through the central Ukraine and on the banks of the Volga.

Looking at us with sad brown eyes, the white-bearded priest told us something of his sufferings during the past twenty-five years. He had been a "traveling priest" during most of this time, with neither altar, nor vestments, nor acknowledged congregation.

"When the Nazi advances frightened the Bolsheviks into opening the churches," he told us, "they paid no particular attention to our ritual. I came back here to my old parish and began to hold services openly. It has taken the MVD several years to get around to us: it is only recently that they have begun to insist that our people, too, become members of the Russian Orthodox churches.

"We have been a minority in Russia since the seventeenth century: our people have a tradition of resistance. We would not join the Orthodox Church when the Czars wanted us to; we will not join it to please the members of the atheist Party of today.

"But oh, my friends," he said, "how tragic that these hard-hearted and unbelieving men should be the ones who try to heal the divisions between us Christians! What a commentary on us, on all of us Christians, that we did not make a united front against the Red and Brown atheism earlier!

"One single apostate is enough to make the Dominions and the Angels weep. One bishop or patriarch who will hitch his chariot to the star of Marx can spread confusion among millions of the simple-hearted and devout."

CHAPTER 16

I Leave Russia

I LEFT my Russian comrades at the Polish border on a cold and windswept day. Autumn was closing down again; the men stood shivering in their ranks. The officers snapped angry orders at their drivers: every morning lately there had been an increasing delay because one of the cold engines refused to start on time. Tempers were worn thin. The soldiers grumbled, "If we were to be sent as occupying forces, why couldn't we get a soft and pleasant city? Vienna, now! Or eastern Germany!"

They were entering Poland as replacements for other troops who would be sent back into Russia—via the "de-intoxicating camps." The men with whom I had been traveling were fresh troop regulars believed to be less susceptible to the lure of foreign luxury than those who had already been in Europe. These replacements were to stay for months, years in the countries "liberated" by the Russians. They were to camp there, as a constant threat whenever a "free election" was ordered. They were to stand by, immobile and approving, when the new policy of religious persecution, postwar style, began.

I checked my papers at the border. I shook hands all

around. I gave a whispered blessing to Kolia and one or two others who had opened their hearts to me on the long march. I turned my face towards the west, and filled my lungs deep with its wintry air.

"This is the air of freedom," I told myself. "This blows from the Europe where man's spirit can expand without limit. The conscience is not hobbled there by the decisions of an atheist state.

"My troubles are at an end."

I spoke too soon.

I entered the railroad station in the little Polish-Czech bordertown and bought a ticket through to Bratislava. It was a long time since I had been in Czecho-Slovakia: the Nazis who had forced me underground had been defeated since then; the Gestapo records no longer held a threat for me. My anti-Nazi activities need not be hushed or covered up. I could regain the use of my own name. So I believed.

It was a strange week that I spent in Bratislava (back in my Roman collar, able to celebrate Mass with the dear luxury of lighted candles and sweet incense). All returning soldiers shared the same baffling, heartbreaking experiences that I knew. There was the joy of seeing old friends and knowing that they had come safely through the war. But there were gaps in our ranks; there were tragic losses. And, as always, it was frequently the hardiest and best who had died, that the rest of us might live.

There was uncertainty as to the fate of many others: had Carl come through? Someone had heard a rumor of his arrest by the Germans in the last month of the war. And Johann, was he still in prison camp in Austria?

Had our friends of the Slovakian forest-maquis scattered to their homes? How had the pro-Soviet government of Prague dealt with the members of our Catholic Action groups?

I found that many evil things remained in Czecho-Slovakia, as in the wake of the war. The little country had lost the enormous area of Ruthenia: everyone I met was eager to tell me, again, how the trick had been played. The Russians had induced Benes to permit a "free election" there; the people of the country would vote as to whether they wished to remain with him or to join the Soviet.

Stefan had seen the "voting" at work.

"The Commissars came to the illiterate Ruthenian villagers," he said. "They brought gifts of salt and tea. They were friendly—oh, as friendly as Red Ridinghood's grandmother. They said to each peasant family, 'The Soviet is giving out presents to our brave Allies. Do you want a cow? A tractor? A dozen sheep? It will cost you nothing, nothing at all. Just make your mark here, on this application. Give us your fingerprints.'

"The people swarmed to sign the documents, which were gathered together, hundreds of thousands of them, and carefully notarized by the Red agents in each town. Then they were presented to Stalin, who sent them to President Benes as evidence.

"For the poor people had not signed a request for a cow: they had made their marks under a petition to join the USSR.

"I tell you, my friend, I read hundreds of these applications as they were passed out. I warned the peasants and they sent the word around: no petitions were signed in any of the villages *I* reached. But it was too late for the word to spread very far. The distances between the towns were too great. Before any friendly outsider could tip the farmers off to the real meaning of the documents, the majority had sealed their fate.

"That was how Russia stole Ruthenia."

In Czecho-Slovakia itself, things were not going well. The Soviet was already hated, in those months of 1945, when the war against the common enemy had barely come to an end. This proud people resented the duplicity with which the Russians had outwitted them and changed their old frontiers. Their hearts were moved by the pitiful conditions of those families whose farms and villages now fell inside the Russian sphere.

Thousands of Ruthenian refugees were fleeing to the west, across the new Russian border, clamoring to escape the dreaded regime of the Soviet. Without a thought, these penniless peasants abandoned the towns which had been their ancestral homes for centuries. They left in the night, barehanded, empty-bellied, seeking the freedom of the West.

On a train near Zhilina I saw these hungry and desperate men and women. Almost all of them were young: the old people had been too sick at heart to move. I asked the refugees what they were doing there, so far inside the Slovakian border.

"Getting as far to the west as we can," they said. "Fleeing the Russian guards."

I spoke to one poor girl who was dressed in an old flour sack, with a hole cut in the top: her last possession. She shivered as she told me of the scenes when the Soviet soldiers had come to her Ruthenian village to raise the new hammer and sickle over the town hall.

"Trucks traveled from home to home that day, seizing all the furniture," she said. "They took our farm animals away with them. They smashed the holy pictures on the walls. They gathered every bit of hidden food that they could find and told us, 'Now you won't need any stock of potatoes or grain. You'll all be working on a collective farm. The state will feed you.' "

She held her thin little hands to try to control their constant shaking; the scenes through which she had passed had made her seem an old and overwrought woman, yet she had the face of a girl of seventeen.

"My mother made me go," she said. "She made my brother leave with me. But we got separated along the way. I don't know what has happened to him now."

"But you are surely safe now?" I asked her gently. "You are back inside the borders of Slovakia."

"No," she said, and she shrank into her corner fearfully as a door slammed open at one end of the train. "No, no, no. The Reds come deep inside Slovakia to search for us and send us back. They may be on this very train.

"That is why we walk the roads for fifty or a hundred miles inside the border before we dare to try the railroad. We are not safe even here."

She was right, that child. Government experts in Prague later showed me the official estimates; more than fifty thousand peasants from Ruthenia had tried to sneak across. Most of them hid in the woods a few miles inside the border. The stronger and more daring made a dash for the Bohemian towns. But the vast majority of both groups were rounded up and "extradited": the captive government of Prague had yielded to the Soviet police the right to search its trains and beat its farms in order to discover these frightened, wretched people and drag them back inside the Soviet.

In Bratislava I soon discovered that the old underground tricks still had their usefulness. One of the first friends I went to see whispered to me, "Come to the old forest meeting place tonight. There is someone there I want you to see."

It was a strange and unhappy experience. I changed, again, to the nonclerical disguise which I had hoped I should never have to wear again. I followed the old, zigzag course across the city which had become a habit during the war: the quick descent from the streetcar after it was already in motion, the rigid wait inside a dark doorway so that any spy who might be following me would have to pass. I entered the forest near the spot where our French friends used to join us from the factory. I groped my way by hooded flashlight to the wartime meeting ground.

Five or six ragged youths sat about a campfire, blankets draped over their shoulders against the autumn cold. My young friend Ferko was there ahead of me. He introduced me to the refugees, all Ruthenian boys who had escaped across the border in the past few months.

"We must have papers to go farther west," they told me. "It is our only chance."

I exchanged glances with Ferko: the forging of false documents had been a commonplace among the underground units of Slovakia during the war. He shook his head at me.

"It is less easy now," he said. "The people we have to hoodwink are Czechs and Slovaks very much harder to fool than the foreigners who ran the Gestapo. The ink has to match more perfectly, the passport paper ought to carry the right watermark. But we have hopes. I am trying to get hold of the passports of all our comrades who were killed during the war. We may be able to change the photographs so that they will pass inspection."

But it was the refugees themselves who did most of the talking that night. They had come from scattered farms and villages in Ruthenia: everywhere the story was the same. The Russian agents had secured the people's votes by false promises of flour or pigs, of shoes or horses.

One boy came from the biggest city of the area, Uzhorod. Here, where a higher proportion of the people were literate, a different technique of subjection had been used.

"They called a mass meeting in the central square to discuss 'food rations,'" he told me. "Everybody was warned to attend: soldiers would come and make things hot for anyone who stayed away that day. All the factory workers were forced to march to the square, straight from their workbenches. Every official, of course, was there."

He poked at the dwindling little fire.

"Well," he said, "in a sense it *was* a conference on food, as the Reds had said. That meeting was to make starvation legal. Only we didn't know that at the time.

"After everybody had gathered in the square and in the streets that led to it, the MVD threw a ring of steel about us. They leveled their tommy guns on the crowd.

"Then the meeting began. The guards had built a platform with loud speakers. The man who took the microphone was not one of our elected officials: he was the chairman of the local Communist Party. He marched up to the platform and said, 'Comrades. We have all gathered together here today to express the deep desire of our hearts: the joining of our little country to our great motherland of the Soviet.

" 'We are fortunate people. If we vote for annexation today, we shall have nothing more to fear. If any counter-revolutionary capitalists are present, the brave Red soldiers on the edges of the crowd will see that they are given the only kind of argument they understand: a mouthful of lead.'

"Nobody spoke. Nobody dared. There was a kind of outraged moan that swept the square, but the chairman pretended not to hear it.

" 'Soldiers,' he said. 'Stand ready, with your hands upon your guns. We'll take the vote. How many counter-revolutionaries here wish to vote against our joining the Soviet?'

"The crowd looked around, into the muzzles of the soldier's guns. They stood silent with fear.

" 'I am proud of you,' he said. 'I'll wire our great leader Stalin that the people of Uzhorod have unanimously voted in favor of being annexed to Russia.'

"That was the way we voted away our future, Father," he said to me, tears choking him. "It was after that shameful scene that the Soviet induced Jan Masaryk, as foreign minister, to sign the paper which turned over our province to the Soviet. Without a shot!"

In 1945, the Czecho-Slovak people had begun openly, happily, to resume their old religious life. They were told that the Christian newspapers could not start up again; but the editors usually accepted, as a valid excuse, the government pleas of insufficient paper. Many monasteries and convents were still closed; but it was understandable that some months must pass before conditions could return to normal.

But then the Czecho-Slovak antireligious persecution began, with Russian "advisors" running it. As soon as the Nazi agents had cleared out, the local Communists had taken over, using the captured German lists of priests and churches, accepting for their own black list the documents drawn up by the Brown despotism in Berlin. It became evident now that the pattern laid down in recent years in Russia itself would also be applied here. The Communists wished to confuse and delude the people by giving them a puppet church. An old and somewhat addled Catholic priest who had held no important ecclesiastical position before the war proved willing to play the Communists' game. He was immediately given a cabinet post and put in charge of the relations between Church and state within the country. He introduced legislation making it impossible for priests to deliver sermons critical of the regime. He assured the devout that they had been misled by the stories which had come out of Russia; that religious freedom within the Soviet was complete. (At the very moment when the father issued these soothing statements, the antireligious terror in Lithuania, Ruthenia, Latvia and the Ukraine was at its height: priests by the hundreds were under arrest for no other crime than loyalty to their God.)

The people ignored the efforts to divide them; they clung to their churches, they listened to the loyal priests who showed them the whole evil scheme by which the Communists hoped to corrupt the Church itself. Printed leaflets (run off on a secret hand press in the Slav languages) reminded the faithful of the antireligious statements made by Stalin, by Marx, by the officials of the Militant Atheists League. These were passed from hand to hand among the Czech and Slovak believers. These leaflets saved thousands from being deluded by the propaganda which would have made them entrust their spiritual life to Stalin's men.

It was during the annual pilgrimage to Levoca, the famous Slovakian shrine, that the Communists first showed their true feelings towards the Church. More than one hundred thousand of the devout had made the pilgrimage from all sections of the country, bringing their little gifts of thanksgiving for the war's end, carrying their medals to be blessed.

It was here, with this great congregation on its knees, that the Slovakian people had a revelation of the true intentions of their enemy: while they knelt before the shrine, a sudden horrible burst of noise shattered their prayers. Fire soared towards heaven from the shrine. The air was thick with bits of wood and glass and fragments of charred human flesh.

The Communists had placed a bomb inside the shrine. The priest and several dozen of the faithful were killed by it. But the bomb accomplished one thing which the Communists had not foreseen: it destroyed, forever, the Slovakians' naïve belief that the Soviet would make genuine peace with God.

There had been in Czecho-Slovakia during the war several student groups who collaborated with the Nazis. They operated under many different names; their organizations overlapped; but the most prominent of these collaborationists were the Hlinka Guard—an organization like the French militia. They knew how to spread themselves thin; to give the impression of immense strength they had issued, from a single headquarters, half a dozen different "student" papers, all of them eulogistic of the Nazi regime. Because of their apparent activity and size, they had deceived many of their countrymen. By the end of the war the very name "student" was suspect. Young men who had fought valiantly against the Nazis for the whole span of their grown-up lives, boys who had been black-listed by the Gestapo and had even suffered jail sentences at their hands, found themselves in the ridiculous situation of being tried as "collaborators with the enemy."

In arranging these arrests on trumped-up charges, the native Communists were extremely active. They took advantage of the ignorance of the Czech and Slovak officials who had been away, during much of the war, with the government in exile in London, to draw up their own lists of men who were opposed to Communism on philosophical and democratic grounds. Even though these men had fought on the Russian side—even though they had been the implacable enemies of the Fascists—their names were handed over to ZOB, the new Communist-run political police as "Nazi collaborators."

Our Catholic Action students and workers had a record of near martyrdom in their opposition to the Nazis: nobody knew this fact better than the Communists who had worked with us and even entrusted their lives to us in the joint underground in the late years of the war. But now the Communist program had changed. Now, it was the Catholics who had become their hated enemy. Now, it was the Christian workers and students who most clearly opposed their plan to make Czecho-Slovakia another Soviet state.

And so I found, in Bratislava, that not all of my missing friends were victims of the Nazis: some of them had been jailed by their own government, for which they had risked their lives throughout the war. One of the first moves of the Communists was an effort to discredit the Church.

For the Czecho-Slovakia of 1945 was a structure at which the busy termites from the east had nibbled away; the superstructure appeared safe and strong to observers in western Europe and America. But the foundations of the country, as an independent state, had been eaten away. In 1948, when the Communist coup swept away the government in a single day, the true state of affairs became apparent to all. But that coup had been in preparation for many years.

CHAPTER 17

Jailed in Prague

My own position was now a curious one. I could admit to nobody that I had spent the last months inside Russia as a priest in disguise; that would have been to court Communist arrest. So I decided to resume my own identity. Addressing Catholic Action groups openly, I still hoped to be able to hide from the omnipresent Comintern the fact that I was the same "Partisan doctor" who had moved about in their country after the war's end. But I was wrong; my life as an outlaw had not ended.

One night I was awakened, in the rectory where I was staying, by a brother who came to my room carrying a kerosene lamp which shook visibly in his nervous hands.

"Police downstairs," he said to me. "They are asking for you."

I hurriedly dressed and, telling him not to worry, went downstairs. Three members of the local Red secret police—ZOB—were waiting for me.

"What do you wish with me at this hour?" I asked.

"Only a little information, Father," said their leader

soothingly. "You will be back here in an hour or less. We have a taxi waiting outside."

I shrugged. The men were armed. There was no way to avoid going with them.

"Where are you taking me?" I asked them, as we passed the porter. I hoped that he would listen to their answer. But it was not informative.

"You will learn," said one of them.

In the dark corner of the taxi, a gun was stuck into my ribs. It was a two-door car. Sitting on the back seat, I was blocked off by the driver, an armed policeman, and by the third man, who turned around to watch me throughout the trip, his revolver aimed at me.

Where would we go? I knew the streets and I tried to follow our progress through the windshield. We twisted rapidly, making many turns, seeking obscure sections of the town. I saw that we were emerging into a suburb; I did not know which one. Then fields and woods and villages appeared and, finally, a large building which might have been an army barracks.

During the trip I had asked nothing, been told nothing.

In the white dawn I found myself marched up the steps to the door of the building, which was barred. A guard on the inside pushed a button to open it, and the great door clanked behind me. I was motioned to follow the leader; the other men walked by my side, their guns still drawn. Down a long corridor of closed doors. Up an iron staircase. Into an office where I was allowed to sit on a straight chair.

"You will stay with us for a while," said one of my guards.

"Good!" I said. "I am entirely at your disposal."

I had decided to play out the little masquerade, to pretend that I had really been brought here for friendly questioning. I acted as if I had noticed no guns, no window bars. Sometimes it is best, with the Communists, to seem very innocent and very dull.

A policeman in unform arrived.

"Go with him," said my guard. The police agent was a simple man. No political agent yet, for the Communists had not then taken over the Czecho-Slovakian police force as they have done today. To the police officer I was, no doubt, a midnight housebreaker. He led me down a circular stairway of dirty concrete and into the low-vaulted cellar, among the furnace pipes. Here, in a small and suffocating little room, he laboriously wrote down my answers to the sort of questionnaire to which the criminal prisoners had to submit.

"Now," he said. "I'll search you. Give me your suspenders, your knife, your shoelaces."

"But, my friend," I said to him. "Why do you wish these things?"

He nodded vaguely towards the left.

"In that very cell out there," he said, "a prisoner hung himself last week by using his belt."

The policeman, after he had searched my clothes, took me to a barred door leading into a wall of solid, foul-smelling darkness. He opened the door, pushed me inside, turned the key behind him and his footsteps grew fainter.

"So," I said to myself. "Not imprisoned by the Nazis, in spite of all my close escapes. Not detained by the Russians, although I spent six months inside their country under an assumed name. It is here, with the war over, in a 'free' and friendly Allied country whose laws I have never broken, that I find myself a prisoner."

I took a timid step forward into the black hole that gaped before my eyes. I stepped on something that moved: a human cry rang out. As my eyes began to pierce the darkness I saw that I was a prisoner in a windowless cell built for solitary confinement, and that its floor was a tangled mass of human bodies. Seven men lay there, writhing in layers and sharing a few feet of fetid air.

The voices came to me. "What are you in for, old boy? Black-market peddling? Got a cigarette?"

I had some cigarettes: I handed them to the grasping fingers and the men became my friends.

"Come on, now, tell us why you're here?" they asked.

I said I did not know, but that I believed myself to be in jail for opposition to the Communists.

"Hard luck," they muttered. "Hard luck. The political prisoners get it the worst of all. All but one of us are politicals here."

"See what it means to oppose the Communists?" said a young man. He lit a match and, opening his mouth wide, pointed to the swollen gums where four or five teeth had recently been knocked out. "They pulled those as a part of my 'interrogation' three nights ago."

Another man spoke. "They made me hold my arms straight out before me for three hours at my last questioning, while they beat them with clubs. Two fingers are broken."

A third man put my hand on his head to feel the great welts from the beating he had received. The fourth told me that he had a black eye, so swollen that he could hardly see through it. "I have got off easy, so far," he said.

The door was suddenly pushed open and another man came catapulting into the overcrowded cell. By now my eyes were accustomed to the darkness, and I could see his face in the light from the corridor. I recognized him. He was a Catholic boy with whom I had worked in the anti-Nazi underground.

We embraced.

When our comrades in misery learned that I was a priest, they treated me with the greatest consideration.

"Father," said one of them, "have you eaten?"

"No," I said.

"We have something tucked away." From under the dirty and flea-covered mattress that lay in one corner, the boy with the broken hands produced a bit of hard black bread. I gratefully took a bite of it and passed it to our new arrival.

"It is still night," said one of the men. "Let's try to sleep."

The only places on the floor not already covered with tortured bodies were close to the foul-smelling water closet, which leaked little pools in one dank corner of the cell. One of the earlier occupants wished to move to this least desirable of places: my maquis friend and I refused. In this hierarchy of misery, the men who were in pain from their beatings must have the one pitiful luxury the cell afforded: a breath of the cleaner air that could be breathed by lying close to the cell door.

It was a miserable night. One of the men suffered from diarrhea, and frequently had to crawl over us. Others lay moaning and nursing their injuries in their dreams. It was not a time for rest.

In the morning I learned more details of the prison life. The guard led us to the bathroom: its only window was covered with a closely woven steel wire covering the heavy metal bars. One of my cell companions whispered to me: "They put that up this week because someone sawed through the old bars and escaped."

As we leaned over the large community basin that served as bathtub, he whispered again, "They killed two men in this tub by throwing them into boiling water just last week."

Back in the cell I began to follow the routine. I learned how certain periods of a day in jail stand out; moments of joy because they are slightly less miserable than the rest. I discovered how the human mind adjusts itself, so that these events are cherished and remembered, as real and solid pleasures might be savored in the outside world.

Morning "coffee," followed our baths, was one of these high points. This was made of ersatz roots, but it was hot and it was black. With it came a thin slice of bread which must last out the day. Luncheon was "soup" with a mealy potato. Dinner was the same. But to the famished, any food is a feast. Warmed and cheered by our meals, we became talkative and friendly at these times.

I was examined twice in the Bratislava jail: in both cases I was led before an officer of ZOB and handed a "confession" of complicity with collaborationists. The charges made were not only untrue; they could not possibly have been true. The events I was supposed to have instigated had happened in towns where I had never been and during periods for which I had iron-clad alibis. But the political police are not interested in ascertaining facts or in hearing the details of a defense. It is their job to make a case against a prisoner, to induce him to sign a paper that will defile him forever in the eyes of those who have trusted him.

"I cannot sign this, for it is not true." Those were almost the only words I spoke to the police officers who investigated me. They were repeated, hour after hour, with a horrible monotony. The scenes were punctuated by occasional assaults upon my person.

"Maybe this will help you to remember," the policeman would say. A stinging blow across my cheek. A crack across the skull with his heavy night stick. A revolver drawn slowly from the holster and laid down, with careful meaning, on the table before me.

On the second occasion the officers tried another method to break me down. They handed me three typewritten "affidavits," signed with the names of men who had worked with me in the Slovakian underground. According to these narratives, our whole resistance movement had been a gigantic collaborationist plot: we had wrecked Allied troop trains and given coded messages to the Germans so that they might arrest the anti-Nazi patriots. It was a tissue of lies; none of my boys could possibly have signed these documents. I told the policeman so.

A few days after this, the door of the cell swung wide and the jailer said to me, "Come now. You are going to leave this place. If you have any packing to do, start it now."

His heavy humor gave me a chance to bid my new friends farewell, to give them my blessing and to accept the messages they asked me to memorize for their friends or families, in case I should be released.

I climbed the circular stairway with a lightened heart.

I believed that I would leave this prison a free man. I thought that some friend in the government had interfered, to prevent this handful of Communists from persecuting me. I had already made plans, before I reached the prison entrance, to plead the cause of all those innocent men I had left in the fetid cell behind me.

I expected to be free.

The car that awaited me at the door was a sinister double of the taxi in which I had arrived. I marched down the steps towards it with two silent guards, one on each side of me. The door of the car swung open. An armed guard stepped out.

"Inside," he said, and accented his meaning by the pressure of his .45 against my back. This did not look like freedom.

We drove all day. At four-hour intervals the car stopped in some quiet village street and one of the three men slipped out for a few minutes, returning with a large can of gasoline for the motor and with loaves of gray bread and onions, which we ate. Sometimes he brought a little black soup, sometimes a bottle of water.

No one spoke to me.

"Where are we going?" I had asked, in the early hours of the drive.

"Shut up. You'll get a chance to do plenty of talking later," said the man who seemed to be in charge.

Twice the drivers changed places. I lost all sense of time. It was light. Then it was dark. Then it was light again. Still we drove through the countryside. Still the silent men sat guarding me. Sometimes I dozed.

Finally I opened my eyes to see the familiar Karol bridge of Prague ahead of us. So! I had been brought to the country's capital. Perhaps I should be taken to a government official, given a chance to tell the story of my mysterious arrest and of the tortures I had undergone in jail? Perhaps the heads of this country, still proud of its "democratic" heritage, would apologize for the carelessness of an overzealous minor official? Perhaps the political prisoners had all been rounded up through an error which was to be set right?

Perhaps. But the men who were escorting me did not look as if they expected to be reprimanded for having exceeded their powers. There was little about their behavior to suggest that the law of "habeas corpus" was weighing on their minds.

I watched the streets. No. We were not making the turn for the government buildings. We were heading, instead, for a part of town I did not know. We were coming to a stop before a building which bore far too much resemblance to the one which I had left behind.

It was another jail.

The Prague prison had one harsh peculiarity not shared with other jails run by Communist Party agents. For here the effort to break down a prisoner's morale began before he was ever led into a cell. The theory—cruelly clever—was that a man would be more frightened of torture before he had established contact with the other inmates and learned the probable limits of the ordeal. The comforting idea that had helped people to face such ordeals before—"If those boys could stand it, so can I"—could not be resorted to here. I did not know whether this place was a common jail or a charnel house from which no man ever emerged alive.

I was led into a bare little room and searched. Then my guard said, "This way, you." He led me to a broad stone corridor where I saw several dozen men standing, each naked, each facing the wall with his arms stretched sidewise, shoulder-high.

"Take off your clothes and stand like these," he said to me. I gave him all I wore and took up the position. "And don't think you can lean against the wall to rest and get away with it," he growled. "We have nasty plans for prisoners who stand less than one foot from the wall."

I stood barefooted in the slime that covered the stones of the corridor, for what must have been two hours. It was a position which became more agonizing with each minute that dragged by. If my arms began to sag, I felt a sharp jab in my back and knew that it was a tommy gun. My muscles strained and ached, the temptation to sway forward and rest my forehead on the wall was almost irresistible.

Behind me I heard a shuffling of many feet: it was, I later learned, the vast body of prisoners returning from the exercise yard. Everyday they were forced to pass in procession down this corridor, to pass the tortured men.

A voice close to my ear said, "Turn around." There stood the guard, my clothing in his hand.

"Carry these and come with me," he said.

I was led down a series of stone steps into a cell which had a smell I recognized too well; the smell of drying human blood. A bare bench bore the blood, still wet, of my predecessor.

"Lie down on that," said the guard.

I took my place. Iron chains were bound around my ankles and my wrists. With another chain the guard began to beat my upturned back. The pain was great. Blood gushed into my eyes and blinded me. I did not know whether he would stop this side of death. My mind fought the agony with prayer. Then the pain ceased.

"Get up."

I staggered to my feet, barely able to stand. While I leaned, gasping, upon the torture bench, the door swung open and another guard walked in. He handed me a paper and a pen.

I brushed the blood and sweat out of my eyes and tried to focus them. The paper declared that I had been a secret agent of the Hapsburg royal family and had worked to destroy the present Czech regime.

"Sign it," said the second guard.

I was too weak to speak. I merely shook my head and dropped the declaration to the floor.

The first guard looked on with professional interest.

"Hot irons?" he asked. There was a moment's pause.

"No, not yet," said the second man. "We'll try another day."

Dressed again and able to walk, bent over with the pains of welts and wounds, I followed the guard up and down a series of corridors to a brightly lighted solitary cell. A ragged pallet lay on the floor; roaches and rats crawled over it. From the bucket in the corner came a sickening odor. The door clanked behind me. I fell down on the mattress into a half-sleep, half-swoon. I do not know how long I lay that way.

Why was I here? I had never been told. The accusations were all in the form of the absurd "confessions" which the officials had tried to get me to sign. Nobody seemed aware of the fact that I had done a dozen things which the Communists who pulled the strings in Czecho-Slovakia might properly resent and fear. Nobody brought up my secret stay in Russia, or my contacts with the Christian opposition to the Communist activities since the end of the war. These men did not seem to have put me in prison for any of the sensible, legitimate reasons I might have expected them to use: that I knew too much, that I was the lifelong enemy of their ideals, that I had organized the youth of the country to oppose them to the end. On these charges they might have kept me in prison for years, and been quite justified, according to their views. Instead, they seemed to have locked me up in the hope that I would, through fear, confess to a long chain of lies. They hoped to discredit me and, through me, the Church to which I belonged.

I had, therefore, a task to do. Here in my windowless cell, alive with crawling, gnawing things, I must forge a will that would be strong enough to stand up under any kind of painful questioning. I must, somehow, through constant prayer and thought prepare myself for the next bout of torture. I must anticipate every probable question, every likely trap, and brace my spirit in advance so as not to be taken by surprise. It occurred to me that I should be very busy in that cell.

When the pain from the beating had dulled I got up, half-blinded by the light, and unsteadily groped my way around. My cell was two steps long and two steps wide. I kept my eyes closed but the light still beat through my eyelids. A brilliant electric bulb on a long wire threw a cruel glare into every corner. It was kept burning day and night to dazzle me. I was to find that the light was never dark.

CHAPTER 18

Christians Behind Bars

THE key turns in the door. A guard tells me to follow him and bring my bucket with me. I trail down the slimy steps: although the sun is beating in through a broad window, it seems half dark after the cruel brilliance of my cell. Another door is opened and I am pushed into a large exercise yard of frozen mud and garbage. There are some fifty or sixty gaunt and ragged figures in the yard.

"Line up," says the harsh voice of a guard. We drag ourselves into a row.

"Shirts off." I look around me: in all the row of famished bodies the ribs stand out. Big welts and fresh scars mark every tortured chest. The men gasp as we are driven through the short gymnastics—a mockery of our living death, for these exercises are required by law from the old prewar days, to keep the prisoners "in a condition of health."

I have been afraid to steal more than a glance at any of the prisoners while the guard stands by, for I do not want to implicate anyone by even a flashing glance of recognition. But now we pull our dirty, torn shirts about us. Now the guard moves back towards the prison wall. We begin our promenade around the yard and I permit myself to look full into the faces of these men.

The dirty, unshaved faces all look much alike at first; except for two men with blackened eyes. Then I look more closely. I recognize Stefan: he was one of the ardent members of the Catholic Action groups. He is only twenty-one, but hardships and suffering have bent him so that he walks like an aged man. And there, a few paces in front of me, is Louis. Our eyes meet. When the half-hour processional is ended we have a few minutes of freedom. Louis sidles up to me.

"The guard who comes on at midnight is one of us," he mutters. Then he drifts away.

Back in my cell in the glaring lights I consider my position as a priest. Can I do anything to help these men? It becomes apparent from the presence of Louis and Stefan that the crime for which many of the prisoners have been assembled here is the crime of believing in the Faith. That faith must be nourished inside these walls.

I had started out my prison career with a Breviary, snatched up from the bedside table through long habit when the midnight summons came and I was taken to the Bratislava jail for "questioning." But the book was taken away from me during the first search; it has never been returned. I have neither a Mass kit nor a Missal. But I have my Rosary!

I was able to smuggle the beads by an old trick familiar to every member of the Christian underground: I kept them rolled up in my hand and raised them above my head with my undershirt while the various police guards searched all my pockets and the linings of my clothes. The Rosary is here, the single visible reminder of the beauty of my Church's liturgy. I look at it, cupped in my hand. It is a cheap Rosary, but it symbolizes all the material aids to worship man has learned to use: here is the stained glass of the Sainte Chapelle and the dome of Saint Peter's, the groined arches of Notre Dame and the Sistine frescoes, compressed in one string of beads.

Man is spirit but he has a body, too, and it is by bending both to the service of his Lord that he fulfills himself. That is why we need stained glass and Rosary beads. That, too, is why I must find a way to bring to these soul-hungering men their physical God; it is the first and biggest thing to do.

I cannot tell when it is midnight inside my cell by any change of light. But I know that it takes ten minutes to say a Rosary. I begin to pray and thus to count the hours. I guess that it was around six o'clock when we left the exercise yard: twice since then my cell door has been opened and a bit of greasy cabbage soup pushed inside the door. I tick off the Rosaries: six to an hour, a hundred and eight, it should be midnight now. I say four more Rosaries for greater safety. Then I set up a noisy hammering on the door of my cell.

A bolt shoots back. A bearded face appears. A pair of curious, suspicious brown eyes appear. It is the midnight guard.

"Louis spoke to you?" I ask. He nods. "Yes. He told me I should trust you."

"Come in," I whisper. The guard shuffles inside the cell. I open my fist and show him the Rosary.

"I am a priest," I tell him. "There are good Catholic

men inside this jail. You must help us. You must make it possible for me to say my Mass and give Communion to them."

He is frightened. He shakes his head emphatically.

"It is impossible," he whispers. "I would like to help you, Father, but they would find out. You cannot see the other prisoners except at exercise time. You cannot possibly say Mass then. No, no. Do not ask me. They would kill us all."

"Listen, my friend," I said to him. "I know I cannot say Mass publicly. But that is not required. If you will bring me a little grape wine and some Hosts, I will say Mass here in the dead of night. You need know nothing about it. I will hide the things securely."

He looked around the bare and brilliantly lighted cell.

"There is no hiding place," he said.

"Bring me a bit of string," I promised him, "and I will hide them. Look. Try to stare up at the light in this cell."

He turned his eyes upwards and dropped them at once.

"You see?" I said. "No one can stand it. The light is too painful. I will attach the little packages to the light bulb. They will be invisible."

He thought.

"Tomorrow," he said, "I will try. Tell me where to get the things for you."

I murmured the name and address of a priest who would understand. Down the corridor a man began to shout. The guard made a quick gesture of silence and slipped out.

The next morning I was called to the office again for questioning. It was the practice in this jail to turn political prisoners over to the ZOB. These men were brutal: some of them had worked as collaborators with the Gestapo and had had a thorough course of training in the methods of the Nazi secret police. But for some reason they did not use physical torture this day as a prelude to my talk; instead I was led into an office where a single smiling, uniformed figure sat at a desk.

"Good morning," he said to me with great politeness. "Please sit down."

He offered me a cigarette. Lighting it, I studied his face. He was a young man with a narrow face, tight, thin lips, and the eyes of a fanatic who has drilled himself to Spartan self-control. He began to talk to me with an air of friendliness.

"I am a member of the Party," he said. "You surely know enough to understand what that means. In Czecho-Slovakia now *I* have the power. These figureheads in the government are window dressing: their fine liberal sentiments will not help you here. We are running Czecho-Slovakia. I advise you not to try to smuggle out any pleas. That will only annoy us, and when we are irritated we can be very disagreeable."

"I am sure of that," I said. "But what are the charges on which you are holding me? You know that I have never been guilty of any of these ridiculous things your men have tried to force me to confess. What do you want of me?"

"Oh, as for that," he said. "We want a very simple thing. We want a written confession that you and your Church are our enemies. That's true enough, isn't it?"

"We are Christians," I told him. "If we are good Christians we can have no enemies—no human enemies. As for your Communist ideals, yes, they are our enemies so far as they are based on a false and atheist conception of man. Yes. That is true."

"Very noble. But if you insist on all the myths of Christianity, you are our eternal enemy," he said. "Until you and your God are as dead as Jupiter and Osiris there can be no lasting truce.

"You know that as well as I. You know that the two systems are completely incompatible. If Christianity and Communism make common cause for a few months, as they did against the Nazis, that is just a matter of tactics. As soon as the Nazis were destroyed the old death struggle between our two systems began again."

"During the war," I said, "your Russian friends did not speak of the reopening of the churches as a provisional matter of expediency or mere tactics. They told the Russian people that from then on they might worship as they pleased. The masses here will not like to discover that they, too, were duped. Their religion is very dear to them. It will require a terror to make them stop practicing their faith, and terror does not inspire confidence. Your Party leaders will incur hate, and yet more hate, the harsher their measures are against the Church. Are you quite sure it is wise to try to rule a people by hatred?"

He shrugged.

"This is all very interesting," he said, "but it is not the point. The point is this: we are going to discredit you and men like you. We are going to make the people believe that all the priests were working with the Nazis. We need a few prominent traitors among the clergy for this purpose.

"You admit that you are the enemy of our Communist

régime. That is practically a confession of treason now. Why not make things more comfortable for yourself and stretch the truth a little? Why don't you sign one of these confessions of conspiracy against the government? Then we will let you go."

"Because they are not true," I said. "Because I never have conspired against the government."

"Oh, come now," he said. "Every time you celebrate a Mass you are showing your opposition to the government of today. Why not express your hatred of us in the form we wish you to?"

"Because it is not true."

"What is truth?" he asked me. And I said, "That is the question Pontius Pilate asked."

That day in the exercise yard I managed to get into line next to Louis when the long promenade began. We had a full half hour in which it was possible to talk by merely keeping the lips from moving, as all prisoners learn to do.

Louis told me the explanation of those bent and dragging bodies which I saw about me. He said, "All of us have been tortured. Some of us are tortured every night. They begin by kicking you in the stomach and hitting you between the eyes. Sometimes they knock out a tooth or two. But the real agony comes later."

Unobtrusively he drew my attention to one of his crippled hands.

"They put a long pencil between my fingers and twisted them on each other until the bones were cracked," he said. "On some of the others they have used an old Oriental device: they twist their noses until the blood runs down their throats and chokes them. All of us, of course, are beaten with belts and chains. Sometimes they beat the soles of our bare feet with sharp sticks.

"But the most dangerous things they do are not physical. They read us declarations signed by our most trusted friends; these implicate us in every kind of plot. They give dates and names and details. Sometimes, after torture, you are so confused that you begin to doubt your own memories; you wonder whether you have really done these things. While your mind is groping and bewildered, a glass of brandy is held beneath your nose, a lighted cigarette is offered you and you are told, 'Just sign this and you can have a drink, a smoke, a good hot meal.' "

I marveled at the courage of these boys who had endured such pain, such persecution and had still the spirit left to give me a warning of what might lie in store for me.

"What are they trying to get from me?" I asked.

"They want you to confess that you were involved in a plot with the Hlinka Guard against the government," he said. "They are trying to implicate the Church, the bishops and even the Vatican authorities.

"Your name has already appeared in half a dozen of the false confessions they are trying to get us all to sign. But do not fear, Father: these are good boys here. They will not give in."

That night the key in my cell door turned gratingly and the friendly guard moved rapidly inside. Without a word he reached into his pocket and produced a half-pint bottle of wine, a second bottle filled with unconsecrated Hosts, a length of strong twine. He locked his hands together, close to the door, and beckoned me to stand on them so that I could reach the cord above the dazzling light and attach the holy contraband as we had agreed.

I made the precious bottles secure. Then I gave him my blessing and my silent thanks. He slipped out of the door again. The Communist prison had its chaplain now.

By standing on tiptoe I was able to unknot the two small bottles and bring down the materials for my Mass.

With the help of whispered consultations in the exercise yard we worked out a system by which the Catholic prisoners might receive the sacraments, under the very eyes of our Communist jailers.

The guard who came at midnight managed to distribute to each Christian prisoner a small bit of tissue paper and a piece of bread. The Christian wrote his confession with these; it was collected, folded, tucked inside the morning hunk of bread which was brought to my cell. I unrolled the confessions, read them and swallowed the papers. I was able to give absolution to these poor boys by meeting their eyes in the exercise yard and winking—the signal we all understood. This method was used for more than forty Catholics.

Those who had confessed had a great desire to receive the Eucharist. This, too, was made possible by our friendly guard. Each night I consecrated Hosts for those who wished to receive the following day: I wrapped each of them in a bit of clean paper smuggled in for the occasion, and the guard put them into the bread that was pushed into the communicant's cell.

My Mass materials were never found. My Christian underground continued all the time I stayed in that cell.

One day I was led from my interrogation down a long corridor I had never seen before. At its end was a heavily bolted door. The guard threw it open and pushed me inside. I found myself in a cell with five men drawn up stiffly at salute. When the door had clanged to behind me, they relaxed. I was now to share their cell.

"Always stand at salute when you hear the guard coming," one of them told me. "Otherwise he beats you."

I threw myself down, exhausted, upon the pile of straw and rags in a corner of the cell. I had been interrogated most of the previous five nights.

One of the young men came close to me. He leaned over with great kindness.

"It is strictly forbidden to lie down during the day," he whispered to me. "The guard has orders to watch us through the peep hole and see that we are standing up at attention whenever he passes. But we have learned how to time his arrival. Lie there and rest now: we'll give you the alert when you have to spring up and be ready for him."

I scarcely heard his voice. My nerves, frayed by the strain and the sleeplessness, took their revenge. I fell into a kind of coma. I was only vaguely conscious of the faces of my cellmates. My brain was no longer receptive to new impressions from the harsh and hostile environment. I could still pray; I could no longer act or speak or think.

Later, however, I revived and looked about at these cellmates. They were pale and sickly men with unkempt beards and tattered, ragged clothes. They were half-frozen and half-starved; I later learned that all in that cell suffered from frostbite. We warmed ourselves by sleeping close together at night; during the day we rested only in uneasy snatches while our friends stood guard.

But it was possible to talk to the other friends in misery. Gradually, I learned their stories. One of them was an old-time Socialist who had refused to join the Communist Party in his region. A second was an aviator who had been indiscreet in telling his friends of the things he had seen in the Russian-occupied countries during the war. All of the men were political prisoners. All had been tortured far more severely than I.

Jan showed me his scarred palms: during his examination the guards had brought red-hot irons, around which they bound his suffering hands "to make him remember." The wounds were festering.

I asked these men whether our cell was served by the friendly guard who came on after midnight. Yes, they said. There was a good man who smuggled messages to the outside and sometimes slipped them a bit of extra bread. One night I determined to establish contact with him and arrange for him to bring me, here, the wine and bread essential for my Mass. After darkness blotted out the little window through which the icy winds blew night and day, I drew out my Rosary and began saying it to mark the hours. When I was sure that twelve-thirty had passed, I rose and banged against the door of the cell with the tin bowl in which our supper had been served.

The guard came. I told him I had been moved and that I wished the materials for my Mass brought to me here.

He shook his head.

"It's too dangerous," he said. "It's too dangerous for both of us. Any one of your cellmates could betray me, and two of them are half-crazy. You can't trust them not to talk. And the others, too. Torture might make them sell us out."

He was right. It was heartbreaking for men as miserable as we to have to doubt each other, to fear that one of us might trade the life of another for a little extra prison privilege. But I had no right to expose these unhappy, unknown prisoners to such a temptation by sharing the secret of my Mass. I begged the guard at least to remove the wine and Hosts from my old cell and see that they were destroyed. He promised that he would.

I made no secret to my cellmates of the fact that I was a priest: each day I watched the moving patch of sun on the wall of our cell and when noon came I produced my hidden Rosary and prayed for an hour. The men watched me in a respectful silence: if they spoke to each other at these times, it was in whispers which could not disturb me. Even one poor man who could not stop counting moved his lips soundlessly while I prayed.

My religious duties had been narrowed, now, to the compass of this small and wretched little cell. It was my task to smuggle hope and charity inside its bars. My greatest enemy in this work was suspense. We did not know what future lay in store for any of us. We were no longer taken downstairs for torture and examination. We sometimes heard the cries of men being dragged through the corridor shortly before dawn, to their death: the executions took place close enough to our window so that we could hear the drop of the bodies from the hangman's noose, the death cry of the condemned man. But nobody came to call us to our death. Nobody brought us word of what the secret police wished to do with us. Nobody let us know whether we were ever to walk out of those cells alive or whether we were to live on, forgotten, until we went wholly mad.

We were able to slip messages to the outside world

through our sympathetic guard; but no answers came back. I smuggled half a dozen tiny capsule-contained notes to be delivered to other priests, to the non-Communist men in the government whom I knew, to the representatives of friendly powers in Prague. For months I did not know whether any of these notes had actually been delivered: the guard was able only to hand them on to whatever priest he found it safest to approach.

I realized that all of us might have to stay in our dank and dreadful cells for months or years. We could not merely stand and stare at the walls without succumbing to despair. And despair is a sin. I must help us all to make a life inside this cell. I must stir the men to some activity which would give continuity to our days and hope to our sorrowing souls.

I said as much to my poor comrades, who had already sunk so deep in lethargy that they were scarcely able to understand my words.

"You are intelligent men," I said. "You have studied and thought in the past. We must all study again. We must save ourselves from self-pity by stretching our minds. Come, now. What shall we study?"

Their brains were dulled by suffering: none of them were able to teach the others, but all of them were able to rouse themselves sufficiently to listen. I said to them, "You have all been interested in social problems; two of you are socialists. We will start with talks on sociology."

For one hour every afternoon I addressed my "class" on social problems. At first their attention wandered; they had the habit of falling into a trance. But Ilya was still fairly alert: the first day, he challenged one of my statements about the Marxian theory of value. While we kept one eye on the door for the guard, while we chafed our numb feet against the cold, we forced our minds to deal with a few of the abstractions of economic theory.

The next day it was a little easier. The talks on sociology became a ritual, a portion of the day marked off from the others, regular sessions which we began when the sun had reached a particular crack on one of the walls.

One day Ilya said, "It is hard to argue socialism without a knowledge of history, and I have spent so little time in school. Can't you give us talks about the history of Europe, too?"

I did. I worked out a course of daily talks on other subjects, too. I began each lecture with a review of the things we had discussed the day before and I always asked whether any of the men wished to question the things I had told them. This proved a useful device: it stirred up their sick and sluggish minds so that they thought about the subjects under discussion in the dreary hours of the day and night. The escape-world of debate and discussion began to win.

During the first few weeks we were only four in the class: then one day the fifth man, Alfred, stopped searching through the window for his wife and joined our discussion of the Crusades. Until that moment he had not spoken a single word. Now, he showed an agile and well-trained mind. The war against Alfred's fantasies was not won in a week. But after a while he spent only a few shamefaced hours a day watching for his wife to appear at the window. In his heart he now realized that he was deluding himself. He recognized his dreams for the drugs they had become.

The sixth man was sicker. We called him "The Count," for we did not know his name, and he counted all the time. He might have been quite alone in the cell, for all the attention he paid to the rest of us. Sometimes "The Count" paced about us in the cramped space, fitting his steps to the numbers he intoned. More often he stood slumped against a corner of the cell, counting, counting, counting.

One sunless, cloudy morning I stood leaning in silence against a wall, mentally preparing the lecture I would give my friends that afternoon. Suddenly I felt a hand tugging at my sleeve. It was "The Count"; his lips were moving, as always, but he was also pointing to the floor.

"What is it?" I asked him.

He pointed vigorously to the floor, to my pocket, to the shadowless wall of the cell. Then, with great difficulty, he controlled himself. Sweat poured from his forehead. His hands were white as they grasped my arm.

"Time to pray," he gasped.

It was the first sign we had had that he knew what was going on about him or could speak except in numerals. I glanced out of the window: it was impossible, without the sun, to know whether noon was really there. But I nodded and thanked "The Count." I drew out my Rosary. Before I knelt I drew him down to his knees beside me. For the duration of the prayers he remained silent. After that, each day, he prayed with me. And I deliberately lengthened the number of prayers a few more each day, so that he might be given those extra moments of peace. One morning, during the prayers, "The Count" began to sob; a great torrent of sorrow broke from his heart and flowed into tears. When it was over, he sank exhausted to the floor and lay there in silence for the rest of the day. He never counted again. Soon "The Count" was attending the lectures with the rest of us.

CHAPTER 19

Back to Freedom

HAD the letters which I smuggled to the outside world ever reached my friends? Had my colleagues begun an investigation of my sudden disappearance, so many months before? I did not know. I had no mail, no direct news of the outside world, no source of information except the prison grapevine. This operated with uncertain success: during our exercise hour one of the prisoners, who worked in the prison bakery, passed on to the rest of us such scraps of news as he had been able to pick up through a grocery boy from the outside world. These items were garbled, confused and sometimes quite inaccurate: they had filtered through the minds of the grocer's boy and the prisoner before they reached my ears, and neither was a political economist.

But one day during our walk in the prison yard, the baker slid into line beside me and whispered, "You're in the news today." "I?" I asked him. "Yes," he said. "The secret police announced that you have been arrested as a Vatican spy. They're going to try you soon."

It was a new phrase, reminiscent of those novels of

eighteenth-century England in which the Jesuit fathers were romanticized as members of a giant international conspiracy. The Vatican employs no spies; the Prague government, some of whose members had known me and my work for twenty years, knew that I was not a spy for any state. But what was behind this yarn seemed evident enough. The Communist-run government was seeking priests whom they might put in the dock in an effort to discredit the Church. My own movements, during the war and after, had been furtive enough to suggest that I had something to hide. I wondered whether the ZOB had decided to make public some of my shifts of identity, my secret movements, and try to prove through these that I was involved in underhand activities. I spent that day in thought. I must decide what I should do if the baker's news proved halfway accurate.

Oddly enough, it turned out to be straightforward. Shortly after midnight I summoned my friendly guard. When he came to the grilling, he verified the story.

"The papers are full of your case," he said. "There is a great to-do about whether you are to be tried in a 'people's' court or a civil court. Tonight's paper says that foreigners are sending protests, trying to help you out. Good luck to you."

It was thanks to an eminent French diplomat, I later learned, that the plans for my trial were actually changed. I had been scheduled for one of the ZOB courts, where summary justice is handed down in star-chamber proceedings. After the intercession of my powerful French friend, the Prague government agreed that I might have a trial by jury.

The next morning I was summoned from the exercise yard and hustled out of the jail. There was the inevitable waiting taxicab. There was the inevitable escort of three gunmen. I was driven to a hotel room where my guards produced a valise filled with clothes I had not seen for many months. They had been seized from the house where I was first arrested in Bratislava.

"You can clean up here for the trial," they said.

I looked into the bathroom mirror. I saw my gaunt, unshaven face. I peeled off my shirt and saw the marks of the heavy chains. My ribs stood out like those of a cardboard skeleton.

And I had been one of the lucky ones among political prisoners! I had been only mildly tortured. I had been imprisoned for a comparatively short time. I had had a spiritual training which enabled me to fight off despair more easily than my friends who still lay on stinking straw, a few miles away from the hotel where I was stepping into a warm and soapy tub. My compassion for the others haunted me.

After my bath I was given a decent meal: white bread, meat stew, real coffee, jam. It seemed the height of luxury. Everything on the way to my trial was like that. It was such a joy to see the sunlight, to gaze at the streets, to see men and women walking freely that I could not take seriously the fact that I was still a prisoner. And a prisoner facing a very serious charge.

What was that charge? It was, I found, another long catalogue of absurdities. Some of my movements during the war were accurately included in it: the prosecution had copies of two of my false identity cards. They had found witnesses willing to swear that I had illegally organized an underground resistance against the Nazis *before* the Communists had any quarrel with them. This was the crux of the indictment: I had not waited for the

Russians to declare war on the Nazis before finding their system evil. I was therefore not a trustworthy friend of the present Czecho-Slovakia, or of Russia.

But the indictment did not stop with this, for such a charge would not have made me a villain in the eyes of the Slovakian and Bohemian public. In order to achieve this end, and in order to smear my Church, the ZOB had gathered together an astonishing array of false affidavits. These were sloppily compiled: they were intended to link me, together with the whole Catholic Action movement, to the collaborationist groups who had supported Hitler. No shred of evidence was introduced to show that our students had ever associated with the German-sponsored organizations. How could it be? We had been sworn enemies of the Nazis from the first.

I stood my trial. I listened to the affidavits and to the cynical ZOB effort to undermine our patriotism. The "informers" whom the ZOB had gathered were a pitiful lot of young boys, collaborationists with the Nazis who had been promised amnesty if they would bear false witness to the association of our Catholic movement with their own.

I was allowed a lawyer who made an honest effort to help me. I sat next to him in court, while the frightened pro-German youths told their fantastic yarns. I whispered to him questions which would obviously show that the boys were lying.

"Ask him if the man he is implicating walks with a limp? Ask him the color of his hair? I am sure he has never even seen him."

The lawyer put the embarrassing question to the witness. It was obvious to the jury that he had invented a pack of lies.

"What was the date of the alleged meeting? How did we arrive there. How many men were present?"

I was able to prove that on the date of my alleged collaboration I had been halfway across the country in another town and had been seen by a dozen reputable witnesses there.

It was a trial run according to the laws of civilized courtroom procedure—a democratic trial. Perhaps it was one of the last to be held in the unhappy countries under Russia's shadow. Thanks to the processes of democratic law, still inscribed in the government lawbooks, thanks to the presence of a jury which judged by the evidence, and thanks to a judge left over from the pre-Communist regime, I had a fair trial.

And I won.

As I gathered my papers and started to leave the courtroom under the eyes of the scowling secret police, the judge leaned down and spoke to me.

"You are leaving here a free man, Father," he said. "I congratulate you. But I wish to warn you: your life cannot be answered for by this court. I advise you to leave the country, and to go at once."

It was obviously sound advice—unanswerable advice. But leaving the country might be quite as dangerous as staying. If I should ask for a passport, if I should try to cross the border openly, one of two things would surely happen. Either the ZOB would arrange for my passport to be refused; or—an even more disagreeable contingency—I would be shadowed and followed across the frontier, and disposed of in some lonely and convenient spot.

I spent that first day of freedom in the familiar game of losing my shadowers: I doubled back across my tracks. I dropped off the rear platforms of streetcars after they were in motion. I took elavators to the fourth floor and walked to the fifth, and darted down the stairs. That night I was sure I had shaken off pursuit. I sought out the suburban home of a good friend, a foreigner whose work included the repatriation of refugees.

"I thought you might be coming here," he said quietly, as he drew me inside his door and pulled the blinds. "I have even drawn a plan for you. You must hide here tonight and tomorrow night. Then we shall get you to safety on Wednesday. This is how we'll do it."

A number of Belgians, refugees who had fled from the Germans into Czecho-Slovakia during the war, were being repatriated on a special train. My friend could arrange a false identity for me as a merchant from Brussels; tomorrow he would arrange to get the necessary papers forged. On Wednesday I was to be driven to the station and smuggled on board the train.

It was a sound plan: that night I soaked from one of my old passports a photograph which showed me wearing a pince-nez with a broad band. The next day my friend's wife bought me glasses of just this kind. With a stiff, old-fashioned turned-down collar and these glasses I looked the part of a respectable merchant, a man too stiff to enter lightly into conversation with the peasants who would make up the majority of travelers on the refugee train. This role would help me to avoid talking and revealing my accent.

On Wednesday morning we set out by car and drove rapidly to the station. We had deliberately planned to arrive at the last possible moment; the refugee train was already moving. I jumped aboard. Boxes, bundles, metal-bound trunks, straw suitcases bulged from every window. Joyous, excited faces waved farewell: these people were glad to be going home.

They were far too much absorbed in their own happiness to notice an unobtrusive merchant with a forbidding pince-nez, who sat in a corner of the carriage, his nose in a book. They were far too busy to inquire what that book might be.

I sighed as I opened my Breviary: it was a long time since I had enjoyed the luxury of reading the daily office. I turned to the appointed Psalm: "*In convertendo Dominus captivitatem Sion . . .*" "When the Lord turned against the captivity of Sion, we became like men consoled. Then was our mouth filled with gladness and our tongue with joy."

It was my farewell chant to Prague, to Czecho-Slovakia, to the lands behind the Iron Curtain. It was my exit from captivity, my entrance to the West.

Freedom lay at the other end of this silver rail over which our train was hurrying. We were leaving many evil and dangerous things behind us; things which may yet destroy the peace and hope of the postwar world. But we were heading for the world where men still know the difference between good and evil and where God's priests are free to speak of Him. My heart sang out to greet the fortunate people I was soon to join, the people who might some day send back the gift of liberty to the imprisoned martyrs I had left behind. I had set my face towards the sun.

(4)

TRENT UNIVERSITY
0 1164 0300388 6

CPSIA information can be obtained
at www.ICGtesting.com
Printed in the USA
LVHW021335220222
711709LV00004B/128